中外文稀有版本文献

《反杜林论》

②

英文版

【德】弗里德里希·恩格斯 ◎ 著

《反杜林论》的出版与传播

（代序）

恩格斯在《反杜林论》中对杜林的批判以及反对杜林主义的斗争，捍卫和发展了马克思主义，不仅使德国社会民主党摆脱了杜林主义的影响，确立了正确的思想理论基础，而且有力地推动了国际工人运动，促进了马克思主义在世界各国的迅速传播和发展。《反杜林论》一书在世界各国广泛的传播，甚至出乎恩格斯的意料，1884年4月11日，恩格斯在获悉《反杜林论》在德国及其他国家，特别是在俄国产生了巨大影响后，写信给伯恩施坦说："对于随书寄来的《杜林》，我费了一点脑筋，后来认为是误寄给我的，也就放心地搁在一边了。我根本没有想到，这是暗示要出第二版。使我很高兴的是，事情果然如此，尤其是现在各方面都告诉我，这本东西产生了完全出乎我意料的影响，特别是在俄国。可见，尽管同不足道的对手进行论战不可避免具有枯燥的性质，但是我们百科全书式地概述了我们在哲学、自然科学和历史问题上的观点，还是起了作用。"130余年来，《反杜林论》以多种语言出版各种版本，这些版本的传播在很大程度上反映了不同时代人们理解《反杜林论》的历史经验。

一 《反杜林论》在俄国及其他国家的出版与传播

众所周知，马克思恩格斯十分重视俄国的革命运动，并与俄国革命家有着密切的联系。1878年7月16日，《反杜林论》刚刚出版一个星期，恩格斯就写信给 B.H.斯米尔诺夫说，前一天已经寄给他了一本"反对杜林的著作"，并请斯米尔诺夫告知拉甫罗夫和洛帕廷的地址，恩格斯想把这本书也邮寄给他们。

1894年，《反杜林论》第三版在斯图加特出版。同一年，沙皇俄国书报审查机关却颁布法令禁止它在俄国出版和传播。禁止的原因在于，恩格斯在其著作中"证明了由于现代资本主义生产方式所造成的不正常的社会经济生活，而导致的社会主义革命的必然性"。因此，《反杜林论》是一本"社会主义教义问答手册"，是民主党人进行宣传的"危险武器"。尽管如此，19世纪80—90年代，《反杜林论》的部分章节还是在俄国被半公开或秘密地发表过几次，并成为"首批俄国马克思主义者的思想武器"。

19世纪80年代初，曾有一本缩略版的《反杜林论》译本在莫斯科的"翻译者和出版者协会"出版。1884年，"劳动解放社"出版了由查苏利奇翻译的小册子《社会主义从空想到科学的发展》，《反杜林论》中的"暴力论"一章也被作为附录收录其中。列宁高度评价了这个译本，认为查苏利奇这个工作是第一次尝试用俄语翻译《反杜林论》的理论财富。19世纪90年代初，莫斯科马克思主义小组成员翻译了一系列《反杜林论》的片段，并发表在杂志上。彼得堡、喀山、莫斯科、萨马拉等许多城市的地下小组都学习和研究恩格斯这部著作，将其中的思想广泛地运用在理论斗争中。值得提及的是，1889年至1893年，列宁在萨马拉生活时期阅读了《反杜林论》，并撰写了关于这部著作的内容概要，但这份概要没能保存下来。

1904年，《反杜林论》俄译本在彼得堡雅科温科出版社出版，印数为2450册。该书的书名为《哲学、政治经济学、社会主义（杜林在科学中实行的变革）》，没有署译者的名字，实际上，它是由孟什维克马尔托夫根据德文第三版翻译的。

1904年10月，《反杜林论》俄文节译本出版。列宁熟悉这个译本。1907年2月，列宁在《卡·马克思致路·库格曼书信集》俄译本序言中指出，"这本书有策杰尔包姆的俄译本，可惜这个译本翻译得很糟，不仅有许多遗漏，而且有不少错误"。1907年，B.雅科温科出版社出版了完整译本的《反杜林论》，标题改为《反杜林论（欧根·杜林先生在哲学中实行的变革）》。

十月革命胜利后，列宁领导的俄共（布）中央十分重视对马克思主义经典文献的收集、整理、翻译和出版，并专门成立马列主义研究院负责此项工作。《反杜林论》属于马克思恩格斯较为大部头的著作，直至1945年第二次世界大战后，马列主义研究院才出版了比较科学和准确的译本，这一版本共印行了10万册。在这个译本中，全部译文都根据1894年出版的《反杜林论》德文第三版校订和修改；在"政治经济学"部分中马克思撰写的第十章也根据保存在马列主义研究院里的手稿复印件校订；被列宁在其著作中引证过的地方，全部采用列宁的译文，正文也都采用列宁的术语。在这个译本的附录中还刊载了《反杜林论》的准备材料以及与该书相关的作品，其中包括第一次用俄文发表的恩格斯的论文《步兵战术及其物质基础》。1948年，该版本再版发行。到1960年前，苏联曾用18种文字出了63种版本的《反杜林论》，总发行量达2461000册。

如前所述，尽管《反杜林论》在俄国产生了广泛的影响，但是，对于一部40余万字的大部头论战性著作来说，一方面，"多数人懒得读像《资本论》那样厚的书"，另一方面，把它翻译成其他文字也极为不易。因此，1880年在法国出版的，根据从《反杜林论》一书中摘录出的三章整理而成的小册子《空想社会主义和科学社会主义》很受世界各国人民的欢迎。这部小册子用平铺直叙的方式阐明了科学社会主义的基本理论，用浅显易懂的语言平实地说明了唯物史观和剩余价值学说的创立使社会主义从空想变为科学的发展过程。正是"这本书在许多优秀的法国人的头脑中引起了真正的革命"。而《反杜林论》第一个不完整的法文单行本是1901年问世的，由保尔·拉法格和劳拉·拉法格翻译，巴黎"拉克"出版社出版。完整版则于1911由贾尔和布里埃出版社出版。此外，1956年出版的法文版《马克思恩格斯全集》也收录了《反杜林论》。

《反杜林论》曾多次被译成英文出版，除了在莫斯科出版的《反杜林论》英文版外，在英美也出版过不少版本的《反杜林论》。例如，美国于1907年在芝加哥首先出版了一部由刘易斯翻译的《反杜林论》。直到1934年，《反杜林论》的全译本才在纽约面世。1936年，英国劳伦斯和威沙特（Lawrence & Wishart）出版社在伦敦出版了该书，1975年再版。此外，《马克思恩格斯全集》英文版和《马克思恩格斯读本》等文集几乎均收录这部名著。

值得提及的是，1935年，《马克思恩格斯全集》历史考证版出版了《〈欧根·杜林先生在科学中实行的变革〉和〈自然辩证法〉》专卷（1935年莫斯科—列宁格勒版）。除收录恩格斯在世时出版过的三个版次《反杜林论》全文外，还发表了恩格斯《〈反杜林论〉的准备材料》和《步兵战术及其物质基础。1700—1870年》。1988年，《马克思恩格斯全集》历史考证版第二版第1部分第27卷发表恩格斯在世时出版过的三个版次《反杜林论》的全文，同时收录的还有恩格斯《〈反杜林论〉的准备材料》，1880年由《反杜林论》改编成的小册子《空想社会主义和科学社会主义》及其1883年德文版《社会主义从空想到科学的发展》。

此外，《反杜林论》还曾在波兰、罗马尼亚、阿尔巴尼亚、南斯拉夫、民主德国、朝鲜民主主义人民共和国和其他一些国家相继被翻译多次出版。

二 《反杜林论》在中国的翻译和传播

百余年来，《反杜林论》在中国得到广泛传播，几代中国读者阅读的该书包括吴亮平译本、中央编译局译本以及其他多种中译本。下面详述之：

1. 吴亮平译《反杜林论》及其重要版本

《反杜林论》被介绍到中国是在五四运动以后。1920年前后，各地共产主义小组相继成立，马克思和恩格斯的著作得到较为广泛的传播。当时，《新青年》《国民》《每周评论》《建设》等进步刊物相继发表介绍马克思主义的文章和马克思主义经典著作的译文。1920年12月，《建设》杂志3卷1号刊载了一篇题为《科学的社会主义与唯物史观》的译文，即是《反杜林论》第三编"社会主义编"的一部分。这篇译文是《反杜林论》一书中最早和我国读者见面的内容。而《反杜林论》第一个中译本在十年后才问世，译者是吴亮平。

吴亮平曾与张闻天、王稼祥、乌兰夫、左权、伍修权、朱瑞、赵一曼等共赴莫斯科中山大学学习，1927年由张闻天等5人介绍加入中国共产党。最初，吴亮平翻译了《社会主义从空想到科学的发展》，这个小册子是《反杜林论》的一部分，从此与《反杜林论》结下不解之缘，产生了要把这部著作完整翻译出版的愿望。随后，吴亮平与张闻天一起合译了马克思的《法兰西内战》、列宁的《社会民主党在民主革命中的两个策略》《国家与革命》等马克思主义经典著作。正是在参与翻译大量马克思主义经典著作的基础上，他收集了关于《反杜林论》的资料，为翻译这一大部头著作做准备。

1929年秋，吴亮平从莫斯科回到上海，在中共中央宣传部工作。1930年5月，由于受到王明的打击，吴亮平被撤职，但他宣传马克思主义的决心没有改变。经地下党员张庆孚介绍，白天他在一所大学代课，维持生计；晚上进行支部规定的革命活动，夜里从事《反杜林论》的翻译。1930年的上海被白色恐怖所笼罩，要秘密翻译一部27万字的理论高深的宏篇巨著，谈何容易！吴亮平遇到的困难是常人难以想象的。时值炎热的盛夏，酷暑难熬，他埋头于简陋的亭子间，挥汗译著。一方面，他时刻提防国民党特务的跟踪盯梢，饮食起居没有规律；另一方面，为了力求译文的准确，吴亮平根据德文原本，参照俄文和日文两种译本进行翻译。在这样的情况下，废寝忘食的吴亮平仅用了三个月的时间就译完了《反杜林论》这部"马克思主义的百科全书"。随后交给了上海江南书店出版。

1930年11月，江南书店出版了吴亮平翻译的《反杜林论》第一个全译本。该书32开横排本，分平装和精装两种。米黄色封面，上端用粗黑体美术字横题书名：反杜林论。下端署有"上海""江南书店印行"等字样。扉页赤字红边，正文横排，共601页。正文前还有写于1930年10月26日的"译者序言"。

《反杜林论》中译本出版不久，吴亮平就被国民党特务逮捕，关押在上海提篮桥监狱。他在监狱中坚贞不屈，团结同牢难友，同敌人进行了不屈不挠的斗争，把敌人的监牢变成了秘密宣传马列主义的特殊学校。吴亮平曾说，《反杜林论》幸好他译得快，不然，就有夭折的危险。如同19世纪德国的俾斯麦实行反社会党人非常法，没有能够禁止《反杜林论》在德国和欧洲的传播一样，《反杜林论》中译本一旦出版，就在中国扎根并得到广泛传播。

吴亮平翻译的《反杜林论》"在三年中间，曾经销行了四五版"，主要的版本有：1931年8月，江南书店再版吴亮平译本。1932年7月，上海笔耕堂重印，改竖排平装本，译者署名"吴理屏"。1937年，上海生活书店重印，竖排平装本，译者署名"吴理屏"，书前有张仲实翻译的V. Posner的《〈反杜林论〉出版六十周年纪念》一文。这对当时的读者了解《反杜林论》一书很有帮助。1938年3月，《反杜林论》又被上海生活书店重印一次，以应当时读者的迫切需要。1939年5月，重庆生活书店重印，封面印有"世界名著译丛之三"字样，书前也收录了张仲实翻译的《〈反杜林论〉出版六十周年纪念》一文和"译者序言"。

1932年，吴亮平被营救出狱。他辗转到中央苏区，从事经济工作。当时，毛泽东非常重视马克思主义著作的翻译和研究，想方设法从各处收集，其中就收集到了吴亮平翻译的《反杜林论》。毛泽东得到这部著作后爱不释手，并多次同吴亮平探讨《反杜林论》中的理论问题，用马克思主义基本理论深入探讨当时中国革命的实际问题。此外，毛泽东不仅注重书的内容，而且还注意译文是否优美。例如"哲学篇"第十一节末尾处，吴亮平用了"太过沉溺于杯中"一句话，毛泽东看了说："这样好，有味。"他还认为吴黎平这个署名很好。

1937年，吴亮平跟随红军经过长征来到延安，继续从事中宣部的工作。1939年，在毛泽东的鼓励下，他花费半年时间，将《反杜林论》的译文根据苏联马克思列宁主义研究院1938年订正的新俄译本、德文原本和英文本重新审校一遍，更正了许多初译时由于地下工作条件恶劣而导致的译文错误。此时，延安已经建立了印刷厂，这个校订本就在1940年8月由解放社出版。全书为竖排32开本，用的是粗糙的通廉纸。书前有译者根据尤琴的文章编译的《〈反杜林论〉内容大要》，以及吴亮平于1940年7月7日写的《〈反杜林论〉中译本出版十年小序》，其中简述了《反杜林论》中译本的十年沧桑，并对该书的内容作了简明的提要勾玄，文中有注释。1978年，吴亮平在《〈反杜林论〉中译本的五十年》一文中写道："《反杜林论》的1940年校订本，对我说来始终具有很大的纪念意义。因为它是我在毛泽东同志的亲自鼓励督促下完成的。假如说，1930年我第一次翻译《反杜林论》时，主要还是出于对马列著作和革命理论的朴素感情（当时我才二十二岁），那么到了这时，我在毛泽东同志教育下，对搞好《反杜林论》这本名著的译本的认识是比较提高了一些。"

直到20世纪80年代，吴亮平翻译的1940年版《反杜林论》还多次被重印，可见他的译本对于《反杜林论》在中国的传播具有重要作用。这些重印的版本是：1947年1月，上海生活书店重印，32开竖排平装本；1949年12月，北京生活·读书·新知三联书店重印，注明初版，32开竖排平装本，封面印有"马列主义理论丛书"字样；1950年11月，生活·读书·新知三联书店重印，注明第二版，大32开，横排平装本，封面印有"马列主义理论丛书"字样；1951年5月，生活·读书·新知三联书店重印，注明上海第四版，大32开，横排平装本，封面印有"马列主义理论丛书"字样，书后附勘误表；1951年6月，生活·读书·新知三联书店重印，注明第三版，大32开，横排平装本，封面印有"马列主义理论丛书"字样，书后附勘误表。

1954年，吴亮平在北京对《反杜林论》的译本作了第二次校订。这次校订是根据1950的俄文本，同时参照德文原本和1954年莫斯科的英文本校译的。校译工作早在1951年就开始了，直到1955年12月才全部完成。他重新翻译了《反杜林论》前十四章。1956年2月，该校译本由人民出版社出版，注明新一版，大32开，横排平装本。书中有著者注、译者注、俄文版编者注，书后有吴亮平写于1955年12月12日的"校译后记"。这一版本到1965年3月共印制了14次之多。1963年9月还出版了十六开大字本。

1973年3月，周恩来总理在一次干部会上谈到，他同毛主席在一次谈话中提到了吴亮平。毛主席讲，吴亮平30年代翻译了《反杜林论》，把马克思主义引入中国，他是第一代马克思主义理论翻译者。后来在陕北为我和斯诺谈话做翻译，把中国共产党和中国革命情况介绍到全世界。大禹治水是用疏导的办法，有进有出，吴亮平在翻译上这一进一出，意义很大，其功不下于大禹治水。此后，毛泽东对吴亮平"其功不在禹下"的评论被广为传播，这促成吴亮平再次较为仔细地校对《反杜林论》。1974年，吴亮平再次对译文根据德文版作了"名词上文字上的校订"后，由人民出版社出版了第二版。这个版本为大32开，横排平装本，书中有著者注、译者注、俄文版编者注，还增加了恩格斯《社会主义从空想到科学的发展》英文版导言。书后附吴亮平写于1973年11月的"校译后记"。该版共印制15次。1980年8月，生活·读书·新知三联书店出版了吴亮平对《反杜林论》的第四次校译本，书后附有吴亮平写于1978年11月的"校译后记"。

2.《反杜林论》中译文的其他版本

新中国成立前，除了吴亮平翻译的《反杜林论》中文全译本之外，还有很多学者翻译了该书的中文摘译文或部分内容。尽管这些译本均不完整，但是对马克思主义基本原理和方法论在中国的传播也起到了不可忽视的历史作用。了解这些译文或译本的内容和版次，有助于思考马克思主义在中国的传播进程。这些译文或译本主要有：

（1）叶作丹摘译《反杜林论》哲学编第七节"自然哲学。有机界"中"达尔文学说部分"，标题为《达尔文学说之基础的要素》，载于1930年6月出版的《马克思学体系》第三册第39—41页。

（2）钱铁如译，《反杜林格论——哲学·经济学·社会主义·批判》（即《反杜林论》），1930年12月上海昆仑书店出版，该译本分为上下册，但现在只见上册，包括三版序言、绪论和哲学编。全书共228页，32开，竖排平装本。正文前有"译者的话"（写于1930年8月30日），书中有译者注。这个译本后来没有再版过。

（3）杜畏之摘译《反杜林论》第二版序言和"概论"部分第1—6自然段，标题为《反杜林论别序》《现代自然科学中之辩证法》，收录于1932年8月出版的《自然辩证法》第159—168、557—560页。

（4）程始仁摘译《反杜林论》"概论"部分，标题为《唯物辩证法与马克思主义》，著者译为"昂格思"。载于1930年4月上海亚东图书馆出版的《辩证法经典》第135—158页。

（5）周建人摘译《反杜林论》第一编第3、6、10、11、12、13节，第二编第2、4节，第三编第2、5节的部分章节和段落，标题为《杜林君在科学中的革命》。载于1948年8月出版的《新哲学手册》第24—84页。

（6）梁武译《新哲学典范》和《新经济学典范》，1949年10月上海文源出版社出版，《新哲学典范》包括：《反杜林论》第一版序言，引论第2节"杜林先生许下了什么诺言"和第一编"哲学编"。全书共127页，32开，竖排平装本。《新经济学典范》包括：《反杜林论》的第二编政治经济学编，书前有写于1949年7月的"编者序"。全书共134页，32开，竖排平装本。

（7）郑易里摘译《〈反杜林论〉的准备材料》第二编第二章和第三

编第一章,标题分别为《奴隶制度》和《傅利叶》,载于1950年9月版《自然辩证法》第374—375、375—376页。

3. 中央编译局编译《反杜林论》各版本

中央编译局在1970年12月编译并出版了《反杜林论》单行本。该文本正文根据《马克思恩格斯全集》德文版第20卷翻译,书后附《社会主义从空想到科学的发展》英文版导言,其正文根据1958年英文版《马克思恩格斯文选》(两卷集)翻译,同时参考了德文本和俄译本。书后还附有注释230条。后来这个译本收入1971年3月出版的《马克思恩格斯全集》第20卷。1972年,这个译本又被收入《马克思恩格斯选集》第3卷。

1995年,中央编译局编译出版《马克思恩格斯选集》中文第二版,其中第3卷收录了根据德文本重新校改的《反杜林论》。1999年,《反杜林论》单行本的第二版出版。这个版本主要采用《马克思恩格斯选集》第二版第3卷中《反杜林论》的译文,同时也根据德文本再次校改过。为了方便研究者对《反杜林论》的深入研读,这版单行本还收录了《〈反杜林论〉的准备材料》和《马克思和恩格斯关于杜林和〈反杜林论〉的书信摘选》。2009年,中央编译局编译出版的《马克思恩格斯文集》第9卷收录《反杜林论》译文,其正文主要根据《马克思恩格斯全集》历史考证版和《马克思恩格斯全集》德文版作了新的审核和修订。在这里还收录了《〈反杜林论〉的准备材料》,恩格斯的《步兵战术及其物质基础。1700—1870年》,以及恩格斯在《社会主义从空想到科学的发展》中对《反杜林论》正文所作的补充和修改。2012年,中央编译局编译出版《马克思恩格斯选集》中文第三版,在第3卷中再次收录《反杜林论》,其译文同《马克思恩格斯文集》的译文。在2013年即将出版的《马克思恩格斯全集》中文第二版第26卷中,《反杜林论》经过与原文再次核校和修改被收录其中,值得提及的是,在这卷中除了在《反杜林论》正文后附了《〈反杜林论〉的准备材料》和《步兵战术及其物质基础。1700—1870年》两篇相关材料外,首次附上了马克思为《反杜林论》政治经济学部分撰写的两篇材料,即《评杜林〈国民经济学批判史〉》和《经济表及若干批注》,恩格斯正是根据这两篇材料写成第二编第十章《〈批判史〉论述》。

此外,民族出版社根据中央编译局翻译的《反杜林论》中译本出版了蒙文版(1972年12月)、藏文版(1973年8月)、维吾尔文版(1972年7月、1978年6月两版)、朝鲜文版(1972年10月)、哈萨克文版(1975年10月)等民族文字译本。新疆人民出版社于1977年3月出版托忒蒙古文版。

《反杜林论》各中译本使恩格斯撰写的这部马克思主义经典著作在中国得到了广泛的传播,在一定程度上反映了中国先进知识分子和马克思主义理论家翻译、研究和传播马克思主义的历程,也在一定程度上反映了中国读者接受、理解和思考马克思主义理论的历程。回顾这一历程,可以帮助我们从文献传播的视角理解中国马克思主义理论发展的学术背景,这对我们进一步促进马克思主义中国化、时代化和大众化无疑具有不可忽视的借鉴意义。

(本文来自2014年中央编译出版社出版的姚颖所著《恩格斯〈反杜林论〉研究读本》有关内容。)

LANDMARKS OF SCIENTIFIC SOCIALISM

"ANTI-DUEHRING"

BY

FREDERICK ENGELS

TRANSLATED AND EDITED BY AUSTIN LEWIS

CHICAGO
CHARLES H. KERR & COMPANY
CO-OPERATIVE

Copyright, 1907
BY CHARLES H. KERR & COMPANY

TABLE OF CONTENTS

CHAPTER I
                                                  PAGE

TRANSLATOR'S INTRODUCTION 5

CHAPTER II

PREFACES 21
    Part I. 21
    Part II. 25
    Part III. 33

CHAPTER III

INTRODUCTION. 34
    I. In General 34
    II. What Herr Duehring Has to Say 48

PART I

CHAPTER IV

    Apriorism 52
    The Scheme of the Universe 61

CHAPTER V

NATURAL PHILOSOPHY 68
    Time and Space 68
    Cosmogony, Physics, and Chemistry 80
    The Organic World 92
    The Organic World (conclusion) 105

CHAPTER VI

MORAL AND LAW 114
    Eternal Truths 114
    Equality. 128
    Freedom and Necessity 144

TABLE OF CONTENTS

Chapter VII

	PAGE
THE DIALECTIC	148
Quantity	148
Negation of the Negation	157
Conclusion	173

PART II

Chapter VIII

POLITICAL ECONOMY	174
I. Objects and Methods	174
II. The Force Theory	182
III. Force Theory (continued)	191
IV. Force Theory (conclusion)	201
V. Theory of Value	212
VI. Simple and Compound Labor	217
VII. Capital and Surplus Value	221
VIII. Capital and Surplus Value (conclusion)	225
IX. Natural Economic Laws — Ground Rent	230
X. With Respect to the "Critical History"	233

PART III

Chapter IX

SOCIALISM	234
Production	234
Distribution	243
The State, The Family, and Education	254

APPENDIX	259

LANDMARKS OF SCIENTIFIC SOCIALISM

CHAPTER I

TRANSLATOR'S INTRODUCTION

When Dr. Eugene Duehring, privat docent at Berlin University, in 1875, proclaimed the fact that he had become converted to Socialism, he was not content to take the socialist movement as he found it, but set out forthwith to promulgate a theory of his own. His was a most elaborate and self-conscious mission. He stood forth as the propagandist not only of certain specific and peculiar views of socialism but as the originator of a new philosophy, and the propounder of strange and wonderful theories with regard to the universe in general. The taunt as to his all-comprehensiveness of intellect, with which Engels pursues him somewhat too closely and much too bitterly, could not have affected Herr Duehring very greatly. He had his own convictions with respect to that comprehensive intellect of his and few will be found to deny that he had the courage of his convictions.

Thirty years have gone since Duehring published the fact of his conversion to socialism. The word "conversion" contains in itself the distinction between the socialism of thirty years ago and that of to-day. What was then a peculiar creed has now become a very widespread notion. Men are not now individually converted

LANDMARKS OF SCIENTIFIC SOCIALISM

to socialism but whole groups and classes are driven into the socialist ranks by the pressure of circumstances. The movement springs up continually in new and unexpected places. Here it may languish apparently, there it gives every indication of strong, new and vigorous life.

The proletariat of the various countries race as it were towards the socialist goal and, as they change in their respective positions, the economic and political fields on which they operate furnish all the surprises and fascinations of a race course. In 1892 Engels wrote that the German Empire would in all probability be the scene of the first great victory of the European proletariat. But thirteen years have sufficed to bog the German movement in the swamps of Parliamentarianism. Great Britain, whose Chartist movement was expected to provide the British proletariat with a tradition, has furnished few examples of skill in the management of proletarian politics, but existing society in Great Britain has none the less been thoroughly undermined. The year before that in which Herr Duehring made his statement of conversion, the British Liberals had suffered a defeat which, in spite of an apparent recuperation in 1880, proved the downfall of modern Liberalism in Great Britain, and showed that the Liberal Party could no longer claim to be the party of the working class. Not only that, but the British philosophic outlook has become completely changed. The nonconformist conscience grows less and less the final court of appeal in matters political. A temporary but fierce attack of militant imperialism coupled with the very general acceptance of an empiric collectivism has sufficed to destroy old ideas and to make the road to victory easier for a determined and relentless working class movement.

TRANSLATOR'S INTRODUCTION

But if thirty years have worked wonders in Europe, and disintegration can be plainly detected in the social fabric, the course of social and political development in the United States has been still more remarkable. In 1875 the country was still a farming community living on the edge of a vast wilderness through which the railroad was just beginning to open a path. Thirty years have been sufficient to convert it into the greatest of manufacturing and commercial states. The occupation of the public lands, the establishment of industry on an hitherto undreamed of scale, the marvellous, almost overnight creation of enormous cities, all these have resulted in the production of a proletariat, cosmopolitan in its character, and with no traditions of other than cash relations with the class which employs it. The purity of the economic fact is unobscured. Hence a socialistic agitation has arisen in the United States, the enthusiasm of which vies with that in any of the European countries and the practical results of which bid fair to be even more striking. This movement has arisen almost spontaneously as the result of economic conditions. It is a natural growth not the result of the preaching of abstract doctrines or the picturing of an ideal state. The modern American proletariat is, as a matter of fact, given neither to philosophic speculation nor to the imagination which is necessary to idealism. Such socialism as it has adopted it has taken up because it has felt impelled thereto by economic pressure.

Hence, apart from all socialistic propaganda, a distinct disintegration-process has been proceeding in modern society. Each epoch carries within itself the seeds of its own dissolution. Things have just this much value, they are transitory, says Engels in his paraphrase of Hegel, and this is in fact the central idea of his dialectic philosophy.

He criticises the work of Duehring from this standpoint. He labors not so much to show that Duehring is mistaken in certain conclusions as to prove that the whole method of his argument is wrong. His diatribes, though the subject matter of his argument requires him to attack the Berlin tutor, are directed chiefly against all absolute theories. "Eternal truth," in the realm of science, equally with that of philosophy, he scouts as absurd. To interpret the history of the time in terms of the spirit of the time, to discover the actual beneath the crust of the conventional, to analyse the content of the formulæ which the majority are always ready to take on trust, and to face the fact with a mind clear of preconceived notions is what Engels set out to do. It cannot be said that he altogether succeeded. No man can succeed in such a task. The prejudices and animosities created by incessant controversy warped his judgment in some respects, and tended on more than one occasion to destroy his love of fair play. The spirit which is occasionally shown in his controversial writing is to be deplored but it may be said in extenuation that all controversies of that time were disfigured in the same way. He pays the penalty for the fault.

Much of the work is valueless to-day because of Engels' eagerness to score a point off his adversary rather than to state his own case. But where the philosopher lays the controversialist on one side for a brief period, and takes the trouble to elucidate his own ideas we discover what has been lost by these defects of temperament. He possesses in a marked degree the gift of clear analysis and of keen and subtle statement.

The socialist movement everywhere arrives some time

TRANSLATOR'S INTRODUCTION

or other at what may be called the Duehring stage of controversy. There are two very distinct impulses towards socialism. The individuals who are influenced by these impulses must sooner or later come into collision, and as a result of the impact the movement is for a time divided into hostile parties and a war of pamphleteering and oratory supervenes. This period has just ended in France. For the last few years the French movement has been divided upon the question of the philosophical foundation of the movement, and the parties to the controversy may be divided into those who sought to justify the movement upon ethical grounds and those who have regarded it as a modern political phenomenon dependent alone upon economic conditions. The former of these parties based its claims to the suffrages of the French people upon the justice of the socialistic demands. It proclaimed socialism to be the logical result of the Revolution, the necessary conclusion from the teachings of the revolutionary philosophers. Justice was the word in which they summed up the claims of socialism, that and Equality, for which latter term as Engels points out in the present work, the French have a fondness which amounts almost to a mania. Hence one party of the French socialist movement chose as a platform those very "eternal truths" which Engels ridicules and which it is the sole purpose of the present work to attack.

To kill "eternal truths" is however by no means an easy matter. Years of habit have made them part of the mental structure of the citizens of the modern democratic or semi-democratic states. Not only in France but to an even greater degree in the English speaking countries these "eternal truths" persist, they form the stock in trade of the clergyman and the ordinary politician. Bernard Shaw directs the shafts of his ridicule against these " eternal truths" and smites with a sarcasm which is more fatal than all the solemn German philosophy which Engels has at his command. But Shaw is not appreciated by the British socialist. The latter cannot imagine that the writer is really poking fun at things so exceedingly serious and so essential to any well constituted man, to a well-constituted Briton in particular. The British socialist is as much in love with " eternal truths " as is the stiffest and most unregenerate of his bourgeois opponents. He therefore toploftily declares that Mr. Shaw is an unbalanced person, a licensed jester. Precisely the same results would attend the efforts of an American iconoclast who would venture to ridicule the " eternal truths which have been handed down to us in documents of unimpeachable respectability, like the Declaration of Independence, and by Fourth of July orators, portly of person and of phrase.

The " eternal truth " phase of socialist controversy seems to be as eternal as the truth, and must necessarily be so as long as the movement is recruited by men who bring into it the ideas which they have derived from the ordinary training of the American citizen.

The other side of the controversy to which reference has been made derived its philosophy from the experience of the proletariat. This modern proletariat, trained to the machine, is a distinct product of the occupation by which it lives. The organisation of industry in the grasp of which the workman is held during all his working hours and manufacture by the machine-process, the motions of which he is compelled to follow have produced in him a mental condition which does not readily respond to any sentimental stimulus. The incessant process from cause to effect endows him with a sort of

TRANSLATOR'S INTRODUCTION

logical sense in accordance with which he works out the problems of life independent of the preconceptions and prejudices which have so great a hold upon the reason of his fellow citizens who are not of the industrial proletariat. Without knowing why he arrives by dint of the experience of his daily toil at the same conclusions as Engels attained as the result of philosophic training and much erudition. The Church is well aware of this fact to her sorrow for the industrial proletarian seldom darkens her portals. He has no hatred of religion, as the atheistic radical bourgeois had, but with a good-natured " non possumus" says by his actions what Engels says by his philosophy.

Revolution is an every day occurrence with the industrial proletarian. He sees processes transformed in the twinkling of an eye. He wakes up one morning to find that the trade which he has learned laboriously has overnight become a drug on the market. He is used to seeing the machine whose energy has enchained him flung on the scrap heap and contemptuously disowned, in favor of a more competent successor whose motions he must learn to follow or be himself flung on the scrap heap also. This constant revolution in the industrial process enters into his blood. He becomes a revolutionist by force of habit. There is no need to preach the dialectic to him. It is continually preached. The transitoriness of phenomena is impressed upon him by the changes in industrial combinations, by the constant substitution of new modes of production for those to which he has been accustomed, substitutions which may make " an aristocrat of labor " of him to-day, and send him tramping to-morrow.

The industrial proletarian therefore knows practically what Engels has taught philosophically. So that when

LANDMARKS OF SCIENTIFIC SOCIALISM

in the course of his political peregrinations he strays into the socialist movement and there finds those who profess a socialism based upon abstract conceptions and " eternal truths " his contempt is as outspoken as that of a Friedrich Engels who chances upon a certain Eugen Duehring spouting paraphrases of Rousseau by the socialistic wayside. Engels simply anticipated by the way of books the point of view reached by the industrial proletarian of to-day by the way of experience, and by the American machine-made proletarian in particular. This is a matter of no mean importance. In the following pages we can detect if we can look beyond and beneath the mere criticism of Duehring, an attitude of mind, not of one controversialist to another merely but of an entire class, the class upon which modern society is driven more and more to rely, to the class which relies upon it.

For their popular support classes and governments rely upon formulæ. When the cry of " Down with the Tsar " takes the place of the humbly spoken " Little Father " what becomes of the Tsardom? When the terms " Liberty " and " Equality " become the jest of the workshop, upon what basis can a modern democratic state depend? This criticism of " eternal truths " is destructive criticism, and destructive of much more than the " truths." It is more destructive than sedition itself. Sedition may be suppressed cheaply in these days of quick-firing guns and open streets. But society crumbles away almost insensibly beneath the mordant acid of contemptuous analysis. So to-day goaded on the one side by the gibes of the machine-made proletariat, and on the other, by the raillery of the philosophic jester, society staggers along like a wounded giant and is only too glad to creep into its cave and to forget its sorrows in drink.

TRANSLATOR'S INTRODUCTION

As for 1875, " Many things have happened since then " as Beaconsfield used to say, but of all that has happened nothing could have given more cynical pleasure to the " Old Jew " than the lack of faith in its own shibboleths which has seized the cocksure pompous society in which he disported himself. The rhetoric of a Gladstone based upon the " eternal truths " which constituted always the foundations of his political appeals would fail to affect the masses to-day with any other feeling than that of ridicule. We have already arrived at the " Twilight of the Idols " at least so far as " eternal truths " are concerned. They still find however an insecure roosting place in the pulpits of the protestant sects.

If blows have been showered upon the political " eternal truths " in the name of which the present epoch came into existence social and ethical ideals have by no means escaped attack. Revolt has been the watchword of artist and theologian alike. The pre-Rafaelite school, a not altogether unworthy child of the Chartist movement, raised the cry of artistic revolt against absolutism and the revolt spread in ever widening circles until it has exhausted itself in the sickly egotism of the " art nouveau." Even Engels, with all his independence and glorification of change as a philosophy, can find an opportunity to fling a sneer at Wagner and the " music of the future." The remnants of early Victorianism cling persistently to Engels. He cannot release himself altogether from the bonds of the bourgeois doctrine which he is so anxious to despise. He is in many respects the revolutionist of '48, a bourgeois politician possessed at intervals by a proletarian ghost, such as he says himself ever haunts the bourgeois. The younger generation without any claims to revolutionism has gone further than he in the denunciation of authority and without the same self consciousness. The scorn of Bernard Shaw for the moguls of the academies and for social ideals is greater than the scorn of Engels for "eternal truths." Says Mr. Shaw, "The great musician accepted by his unskilled listener is vilified by his fellow musician. It was the musical culture of Europe that pronounced Wagner the inferior of Mendelssohn and Meyerbeer. The great artist finds his foes among the painters and not among the men in the street. It is the Royal Academy that places Mr. Marcus Stone above Mr. Burne Jones. It is not rational that it should be so but it is so for all that. The realist at last loses patience with ideals altogether and finds in them only something to blind us, something to numb us, something to murder self in us. Something whereby instead of resisting death we disarm it by committing suicide." Here is a note of modernity which Engels was hardly modern enough to appreciate and yet it was written before he died.

Nietzsche, Tolstoy and a host of minor writers have all had their fling at "eternal truths" and modern ideals. The battle has long since rolled away from the ground on which Engels fought. His arguments on the dialectic are commonplaces to-day which it would be a work of supererogation to explain to anyone except the persistent victim of Little Bethel. The world has come to accept them with the equanimity with which it always accepts long disputed truths.

The sacred right of nationality for which men contended in Engels' youth, as a direct consequence of political "eternal truths" has been ruthlessly brushed aside. The philosopher talks of the shameful spoliation of the smaller by the larger nations, a moral view of commercial progress, which an age, grown more impatient of "eternal truths" than Engels himself simply ignores,

TRANSLATOR'S INTRODUCTION

and moves on without a qualm to the destruction of free governments in South Africa. Backward and unprogressive peoples jeer, it is true, and thereby show their political ineptitude, for even the American Republic, having freed the negro under the banner of "eternal truth" annexes the Philippines and raids Panama in defiance of it.

And so since the days of 1875 the world has come to accept the general correctness of Engels' point of view.

The enemy which Engels was most anxious to dislodge was "mechanical socialism," a naïve invention of a perfect system capable of withstanding the ravages of time, because founded upon eternal principles of truth and justice. That enemy has now obeyed the law of the dialectic and passed away. Nobody builds such systems, nowadays. They have ceased their building however not in obedience to the commands of Friedrich Engels but because the lapse of time and the change in conditions have proved the dialectic to the revolutionist. With the annihilation of "eternal truths," system building ceased to be even an amusing pastime. The revolutionist has been revolutionized. He no longer fancies that he can make revolutions. He knows better. He is content to see that the road is kept clear so that revolutions may develop themselves. Your real revolutionist, for example, puts no obstacle in the path of the Trust, he is much too wise. He leaves that to the corrosion of time and the development of his pet dialectic. He sees the contradiction concealed in the system which apparently triumphs, and in the triumph of the system he sees also the triumph of the contradiction. He waits until that shadowy proletariat which haunts the system takes on itself flesh and blood and shakes the system with which it has grown up. But this waiting for the development of the inevitable is weary work to those who want to realise forthwith, so they, unable to confound the logic of Engels, attack the "abstractions" on which his theory is founded. They still oppose their "eternal truths" to the dialectic.

Thus in England, where the strife between the two parties in the socialist movement has lately been waged with a somewhat amusing ferocity, Engels is charged with a wholesale borrowing from Hegel. In any other country than England this would not be laid up against a writer, but the Englishman is so averse to philosophy that the association of one's name with that of a philosopher, and a German philosopher in particular, is tantamount to an accusation of keeping bad company. But a glance at the following pages should tend to dispose of so romantic a statement which could, in fact, only have been made by those who know neither Hegel nor Engels.

That Hegel furnished the original philosophic impetus to both Marx and Engels is true beyond question, but the impetus once given, the course of the founders of modern socialism tended ever further from the opinions of the idealistic philosopher. In fact Engels says somewhat self consciously, not to say boasts, that he and his followers were pioneers in applying the dialectic to materialism. Whatever accusation may be made against Engels, this much is certain that he was no Hegelian. In fact both in the present work and in "Feuerbach" he is at great pains to show the relation of the socialist philosophy as conceived by himself and Marx to that of the great man for whom he always kept a somewhat exaggerated respect, but from whom he differed fundamentally. Engels' attack upon the philosophy of Duehring is based upon dislike of its idealism, the funda-

TRANSLATOR'S INTRODUCTION

mental thesis upon which the work depends being entirely speculative. Duehring insisted that his philosophy was a realist philosophy and Engels' serious arguments, apart from the elaborate ridicule with which he covers his opponent and which is by no means a recommendation to the book, is directed to show that it is not realist, that it depends upon certain preconceived notions. Of these notions some are axiomatic, as Duehring claims, that is they are propositions which are self evident to Herr Duehring but which will not stand investigation. Others again are untrue and are preconceptions so far as they are out of harmony with established facts.

Much of Engels' work is out of date judged by recent biological and other discoveries, but the essential argument respecting the interdependence of all departments of knowledge, and the impossibility of making rigid classifications holds good to-day in a wider sense than when Engels wrote. Scientific truths which have been considered absolute, theories which have produced approximately correct results, have all been discredited. The dogmas of science against which the dogmatic ecclesiastics have directed their scornful contempt have shared the same fate as the ecclesiastical dogmas. Nothing remains certain save the certainty of change. There are no ultimates. Even the atom is suspect and the claims of the elements to be elementary are rejected wholesale with something as closely resembling scorn as the scientist is ever able to attain. A scientific writer has recently said " What is undeniable is that the Daltonian atom has within a century of its acceptance as a fundamental reality suffered disruption. Its proper place in nature is not that formerly assigned to it. No longer ' in seipso totus, teres, atque rotundus ' its reputation for inviolability and indestructibility is gone for ever. Each of these supposed 'ultimates' is now known to be the scene of indescribable activities, a complex piece of mechanism composed of thousands of parts, a star-cluster in miniature, subject to all kinds of dynamical vicissitudes, to perturbations, accelerations, internal friction, total or partial disruption. And to each is appointed a fixed term of existence. Sooner or later the balance of equilibrium is tilted, disturbance eventuates in overthrow; the tiny exquisite system finally breaks up. Of atoms, as of men, it may be said with truth ' Quisque suos patitur manes."

The discovery of radium was in itself sufficient to revolutionise the heretofore existing scientific theories and the revolution thereby effected has been enough to cause Sir William Crookes to say, " There has been a vivid new start, our physicists have remodelled their views as to the constitution of matter." In his address to the physicists at Berlin the same scientist said, " This fatal quality of atomic dissociation appears to be universal, and operates whenever we brush a piece of glass with silk; it works in the sunshine and raindrops in lightnings and flame; it prevails in the waterfall and the stormy sea " and a writer in the Edinburgh Review (December, 1903) remarks in this connection " Matter he (Sir William Crookes) consequently regards as doomed to destruction. Sooner or later it will have dissolved into the 'formless mist' of protyle and 'the hour hand of eternity will have completed one revolution.' The 'dissipation of energy' has then found its correlative in the 'dissolution of Matter.'"

The scope of this revolution may only be gauged by the fact that one writer ("The Alchemy of the Sea," London " Outlook," Feb. 11, 1905) has ventured to say, and this is but one voice in a general chorus: " To-day

TRANSLATOR'S INTRODUCTION

no one believes in the existence of elements; no one questions the possibility of a new alchemy; and the actual evolution of one element from another has been observed in the laboratory — observed by Sir William Ramsey in London, and confirmed by a chemist in St. Petersburg." Helium being an evolution of radium and it is expected furthermore that radium will prove to be an evolution of uranium and so there is a constant process as the writer points out of what was formerly called alchemy the transmutation of one metal into another.

It is clear that in face of these facts the arguments of Engels possess even greater force at the present day than when they were enunciated and that the old hard and fast method of arguing from absolute truths is dead and done for.

Only statesmen see fit to still harp on the same phrases which have become as it were a part of the popular mental structure and by constant appeals to the old watchwords to obscure the fact of change. Were one not acquainted with the essential stupidity of the political mind and the lack of grasp which is the characteristic of statesmen, it might be imagined that all this was done with malice aforethought and that there was a sort of tacit conspiracy on the part of the politicians to delude the people. But experience of the inexcusable blunders and the inexplicable errors into which statesmen are continually driven forces the conclusion that they are in reality no whit in advance of the electorate and that only now and then a Beaconsfield appears who can understand the drift of events. Such a man is the " revolutionist " which Beaconsfield claimed himself to be. But what shall we say of the President of the country that has attained the highest place in industrial progress among the nations, whose whole history is a verification of the truth of the dialectic and who can still appeal to "individualism" as a guiding principle of political action? It is a wanton flying in the face of the experience of the last quarter of a century and such rashness will require its penalty. "Back to Kant" appears to be the hope of reactionary politicians as well as of reactionary philosophers.

CHAPTER II

I

PREFACES

The following work is by no means the fruit of some "inward compulsion," quite the contrary.

When three years ago, Herr Duehring suddenly challenged the world, as a scholar and reformer of socialism, friends in Germany frequently expressed the wish that I should throw a critical light upon these new socialist doctrines, in the central organ of the Social Democratic Party, at that time the "Volkstaat." They held it as very necessary that new opportunity for division and confusion should not be afforded in a party so young and so recently definitely united. They were in a better condition than myself to comprehend the condition of affairs in Germany, so that I was compelled to trust to their judgment. It appeared furthermore that the proselyte was welcomed by a certain portion of the socialist press, with a warmth, which meant nothing more than kindliness to Herr Duehring, but it was seen by a portion of the party press that a result of this kindly feeling towards Herr Duehring was the introduction unperceived of the Duehring doctrine. People were found who were soon ready to spread his doctrine in a popular form among the workingmen, and finally Herr Duehring and his little sect employed all the arts of advertisement and intrigue to compel the "Volksblatt" to change its attitude respecting the new teachings which put forth such tremendous claims.

LANDMARKS OF SCIENTIFIC SOCIALISM

However, a year elapsed before I could make up my mind to engage in so disagreeable a business to the neglect of my other labors. It was the sort of thing one had to get through as quickly as possible, once it was begun. And it was not only unpleasant but quite a task. The new socialist theory appeared as the last practical result of a new philosophic system. It therefore involved an investigation of it in connection with this system and therefore of the system itself. It was necessary to follow Herr Duehring over a wide expanse of country where he had dealt with everything under the sun, yea, and more also. So there came into existence a series of articles which appeared from the beginning of 1877 in the successor of the " Volkstaat," the " Vorwaerts " of Leipsic, and are collected here.

It was my object which extended the criticism to a length out of all proportion to the scientific value of the matter and, therefore, of Herr Duehring's writings. There are two further reasons in extenuation of this lengthiness. In the first place it gave me an opportunity of developing my views, in a positive fashion, with respect to matters which are connected with this, though very different, and which are of more general scientific and practical interest to-day. I have taken the opportunity to do so in every chapter, and, as this book cannot undertake to set up a system in opposition to that of Herr Duehring, it is to be hoped that the reader will not overlook the real significance of the views which I have set forth. I have already had sufficient proof that my labors have not been altogether in vain in this regard.

On the other hand the " system-shaping " Herr Duehring is by no means an exceptional phenomenon in Germany these days. Nowadays in Germany systems of cosmogony, of natural philosophy in particular, of

PREFACES

politics, of economics, etc., are in the habit of shooting up over night like mushrooms. The most insignificant Doctor of Philosophy, nay, even the student, has no further use for a complete " system." In the modern state, it is predicated that every citizen is able to pass judgment on all the questions upon which he is called upon to vote; in political economy it is assumed that every consumer is thoroughly acquainted with all commodities, which he has occasion to buy to maintain himself withal, and the same idea is also held as regards knowledge. Freedom of knowledge demands that a person write of that which he has not learned and proclaim this as the only sound scientific method. But Herr Duehring is one of the most conspicuous types of those absurd pseudo-scientists, who to-day occupy so conspicuous a place in Germany and drown everything with their noisy nonsense. Noisy nonsense in poetry, in philosophy, in political economy, in writing history: noisy nonsense in the professor's chair and tribune; noisy nonsense too in the claims to superiority and intellectuality above the vulgar noisy nonsense of other nations, noisy nonsense the most characteristic and mightiest product of German intellectual activity, cheap and bad, like other German products, along with which, I regret to say, they were not exhibited at Philadelphia.

So, German socialism, particularly since Herr Duehring set the example, beats the drum, and produces here and there one who prides himself upon a " science " of which he knows nothing. It is this, a sort of child's disease which marks the first conversion of the German university man to social democracy and is inseparable from him, but it will soon be thrust aside by the remarkable sound sense of our working class.

It is not my fault that I am obliged to follow Herr

LANDMARKS OF SCIENTIFIC SOCIALISM

Duehring into a realm in which I can at the very most only claim to be a dilettante. On such occasions I have for the most part limited myself to placing the plain incontrovertible facts in contrast with the false or crooked assertions of my opponent, as in relation to jurisprudence and many instances with regard to natural science. In other places he indulges in universal views on the subject of natural science theories and therefore on a field where the professional naturalist must range out of his own particular specialty to neighboring regions, where he, according to Herr Virchow's confessions is just as good a "half-knower" as the rest of us. For slight deficiencies and unavoidable errors in the publication I hope that the same indulgence will be extended to me as has been shown the other side of the controversy.

Just as I was completing this preface I received the publishers' notice of a new important book by Herr Duehring. "New Foundations for rational Physics and Chemistry." Although I am very well aware of my deficiencies in physics and chemistry I still believe that I know my Duehring well enough, without having read the book, to venture to say that the laws of physics and chemistry there set forth are worthy of being placed alongside of Herr Duehring's former discoveries and the laws of economics, scheme of the universe, etc., examined in my writings and proved to be misunderstood or commonplace, and that the rhigometer, an instrument constructed by Herr Duehring for measuring temperature will be found to serve not only as a measure for high or low temperature but of the ignorance and arrogance of Herr Duehring. *London, 11 June, 1878.*

II

It came to me as quite a surprise that a new edition of this work was called for. The special views which it criticised are practically forgotten to-day. The work itself has not only been placed before many thousands of readers by its serial publication in "Vorwaerts" of Leipsic in 1877 and 1878, but it has also been published in large editions in its entirety. How then can there be any further interest in what I have to say about Herr Duehring?

In the first place, I fancy, that it is owing to the fact that this book, as indeed, all my writings at that time, was prohibited in Germany soon after the publication of the anti-Socialist laws. Whosoever was not fettered by the inherited officialdom of the countries of the Holy Alliance should have clearly seen the effect of this measure — the double and treble sale of the prohibited books, and the advertisement of the impotence of the gentlemen in Berlin, who issued injunctions and could not make them effective. Indeed the amiability of the Government was the cause of the publication of several new editions of my shorter writings, as I am able to affirm. I have no time for a proper revision of the text and so allow it to go to press, just as it is.

But there is still an additional circumstance. The "system" of Herr Duehring here criticised spreads over a very extensive theoretical ground and I was compelled to pursue him all over it and to place my ideas in antagonism to his. Negative criticism thereupon became

LANDMARKS OF SCIENTIFIC SOCIALISM

positive; the polemic developed into a more or less connected exposition of dialectic methods and the socialist philosophy, of which Marx and myself are representative, and this in quite a number of places. These our philosophic ideas have had an incubation period of about twenty years since they were first given to the world in Marx's " Misere de la Philosophie " and the Communist Manifesto until they obtained a wider and wider influence through the publication of " Capital " and now find recognition and support far beyond the limits of Europe in all lands where a proletariat exists together with progressive scientific thinkers. It seems that there is also a public whose interests in this matter are sufficient to induce them to purchase the polemic against Duehring's opinions, in spite of the fact that it is now without an object, and who evidently derive pleasure from the positive development.

I must call attention to the fact, by the way, that the views here set out were, for by far the most part, developed and established by Marx, and only to a very slight degree by myself, so that it is understood that I have not represented them without his knowledge. I read the entire manuscript to him before sending it to press and the tenth chapter of the section on Political Economy was written by Marx and unfortunately had to be somewhat abbreviated by me.

It was our wont to mutually assist each other in special branches of work.

The present edition is with the exception of one chapter an unchanged edition of the former. I had no time for revision although there was much in the mode of presentation which I wanted altered. But there is incumbent upon me the duty of preparing for publication the manuscripts which Marx left, and this is much more

PREFACES

important than anything else. Then my conscience rebels against making any changes. The book is controversial and I have an idea that it is unfair to my antagonist for me to alter anything when he cannot do so. I could only claim the right to reply to Herr Duehring's answer. But what Herr Duehring has written with respect to my attack I have not read and shall not do so, unless obliged. I am theoretically done with him. Besides I must observe the rules of literary warfare all the more closely as a despicable wrong has since been inflicted upon him by the University of Berlin. It has been chastised for this, indeed. A university which so degrades itself as to refuse permission to Herr Duehring to teach under the known circumstances should not be surprised if a Herr Schwenninger is forced upon it under circumstances just as well known.

The one chapter in which I have permitted myself any explanations is the Second of the Third Section "Theory." Here where the sole concern is the presentation of a most important part of the philosophy which I represent, my antagonist cannot complain if I put myself to some trouble to speak popularly and to generalise. This was undoubtedly a special occasion. I had made a French translation of three chapters of the book (the First of the Introduction and the First and Second of the Third Section) into a separate pamphlet for my friend Lafargue, and the French edition afterwards served as a basis for one in Italian and one in Polish. A German edition was provided under the title "The Development of Socialism from Utopia to Science." The latter has exhausted three editions in a few months and has also made its appearance translated into Russian and Danish. In all these publications only the chapter in question was added to and it would have been pedantic in me if I had confined myself to the actual wording of the original in the new edition in spite of the later and international form which it had assumed.

Where I wished to make changes had particular reference to two points. In the first place with regard to primitive history, as far as known, to which Morgan was the first to give us the key in 1877. In my book "The Origin of the Family, Private Property and the State," Zurich, 1884, I have since had an opportunity of working up material more lately accessible which I employed in this later work. In the second place, as far as that portion which is concerned with theoretical science is concerned, the presentation of the subject is very defective and a much more definite one could now be given. If I did not allow myself the right of improving it now, I should be in duty bound to pass criticism on myself instead of the other.

Marx and I were probably the first to import the well known dialectic of the German idealistic philosophy into the materialistic view of nature and history. But to a dialectical and at the same time materialistic view of nature there pertains an acquaintance with mathematics and natural science. Marx was a sound mathematician but the sciences we only knew in part, by fits and starts, sporadically. After I retired from mercantile pursuits and went to London and had time, I made as far as possible a complete mathematical and scientific "molting," as Liebig calls it, and spent the best part of eight years on it. I was occupied with this molting process when it chanced that I was called upon to busy myself with Herr Duehring's so-called philosophy. If, therefore, I often fail to find the correct technical expression, and am a little awkward in the field of natural science it is only too natural. On the other hand the

PREFACES

consciousness of insecurity which I have not yet got over has made me cautious. Actual blunders respecting facts up to the present known, and incorrect presentations of theories thus far recognised cannot be proved against me. In this relation just one great mathematician, who is laboring under a mistake, has complained to Marx in a letter that I have made a mischievous attack upon the honor of the square root of minus one.

As regards my review of mathematics and the natural science it was necessary for me to reassure myself on some special points — since I had no doubts about the truth of the general proposition — that in nature the same dialectic laws of progress fulfill themselves amid all the apparent confusion of innumerable changes as dominate the apparently accidental in nature; the same laws whose threads traverse the progressive history of human thought, and little by little come to the consciousness of thinking men. These were first developed by Hegel in a comprehensive fashion but in a mystical form. Our efforts were directed towards stripping away this mystical form and making them evident in their full simplicity and universal reality. It was self evident that the old philosophies of nature — in spite of all their actual value and fruitful suggestiveness — could be of no value to us. There was an error in the Hegelian form, as shown in this book, in that it recognised no progression of nature in time, no "one after another" (Nacheinander) but merely "one besides another" (Nebeneinander). This was due on the one hand to the Hegelian system itself which ascribed to the Spirit (Geist) alone a progressive historical development, but on the other hand, the general attitude of the natural sciences was responsible. So Hegel fell far behind Kant in this respect for the latter had al-

LANDMARKS OF SCIENTIFIC SOCIALISM

ready by his nebular hypothesis proclaimed the origin and, by his discovery of the stoppage of the rotation of the earth through the tides, the destruction of the solar system. And finally, I could not undertake to construct the dialectical laws of nature but to discover them in it and to develop them from it.

To do this entirely and in each separate division is a colossal task. Not only is the ground to be covered almost immeasurable but on this entire ground natural science is involved in such tremendous changes that even those who have all their time to give can hardly keep up with it. Since the death of Marx however my mind has been occupied by more pressing duties and so I had to interrupt my work. I must, for the moment, confine myself to the hints in the work before us and wait for a later opportunity to correct and publish the results obtained, probably together with the most important manuscripts on mathematics left behind by Marx.

But the advance of theoretical science makes my work in all probability, in a great measure, or altogether, superfluous. Since the revolution which overturned theoretical science the necessity of arranging the accumulation of purely empirical discoveries has caused the opposing empiricists to pay more and more attention to the dialectical character of the operations of nature. The old stiff antagonisms, the sharp impassable frontier lines are becoming more and more abolished. Since the last "true" gases have been liquefied, since the proof that a body can be put in a condition in which liquid and gaseous forms cannot be differentiated, aggregate conditions have to the last remnant lost their earlier absolute character. With the statement of the kinetic theory of gases that, in gases, the squares of the speeds with which the separate gas molecules move are in inverse ratio

PREFACES

to the molecular weights, under the same temperature, heat takes its place directly in the series of such measurable forms of motion. Ten years ago the newly discovered great fundamental law of motion was still understood as a mere law of the conservation of energy, as a mere expression of the indestructibility and uncreatibility of motion, and therefore merely on its quantitative side. That narrow negative expression has been more and more subordinated to the transformation of energy, in which the qualitative content of the process is duly recognised and the last notion of an extramundane Creator is destroyed. That the quantity of motion (of energy, so called) is not changed when it is transformed into kinetic energy (mechanical force, so called), into electricity, heat, potential static energy need not now be preached any longer as something new, it served as the foundation, once attained, of many valuable investigations of the process of transformation itself, of the great fundamental process, in the knowledge of which is comprehended the knowledge of all nature. And since biology has been treated in the light of the theory of evolution it has abolished one stiff line of classification after another in the realm of organic nature. The entirely unclassified intermediate conditions increase in number every day. Later investigations throw organisms out of one class into another, and marks of distinction which have become articles of faith lose their individual reality. We have now mammals which lay eggs and, if the news is established, birds also which go on all fours. It was already observed, before the time of Virchow, as a conclusion of the discovery of the cell, that the identity of the individual creature is lost, scientifically and dialectically speaking, in a federation of cells, so the idea of animal (and therefore human) individuality is still further complicated by the discovery of the amœba in the bodies of the higher animals constituting the white blood corpuscles. And these are just the things which were considered polar opposites, irreconcilable and insoluble, the fixed boundaries and differences of classification, which have given modern theoretical science its limited and metaphysical character. The knowledge that these distinctions and antagonisms actually do occur in nature, but only relatively, and that on the other hand that fixity and absoluteness are the products of our own minds — this knowledge constitutes the kernel of the dialectic view of nature. The view is reached under the compulsion of the mass of scientific facts, and one reaches it the more easily by bringing to the dialectic character of these facts a consciousness of the laws of dialectic thought. At all events, the scope of science is now so great that it no longer escapes the dialectic comprehension. But it will simplify the process if it is remembered that the results in which these discoveries are comprehended are ideas, that the art of operating with ideas is not inborn, moreover, and is not vouchsafed every day to the ordinary mind, but requires actual thought, and this thought has a long history crammed with experiences, neither more nor less than the accumulated experiences of investigation into nature. By these means, then, it learns how to appropriate the results of fifteen hundred years development of philosophy, it gets rid of any separate natural philosophy which stands above or alongside of it and the limited method of thought brought over from English empiricism.

London, 22nd September, 1885.

III

The following new edition is, with the exception of a very few changes in form of expression, a reproduction of the former. Only in one chapter, namely in the Xth. of the Second Section (that on Critical History) I have allowed some important emendations, for the following reasons. As has been stated already in the preface to the second edition, this chapter is in all its essentials, the work of Marx. In its first form, which was intended as an article in a review, I was compelled to abbreviate the manuscript of Marx very much, particularly in those points in which the criticism of Herr Duehring's propositions is subordinate to the particular development of the history of economics. But these are just the portions of the manuscript which constitute the greatest and most important of, as regards its permanent interest, part of the work. The places in which Marx gives their appropriate place in the genesis of political economy to such writers as Petty, North, Locke and Hume, I consider myself obliged to give as literally and completely as possible, and still more so, his explanation of the "economic tableaux" by Quesnay, the insoluble riddle of the sphinx to all economists. I have omitted however that part which dealt solely with the writings of Herr Duehring as far as the connection permitted. For the rest, I am perfectly well satisfied with the extent to which the views represented in this work, have made their way into the minds of the working class and the scientists throughout the world since the publication of the former edition.

F. ENGELS.

London, 23d May, 1894.

CHAPTER III

INTRODUCTION

I. In General

Modern socialism is in its essence the product of the existence on the one hand of the class antagonisms which are dominant in modern society, between the property possessors and those who have no property and between the wage workers and the bourgeois; and, on the other, of the anarchy which is prevalent in modern production. In its theoretical form however it appears as a development of the fundamental ideas of the great French philosophers of the eighteenth century. Like every new theory it was obliged to attach itself to the existing philosophy however deeply its roots were embedded in the economic fact.

The great men in France who cleared the minds of the people for the coming revolution were themselves uncompromisingly revolutionary. They did not recognise outside authority of any kind whatsoever. Religion, natural science, society, the state, all were subjected to the most unsparing criticism, and everything was compelled to justify its existence before the judgment seat of reason or perish. Reason was established as the one and universal measure. It was the time when, as Hegel said, the world was turned upside down, first in the sense that the human mind and the principles arrived at by process of thought were claimed as the foundations of all human actions and social relations, but later also, in the wider sense, that the reality which con-

INTRODUCTION

tradicted these theories had indeed to be turned upside down. All forms of society and the state existent heretofore, all survivals of old notions, were thrown into the lumber room as unreasonable. Up to that time the world had only allowed itself to be led by prejudice. All that had been done deserved merely pity and contempt. Now for the first time day broke: from now on, superstition, injustice, tyranny and privilege should be replaced by eternal truth, eternal justice, equality founded on natural rights and the inalienable rights of man.

We now know that the rule of reason was nothing more than the rule of the bourgeoisie idealised, that eternal right found its realisation in bourgeois justice, that equality was materialised in bourgeois equality before the law, that when the rights of man were proclaimed bourgeois rights of property were proclaimed at one and the same time, and that the state of reason, Rousseau's Social Contract, could only come into existence as the bourgeois democratic republic. To such a slight extent could the great thinkers of the eighteenth century, just as their predecessors, prevail over the limits which their own epoch had placed upon them.

But besides the antagonism between feudal baron and bourgeois there existed the general antagonism between the robbers and the robbed, between the rich idlers and the toiling poor. It was just this antagonism which made it possible for the leaders of the bourgeoisie to pose as the representatives not merely of a special class but of the whole of suffering humanity. Furthermore the bourgeoisie was saddled with an antithesis right from the start. Capitalists cannot exist without laborers, and, in proportion, as the members of the gilds in the Middle Ages developed into the modern bourgeois, the journey-

LANDMARKS OF SCIENTIFIC SOCIALISM

men of the gilds and the day laborers, on their part, developed into the proletariat. And though the bourgeois, as a general rule, might claim to represent also the interests of the different working classes of the period, still, independent movements of the latter classes broke out in connection with each great movement on the part of the bourgeoisie; such working classes being the more or less developed predecessors of the modern proletariat. Thus there came into being at the time of the German Reformation and the Peasant War, the party of Thomas Munzer, in the great English Revolution the Levellers, and in the great French Revolution, Baboeuf.

Besides these revolutionary demonstrations of a class still undeveloped, occurred certain theoretical manifestations of a corresponding nature. Thus in the sixteenth and seventeenth centuries, utopian pictures of an ideal social condition, in the eighteenth century, absolutely communistic theories (Morelly and Mably). The demand for equality was confined no longer to political rights, it had to be extended to the social condition of individuals; the demand was made for the abolition not merely of class privileges but of class distinctions also. An ascetic communism patterned on that of Sparta was the first form which the new teachings assumed. Then came the three great utopians — Saint Simon, in whose eyes bourgeois aims possessed a certain merit as well as those of the proletariat: then Fourier and Owen, who, in the land of the most highly developed capitalistic production, and under the influence of the antagonisms which arise therefrom, developed in direct relation to French materialism their proposals which tended to the abolition of class distinctions.

One common feature pertaining to all the three is the fact that they did not appear as the representatives of

INTRODUCTION

the interests of the proletariat which had been in the meantime developed through the historical process. Like the philosophers, their ambition is not to free a particular class but the whole world. Like them they wish to introduce the government of reason and eternal justice. But there is a world of difference between their government and that of the philosophers. According to the philosophers, the bourgeois world as it exists is unreasonable and unjust and is destined for the rubbish heap, just as feudalism and all other earlier forms of society. The reason that true justice and reason have not dominated the world is because up to the present man has not properly comprehended them. That a man of genius has appeared and that the truth concerning these things should have now been made clear are not results arising from a combination of historical progress and necessity, but a mere piece of luck. He might just as well have been born five hundred years earlier and saved mankind the mistakes, conflicts and sorrows of five hundred years.

This is actually the idea of all English and French socialists and of the earlier German socialists, Weitling included. According to this view, socialism is the expression of absolute truth, reason, and justice, and only has to be perceived in order to vanquish the world by reason of its truth. Hence, absolute truth, reason, and justice vary according to each founder of a school, and therefore with each one, the variety of absolute truth, reason and justice is dependent, in turn, upon the subjective temperament of that founder, his conditions of life, the extent of his knowledge and mental discipline, so that in this conflict of absolute truths there is no possible solution save that they rub each other smooth by mutual contact. Hence nothing could result from

LANDMARKS OF SCIENTIFIC SOCIALISM

it except a sort of eclectic, average socialism, which is, as a matter of fact, up to the present, the prevailing notion in the minds of the great majority of socialist agitators in France and England — a mixture admitting of manifold shades, of a few notable critical utterances, economic teachings and pictures of a future state of society by leaders of different sects, a mixture which flows all the easier in proportion as the sharp precise corners are rubbed off the separate notions in the stream of debates, just as pebbles become round in a brook.

In order that a science can be made out of socialism it is first necessary that it be placed on a sound basis.

Meanwhile, close to and just after the French philosophy of the eighteenth century, the new German philosophy arose and culminated in Hegel. Its greatest service was the restoration of the dialectic as the highest form of thought. The old Greek philosophers were all natural dialecticians, and the most universal intellect among them, Aristotle, was already the discoverer of the essential forms of dialectic thought. On the other hand, subsequent philosophy although in it there were brilliant exponents of the dialectic (e. g. Descartes and Spinoza), was more and more involved in the socalled metaphysical mode of thought, chiefly owing to English influence which completely mastered the French philosophers, at least of the eighteenth century. Outside of the strict frontiers of philosophy, masterpieces of the dialectic might be found occasionally of which I can only recall " Rameau's Nephew " by Diderot, and the treatise upon the origin of human inequality by Rousseau.

We now give briefly the essential features of the two modes of thought: we will return to them more fully later.

If we examine nature, the history of man or our own

INTRODUCTION

intellectual activities, we have presented to us an endless coil of interrelations and changes in which nothing is constant whatever be its nature, time or position, but every thing is in motion, suffers change, and passes away. This original, naïve and very nearly correct philosophy of the world is that of the old Greek philosophers and was first put in a very clear form by Heraclitus. Everything is and yet is not, since everything is in a state of flux, is comprehended as undergoing constant modification, as eternally existing and disappearing. But this philosophy, correct as it is as regards phenomena in general, viewed as a picture, is insufficient to explain the individual phenomena of which the picture of the universe is composed, and as long as we cannot do that we are not clear about the general picture. In order to study these individual phenomena we are obliged to take them out of their natural or social connection, and examine each of them by itself according to its own form and its particular origin and development. This is the task of natural science and historical investigation, branches of discovery to which the Greeks of classical times assigned a subordinate place for very good reasons, since they, first of all, had to collect the material. The beginning of an exact observation of nature was made first by the Greeks of the Alexandrine period, and was later developed further by the Arabs in the Middle Ages. True natural science hence dates from the second half of the fifteenth century, and from then on has advanced at a constantly growing rate. The dissection of nature into its separate parts, the separation of different natural events and natural conditions into certain classes, the examination of the interiors of organic bodies with respect to their manifold anatomical forms, furnished the fundamental reasons for the progress in a knowledge of nature which the last four hundred years have brought in their train. But it has caused us occasionally to drop into the habit of regarding natural phenomena and events as entities, apart from the great universal interrelations, and therefore not as moving but quiescent, not as changeable in their essence but fixed and constant, not in their life but in their death. And hence, just as happened with Bacon and Locke, this point of view has been carried over from science into philosophy, and has constituted the specially narrow view of the last century, the metaphysical mode of thought.

For the metaphysician, things and their pictures in the minds, concepts, are separate entities, one following the other without any regard to each other, stable, rigid, eternally fixed objects of investigation. The metaphysician thinks in antitheses. His conversation is "Yea, yea; Nay, nay" and whatsoever is more than these cometh of evil. For him a thing exists or it does not exist, a thing can never be itself and something else at the same time; positive and negative are mutually exclusive, cause and effect stand in stiff antagonism to each other. This method of thought seems at the first glance to be quite plausible because it is in accordance with sound common sense. But sound common sense, respectable fellow though he may be in his own home surrounded by his four walls, meets with strange adventures when he betakes himself into the wide world of investigation; and the metaphysical way of looking at things, sound and useful as it is, under given conditions, runs sooner or later into a stone wall, beyond which it is one-sided, stupid and abstract, and loses itself in insoluble contradictions. Because it omits to notice the interrelations of the individual phenomena, their existence, their coming and their going, their static

INTRODUCTION

and mobile conditions, and so to speak does not see the forest for trees. We know for example, with sufficient certainty for every day affairs, whether an animal is alive or dead, but, on closer examination, we find that this is sometimes no easy matter to decide, as jurists know very well and have gone indeed to great pains to discover a rational border line beyond which the killing of a child in the womb of its mother is murder. It is just as impossible too to fix the precise moment of death, for physiology shows that death is not a single and sudden event but a very slow process. Just so is every organic being at the same moment itself and not itself. Every moment it takes up matter coming to it from the outside and throws off other matter, every moment its body-cells die and are recreated. Indeed after a longer of shorter period the whole material of the body is renewed through the taking up of other particles of matter so that each organic being is at the same time itself and something else. We find also if we look at the matter more closely that the two poles of an antithesis, positive and negative, are just as inseparable as they are antagonistic, and that they, in spite of all their fixed antagonisms permeate each other, also that the cause and effect are concepts which can only realise themselves in relation to a particular case. However when we come to examine the separate case in its general relation to the world at large they come together and dissolve themselves in face of the working out of the universal problem, for, here, cause and effect exchange places, what was at one time and place effect becoming cause and vice versa.

All these phenomena and thought-concepts do not fit into the frame of metaphysical philosophy. According to the dialectic method of thinking which regards things

LANDMARKS OF SCIENTIFIC SOCIALISM

and their concepts in relation to their connection with each other, their concatenation, their coming into being and passing away, phenomena, like the preceding, are so many confirmations of its own philosophy. Nature is the proof of the dialectic, and we must give to modern science the credit of having furnished an extraordinary wealth and daily increasing store of material towards this proof, and thereby showing in the last instance things proceed dialectically and not in accordance with metaphysical notions. But as the scientists who have learned to think dialectically may be still easily counted, the chaos arising from the confusion between actual results and an antiquated mode of thought is thus explained, and this confusion is to-day dominant in theoretical science, and drives teachers and pupils, writers and readers to despair.

A correct notion of the universe, of the human race, as well as of the reflection of this progress in the human mind can only be had by means of the dialectic method, together with a steady observation of the change and interchange which goes on in the universe, the coming into existence and passing away, progressive and retrogressive modification.

And the later German philosophy has proceeded from this standpoint. Kant began his career in this way by abolishing Newton's conception of a stable solar system which persisted after receiving its first impulse, in favor of a historical process, to wit, the origin of the sun and all the planets from a rotating mass of nebulæ. From this concept he drew the conclusion that, granted this origin, the future dissolution of the solar system is inevitable. His theory was mathematically proved by Laplace half a century later, and half a century later still the spectroscope discovered the existence of such

INTRODUCTION

glowing masses of gas in space in different stages of condensation.

This later German philosophy found its conclusion in the philosophy of Hegel where for the first time, and this is his greatest service, the entire natural, historical and spiritual universe was regarded as a process, that is, as in constant progress, change, transformation and development, and the attempt was made to show the more subtle relations of this process and development. From this historical point of view the history of mankind no longer appeared as a barren confusion of mindless forces, all alike subject to rejection before the judgment seat of the most recently ripened philosophy, and which, at the very best, man puts out of his mind as soon as possible, but as the development-process of humanity itself, to follow the process of which, little by little, through all its ramifications, and to establish the essential laws of which, in spite of all apparent accidents, is now the task of philosophic thought.

It is immaterial at this place that Hegel did not solve this problem. His epoch-making service was to have proposed it. It is a problem, moreover, which no individual can solve. Though Hegel, next to Saint Simon, was the most universal intellect of his time he was still limited, in the first place, through the necessarily narrow grasp of his own knowledge and in addition through the limitations of the contemporary conditions of knowledge. There was a third reason, too. Hegel was an idealist, that is he regarded thought not as a mere abstract representation of real phenomena, but, on the contrary, phenomena and their development appeared to him as the representations of the Idea which existed before the world. The result was an inversion of everything, the actual interrelations of the universe were turned completely upside down, and though of these interrelations, many single ones were set out justly and correctly by Hegel, much of the detail is patched, labored, made up, in short, incorrect. The Hegelian system was, to speak briefly, a colossal miscarriage, and the last of its kind. It rested on an incurable contradiction; on the other hand, it actually proclaimed the historical conception according to which human history is a process of development, which, in its very nature, cannot find its intellectual conclusion in the discovery of a so-called absolute truth, on the other hand it declared itself to be the central idea of just such an absolute truth. An all embracing and determined knowledge of nature and history is in absolute contradiction with the foundations of dialectic thought, but it is not denied, on the contrary, it is strongly affirmed, that the systematic knowledge of the entire external world may from age to age make giant strides.

The total perversion of modern German idealism of necessity drove men to materialism, but not, and this is well worth noting, to the mere metaphysical mechanical materialism of the eighteenth century. In contradiction to the naïvely simple revolutionary pushing on one side of all earlier history, modern materialism sees in history the process of the development of society, to discover the laws of whose development is its task. In contradistinction to the conception of nature which prevailed among the French philosophers, as well as with Hegel, as something moving in a narrow circle with an eternal and unchangeable substantial form, as Newton conceived it, and with invariable species of organic beings, as Linnæus thought, materialism embraces the more recent discoveries of natural science, according to which nature has also a history in time. For the forms of the worlds, like the

INTRODUCTION

species of organisms by which they are inhabited under suitable conditions, come into being and pass away, and the cycles of their progress, in so far as it is permissible to use the term, take on eternally more magnificent dimensions. In either case it is entirely dialectic and no longer forces a static philosophy upon the other sciences. As soon as the demand is made upon each separate branch of science that it make clear its relation to things in general, and science as a whole, the individual science thereupon becomes superfluous. Of all philosophy up to the present time the only peculiar property which remains as its characteristic is the study of thought and the formal laws of thought — logic and the dialectic. All else belongs to the positive sciences of nature and history.

While the revolution in natural science was only able to be completely carried out in proportion as investigation furnished the necessary positive material, there were known a multitude of earlier historical facts which gave a distinct bias to the philosophy of history. In 1831 in Lyons the first purely working class revolt occurred. The first national working class movement, that of the English Chartists, reached its height between 1838 and 1842. The class war between the proletariat and the bourgeoisie proceeded historically in the most advanced European countries just in proportion as the newly developed greater industry has progressed, on the one hand, and the political power of the bourgeoisie on the other. The teachings of the bourgeois economists with respect to the identity of the interests of capital and labor and with respect to the universal peace and well being which would follow as a matter of course from the adoption of free trade were more and more contradicted by facts. All these things could be as little ig-

LANDMARKS OF SCIENTIFIC SOCIALISM

nored as the French and English socialism which was their theoretical though very insufficient expression. But the old idealistic philosophy of history which was as yet by no means laid aside knew nothing of class wars dependent upon material interests, and nothing of material interests, specially. Production, like all economic phenomena only occupied a subordinate position as a secondary element of the history of civilisation." The new facts, moreover rendered necessary a new investigation of all preceding history and then it became evident that all history up to then had been a history of class struggles and that these mutually conflicting classes are the results of a given method of production and distribution at a given period, in a word, of the economic conditions of that epoch. Hence, that the economic structure of society at a given time furnishes the real foundations upon which the entire superstructure of political and juristic institutions as well as the religious, philosophical and other abstract notions of a given period are to be explained in the last instance. Idealism was thereupon driven from its last refuge, the philosophy of history; a materialistic philosophy of history was set up, and the path was discovered by which the consciousness of man could be shown as springing from his existence rather than his existence from his consciousness.

But the socialism which had existed so far was just as incompatible with the materialistic conception of history as was the naturalistic French materialism with the dialectic and the modern discoveries in natural science. The then existing socialism criticised the prevailing capitalistic methods of production and their results but it could not explain them and thus could not match itself against them, it could only brush them on one side as

INTRODUCTION

being bad. But it was necessary to show, on the one hand, the capitalistic methods of production in their historical connection, and their necessity at a given historical epoch and therefore the necessity of their ultimate disappearance. On the other hand their inner character had to be explained and this was all the more concealed for criticism had up to then been chiefly engaged in pointing out the evil results flowing from them rather than in destroying the thing itself. This was made clear by the discovery of surplus value.

It was shown that the appropriation of unpaid labor is the basis of the capitalistic mode of production and the robbery of the worker is carried out by its means; that the capitalist, although he buys the labor-force of the worker at the full value which it possesses in the market as a commodity, yet derives more from it than he has paid for it, and that in the last instance this surplus creates the total amount of value from which the capital steadily increasing in the hands of the capitalistic class is amassed. The phenomenon not only of capitalistic production but of the creation of capital has thus been explained.

For these two great discoveries, the materialistic conception of history and the disclosure of the mystery of capitalistic production we must thank Marx. Granted these, socialism became a science, which thereupon had to busy itself in the working out of these ideas in their individual aspects and connections.

Thus matters stood in the realm of theoretical socialism and the dead philosophy (of metaphysics Ed.) when Herr Eugene Duehring, with no slight impressement sprang up before the public and announced that he had accomplished a complete revolution in political economy and socialism.

Let us now see what Herr Duehring promises and — how he keeps his promis,

II. *What Herr Duehring Has to Say*

Up to now, the notable writings of Herr Duehring are his " Course of Philosophy," his " Course of Political and Social Science " and his " Critical History of Political Economy and Socialism." The first work is the one which particularly claims our attention.

Right on the first page Herr Duehring announces himself as " one who claims to represent this power (of philosophy) at the present time and its unfolding in the undiscoverable future." He discovers himself, therefore, as the one true philosopher for the present and the hidden future. Whoso differs from him differs from truth. Many people even before Herr Duehring, have thought this about themselves or something like it, but, with the exception of Richard Wagner, he is the first who has allowed himself to say it right out. And, as a matter of fact, the truth, as it is handled by him is " a final truth of the last instance." Herr Duehring's philosophy is " the natural system, or the philosophy of reality. . . . Reality is so understood as to exclude every sudden impulse towards an unreal and subjectively limited comprehension of the universe." The philosophy is therefore so shaped as to exclude Herr Duehring himself from the somewhat obvious limitations of his own personal, subjective narrowness. It is quite necessary to explain how this miracle is worked, if he is in a position to lay down unquestionable

INTRODUCTION

truths of the last instance, though, for our part, we cannot discover any particular merit in them. This "natural system of valuable knowledge" has "with great profundity established the foundation forms of existence." Out of his real critical attitude proceed the elements of a real critical philosophy, based on the realities of nature and life, which does not allow of any merely imaginary horizon but in its mighty revolutionary progress opens up the earth and heaven of external and inner nature; it is a "new method of thought" and its results are "from the bottom up, peculiar results and philosophies . . . system-shaping ideas . . . fixed truths." We have in it before us "a work which must seek its force in the concentrated initiative," whatever that may mean; an "investigation reaching to the roots . . . a rooted science . . . a severely scientific conception of things and men . . . a comprehensive thorough effort of the mind . . . a creative sketch of suppositions and conclusions from overmastering ideas . . . the absolute fundamental." In the realm of political economy he gives us not only "historical and systematic comprehensive efforts" of which the historical are moreover distinguished by "my presentation of history in the grand style" and those in political economy have produced "creative movements," but closes with a special completely elaborated scientific scheme for a future society which is "the actual fruit of a clear and basic theory," and is therefore just as free from the possibility of error and as individual as Duehring's philosophy . . . for "only in that socialistic structure which I have disclosed in my "Course of Political and Social Science" can a true ownership arise in place of the present apparent private property which rests on force such an ownership as must be recognised in the future."

These flowers of rhetoric from the praises of Herr Duehring by Herr Duehring might be increased tenfold with ease. They must cause a doubt to arise in the mind of the reader whether he is reading the words of a philosopher or of a — but we must ask him to withhold his judgment until he shall have learnt the aforesaid grasp of the root of things by a closer acquaintance. We only quote the foregoing flowery remarks to show that we have to do with no ordinary philosopher and socialist who simply speaks what he thinks and leaves the future to decide with respect to their value, but with an extraordinary personality like the Pope whose individual teachings must be received if the damnable sin of heresy is to be avoided. We have not by any means to deal with the kind of work which abounds in all the socialist writings, and the later German ones, in particular, works in which people of varying calibre seek to explain in the most naïve fashion their notions of things in general and for an answer to whom there is more or less material available. But whatever may be the literary or scientific deficiencies of these works their goodwill towards socialism is always manifest. On the other hand, Herr Duehring presents us with statements which he declares to be final truths of the last instance, exclusive truths, according to which any other opinion is absolutely false. Thus he owns the only scientific methods of investigation, and all others are unscientific in comparison. Either he is right and we are face to face with the greatest genius of our time, the first superhuman, because infallible, man; or he is wrong, and then, since our judgment may always be at fault, benevolent regard for his possible

INTRODUCTION

good intentions would be the deadliest insult to Herr Duehring.

When one is in possession of final truths of the last instance and the only absolutely scientific knowledge one must have a certain contempt for the rest of erring and unscientific humanity. We cannot therefore be surprised that Herr Duehring employs very abusive terms with regard to his predecessors, and that only a few exceptional people, recognised by him as great men, find favor in face of his comprehension of fundamental truths.

(Then follows a list of the epithets applied by Duehring to philosophers, naturalists, Darwin, in particular, and to the socialist writers. This list has been omitted as it contributes nothing of value to the general discussion and is only useful for the particular controversial matter in hand. Ed.)

And so on — and this is only a hastily gathered bouquet of flowers from Herr Duehring's rose garden. It will be understood that if these amiable insults which should be forbidden Herr Duehring on any grounds of politeness, are found somewhat disreputable and unpleasant, they are, still, final truths of the last instance. Even now we shall guard against any doubt of his profundity because we might otherwise be forbidden to discover the particular category of idiots to which we belong. We have but considered it our duty on the one hand to give what Herr Duehring calls " The quintessence of a modest mode of expression," and on the other hand, to show that in Herr Duehring's eyes the objectionableness of his predecessors is no less firmly established than his own infallibility. Accordingly if all this is actually true we bow in reverence humbly before the mighty genius of modern times.

CHAPTER IV

PHILOSOPHY

Apriorism

Philosophy is, according to Herr Duehring, the development of the highest forms of consciousness of the world and life, and embraces, in a wider sense, the principles of all knowledge and volition. Wherever a series of perceptions, or motives or a group of forms of life becomes a matter of consideration in the human mind the principles which underly these forms, of necessity, become an object of philosophy. These principles are single, or, up to the present, have been considered as single ingredients out of which are composed the complexities of knowledge and volition. Like the chemical composition of material bodies, the entire universe may be also resolved into fundamental forms and elements. These elementary constituents and principles serve, when once discovered, not only for the known tangible world but for that also, which is unknown and inaccessible. Philosophical principles therefore constitute the last complement required by the sciences in order that they may become a uniform system by means of which nature and human life are explained. In addition to the examination of the fundamental forms of all existence, philosophy has only two particular objects of investigation, Nature and Humanity. Hence our material may be classified into three main groups,— a general scheme of the universe, the teaching of the principles of nature and finally the principles which regulate Humanity. This

PHILOSOPHY

arrangement at the same time comprises an inner logical order, for the formal principles which are true for all existence take precedence, and the concrete realms in which these principles display themselves follow in the gradation of their successive arrangements. So far, this is Herr Duehring's conception of things given almost in his very words.

He is therefore engaged with principles, formal conceptions, which are subjective and not derived from the knowledge of external phenomena, but which are applied to Nature and Humanity, as the principles according to which Nature and Humanity must regulate themselves. But how are these subjective principles derived? From thought itself? No, for Herr Duehring himself says: the purely ideal realm is limited to logical arrangements and mathematical conceptions (which latter as we shall later see is false). Logical arrangements can only be referred to forms of thought, but we are engaged here only with forms of existence, the external world, and these forms can never be created by thought nor derived from it but only from the external world. Hereupon the entire matter undergoes a change. We see that principles are not the starting point of investigation but the conclusion of it, they are not to be applied to nature and history but are derived from them. Nature and Humanity are not steered by principles, but principles are, on the other hand, only correct so far as they correspond with nature and history. That is just the materialistic conception of the matter, and the opposite, that of Herr Duehring is the idealistic conception, it turns things upside down and constructs a real world out of the world of thought, arrangements, plans and categories existing from everlasting before the world, just like Hegelianism.

LANDMARKS OF SCIENTIFIC SOCIALISM

As a matter of fact, we prefer Hegel's "Encyclopedia," with all its fever phantoms, to the "final truths of the last instance" of Herr Duehring. In the first place, according to Herr Duehring we have the general scheme of the universe which by Hegel is called "logic." Then according to both of them we have the application of this scheme to nature by means of the logical categories, the philosophy of nature, and finally their application to Humanity, by what Hegel calls "the Philosophy of the Spirit." "The inner logical arrangement" of Duehring's scheme brings us therefore logically back to Hegel's "Encyclopedia" from which it is taken with a fidelity which would move that Wandering Jew of the Hegelian school, Professor Michelet of Berlin, to tears.

Such a result follows if one takes it for granted that "consciousness," "thought," is something which has existed from the beginning in contradistinction to nature. It would then be of the greatest importance to bring consciousness and Nature, thought and existence, into harmony, to harmonise the laws of thought and the laws of Nature. But one enquires further what are thought and consciousness and whence do they originate. It is consequently discovered that they are products of the brain of man, and that Humanity is itself a product of nature which has developed in and along with its environment; wherefore it becomes self-apparent that the products of the brain of man being themselves, in the last instance, natural products, do not contradict all the rest of Nature but correspond with it.

But Herr Duehring cannot allow so simple a treatment of the subject. He thinks not only in the name of Humanity which would be quite a large affair, but in the name of the conscious and thinking beings of the whole universe. Indeed, it would be "a degradation of the

PHILOSOPHY

foundation concepts of knowledge and consciousness if one should wish to exclude or even to throw suspicion upon their sovereign value and undoubted claims to truth by means of the epithet 'human.'" In order that there may be no suspicion that upon some heavenly body or other twice two may make five, Herr Duehring does not venture to call thought a human attribute, and therefore he is obliged to separate it from the only true foundation on which it rests, as far as we are concerned, namely, from man and nature, and thereby falls, without any possibility of getting out, into an "ideology" which causes him to play baby to Hegel. It is self-evident that one cannot build materialistic doctrines on foundations so ideological. We shall see later that Herr Duehring is compelled to push nature to the front as a conscious agent and, therefore, as that, which people in plain English call God.

Indeed, our philosopher had other motives in shifting the foundation of reality from the material world to that of thought. The knowledge of this general scheme of the universe, of these formal principles of being is just the foundation of Herr Duehring's philosophy. If we derive the scheme of the universe not from our own brain, but merely by means of our own brain, from the material world, we need no philosophy, but simply knowledge of the world and what occurs in it, and the results of this knowledge likewise do not constitute a philosophy, but positive science. In such a case, however, Herr Duehring's entire book would have been love's labor lost.

Further, if no philosophy, as such, is longer required there is no longer the necessity of any philosophy of nature even. The view that all the phenomena of nature stand in systematic mutual relations compels science to

LANDMARKS OF SCIENTIFIC SOCIALISM

prove this systematic interconnection in all respects, in single cases as well as in the entirety. But an appropriate creative, scientific representation of this mutual connection in such a way as to show the composition of an exact thought-picture of the system of the universe in which we live remains not only for us but for all time an impossibility. Should such a final conclusive system of the interconnection of the various activities of the universe, physical, as well as intellectual and historical, ever be brought to completion at any point of time in the history of the human race, human knowledge would forthwith come to an end and future historical progress would be cut off from the very moment in which society was directed in accordance with the system, which would be an absurdity, mere nonsense.

Man is therefore confronted by a contradiction, on the one hand he is obliged to study the interconnections of the world-system exhaustively, and, on the other hand, he is unable to fully accomplish the task either as regards himself or as regards the system of nature. This contradiction, however, does not consist solely in the nature of the two factors World and Man; it is the main lever also of universal intellectual progress and is solved every day and for ever in an endless progressive development of humanity, just as mathematical problems find their solution in an endless progression of a recurring decimal. As a matter of fact also every concept of the universe is subject to objective limitations owing to the conditions of historical knowledge, and subjectively in addition owing to the physical and mental make up of the author of the concept. But Herr Duehring exhibits a mode of thought which is confined in its application to a limited and subjective idea of the universe. We saw earlier that he was omnipresent, in all

PHILOSOPHY

possible forms of the universe, now we see that he is omniscient. He has solved the final problems of science and has nailed up tight all future knowledge.

Herr Duehring considers that he can, as with the fundamental forms of existence, produce aprioristically by means of his own cogitations the whole of pure mathematics without making any use of the experience which is afforded us in the objective world. In pure mathematics the understanding is engaged " in its own free creations and imaginations "; the concepts of number and form are " self-sufficient objects proceeding from themselves " and so have " a value independent of individual experience and actual objective reality."

That pure mathematics has a significance independent of particular individual experience is quite true as are also the established facts of all the sciences and indeed of all facts. The magnetic poles, the formation of water from oxygen and hydrogen, the fact that Hegel is dead and that Herr Duehring is alive, are facts independent of my experience or that of any other single individual, and will be independent of that of Herr Duehring himself, as soon as he shall sleep the sleep of the just. But in pure mathematics the mind is not by any means engaged with its own creations and imaginings. The concepts of number and form have only come to us by the way of the real world. The ten fingers on which men count and thereby performed the first arithmetical calculations are anything but a free creation of the mind. To count not only requires objects capable of being counted but the ability, when these objects are regarded, of subtracting all qualities from them except number and this ability is the product of long historical development of actual experience. The concept form is, like that of number, derived exclusively

LANDMARKS OF SCIENTIFIC SOCIALISM

from the external world and is not a purely mental product. To it things possessed of shape were necessary and these shapes men compared until the concept form was arrived at. Pure mathematics considers the shapes and quantities of things in the actual world, very real objects. The fact that these objects appear in a very abstract form only superficially conceals their origin in the world of external nature. In order to understand these forms and qualities in their purity it is necessary to separate them from their content and thus one gets the point, without dimensions, the line, without breadth and thickness, a and b, x and y, constants and variables, and we finally first arrive at independent creations of the imagination and intellect, imaginary magnitudes. Also the apparent derivation of mathematical magnitudes from each other does not prove their aprioristic origin, but only their rational interconnection. Before one attained the concept that the form of a cylinder was derived from the revolution of a rectangle round one of its sides, he must have examined a number of rectangles and cylinders even if of imperfect form. Like all sciences, mathematics has sprung from the necessities of men, from the measurement of land and the content of vessels, from the calculation of time and mechanics. But, as in every department of thought, at a certain stage of development, laws are abstracted from the actual phenomena, are separated from them and set over against them, as something independent of them, as laws, which apparently come from the outside, in accordance with which the material world must necessarily conduct itself. So, it has happened in society and the state, so, and not otherwise, pure mathematics though borrowed from the world is applied to the world, and

PHILOSOPHY

though it only shows a portion of its component factors is all the better applicable on that account.

But as Herr Duehring imagines that the whole of pure mathematics can be derived from the mathematical axioms, "which according to purely logical concepts are neither capable of proof nor in need of any, and without empirical ingredients anywhere and that these can be applied to the universe, he likewise imagines, in the first place, the foundation forms of being, the single ingredients of all knowledge, the axioms of philosophy, to be produced by the intellect of man; he imagines also that he can derive the whole of philosophy or plan of the universe from these, and that his sublime genius can compel us to accept this, his conception of nature and humanity. Unfortunately nature and humanity are not constituted like the Prussians of the Manteuffel regime of 1850.

The axioms of mathematics are expressions of the most elementary ideas which mathematics must borrow from logic. They may be reduced to two.

(1) The whole is greater than its part; this statement is mere tautology, since the quantitatively limited concept, "part," necessarily refers to the concept, "whole,"— in that "part" signifies no more than that the quantitative "whole" is made up of quantitative "parts." Since the so-called axiom merely asserts this much we are not a step further. This can be shown to be a tautology if we say "The whole is that which consists of several parts—a part is that several of which make up a whole, therefore the part is less than the whole." Where the barrenness of the repetition shows the lack of content all the more strongly.

(2) If two magnitudes are equal to a third they are equal to one another; this statement is, as Hegel has

LANDMARKS OF SCIENTIFIC SOCIALISM

shown, a conclusion, upon the correctness of which all logic depends, and which is demonstrated therefore outside of pure mathematics. The remaining axioms with regard to equality and inequality are merely logical extensions of this conclusion. Such barren statements are not enticing either in mathematics or anywhere else. To proceed we must have realities, conditions and forms taken from real material things; representations of lines, planes, angles, polygons, spheres, etc., are all borrowed from reality, and it is just naive ideology to believe the mathematicians, who assert that the first line was made by causing a point to progress through space, the first plane by means of the movement of a line, and the first solid by revolving a plane, etc. Even speech rebels against this idea. A mathematical figure of three dimensions is called a solid — corpus solidum — and hence, according to the Latin, a body capable of being handled. It has a name derived, therefore, by no means from the independent play of imagination but from solid reality.

But to what purpose is all this prolixity? After Herr Duehring has enthusiastically proclaimed the independence of pure mathematics of the world of experience, their apriorism, their connection with free creation and imagination, he says " it will be readily seen that these mathematical elements (number, magnitude, time, space, geometric progression), are therefore ideal forms with relation to absolute magnitudes and therefore something quite empiric, no matter to what species they belong." But " mathematical general notions are, apart from experience, nevertheless capable of sufficient characterization," which latter proceeds, more or less, from each abstraction, but does not by any means prove that it is not deprived from the actual. In the scheme of the

PHILOSOPHY

universe of our author pure mathematics originated in pure thought, in his philosophy of nature it is derived from the external world and then set apart from it. What are we then to believe?

The Scheme of the Universe.

"All-comprehending existence is sole. It is sufficient to itself and has nothing above or below it. To associate a second existence with it would be to make it just what it is not, a part of a constituent or all-embracing whole. When we conceive of our idea of soleness as a frame there is nothing which can enter into this, nothing which retains twofoldness can enter into this concept of unity. But nothing can alienate itself from this concept of unity. The essence of all thought consists in uniting the elements of consciousness in a unity. The indivisible concept of the universe has arisen by comprehending everything, and the universe, as the word signifies, is recognised as something in which everything is united into one unity."

So far Herr Duehring is quoted. The mathematical method, "Everything must be decided on simple axiomatic foundation principles, just as if it were concerned with the simple principles of mathematics," this method is for the first time here applied.

"The all-embracing existence is sole." If tautology, simple repetition in the predicate of what has been stated in the subject, if this constitutes an axiom, then we have a splendid specimen. In the subject Herr Duehring tells us that existence comprehends everything, in the predicate he explains intrepidly that there is nothing outside it. What a system-shaping thought. It is indeed system-shaping until we find six lines further down that Herr Duehring has transformed the sole-

LANDMARKS OF SCIENTIFIC SOCIALISM

ness of being by means of our idea of unity into its one-ness. As the work of all thought consists in the bringing together of all thought into a unity so is existence, as soon as it is conceived, thought of as a unity, an indivisible concept of the universe, and because existence so conceived is the sole universal concept, so is real existence, the real universe, just as much an indivisible unity, and consequently " the beings in the beyond have no further place as soon as the mind has learned to comprehend existence in the homogeneous universality."

That is a campaign with which in comparison Austerlitz and Jena, Koeniggratz and Sedan sink in insignificance. In a couple of expressions after we have set the first axiom moving we have abolished, put away, and destroyed all the inhabitants of the spirit-world, God, the heavenly hierarchies, heaven, hell and purgatory as well as the immortality of the soul.

How do we arrive at the idea of the unity of existence from that of its soleness? As a matter of fact, we generally conceive it. As we spread out our idea of unity as a frame around it the concept of existence becomes the concept of unity., for the existence of all thought consists in the bringing of elements of consciousness into unity.

This last statement is simply false. In the first place thought consists in the decomposition of objects of consciousness into their elements as well as in the uniting of mutually connected elements into a unity. There can be no synthesis without analysis. In the second place, thought can, without error, only bring those elements of consciousness into a unity in which or in the actual prototypes of which this unity already existed beforehand. If I comprehend a shoebrush under the

PHILOSOPHY

class mammal, it does not thereupon become a milk-giver. The unity of existence is therefore just the thing which had to be proved in order to justify his concept of thought as a unity, and if Herr Duehring assures us that he regards existence as a unity and not as twofold he tells us nothing more than that he himself personally thinks so.

To give a clear explanation of his method of reasoning, it is as follows, "I begin with existence. Therefore I think of existence. The idea of existence is an idea of unity. Thought and existence must therefore belong together, they answer one another, they mutually cover each other. Therefore existence is in reality a unity and there are no beings beyond." But if Herr Duehring had spoken thus plainly instead of entertaining us with oracular statements, the ideology of his argument would have been completely exposed. To attempt to undertake to prove from the identity of thought and existence the reality of the result of thought, that indeed were one of the fever-phantoms of a Hegel.

If his entire method of proof were really correct Herr Duehring would not have gained a single point over the spiritists. The spiritists would curtly reply, "The universe is simple from our standpoint also. The division into the hither and the beyond only exists from our special earthly original sin standpoint. In its essence, that is God, the entire universe is a unity." And they will take Herr Duehring with them to his beloved heavenly bodies. and will show him one or more where no original sin can be found. and where there is therefore no antagonism between the hither and the beyond, and the oneness of the universe is a demand of faith.

The most comical thing about the matter is that Herr Duehring in order to prove the non-existence of God from his concept of existence, furnishes the ontological proof of God's existence. This runs as follows — If we think of God we think of Him as the concept of complete perfection. To the idea of perfection existence is a first essential, since a non-existent being is of necessity imperfect. We must therefore add existence to the perfections of God. Therefore God must exist. Thus Herr Duehring reasons exactly. If we think of existence we think of it as a concept. What is united into a concept is a unity, therefore existence would not correspond with its concept if it were not a unity. Therefore it must be a unity, therefore there is no God, etc.

If we speak of existence and merely of existence, the unity can only consist in this that all objects with which it is concerned are — exist. They are comprised under the unity of this common existence, and no other, and the general dictum that they all exist cannot give them any further qualities, common or not common, but excludes all such from consideration in advance. For as soon as we take a step beyond the simple fact that existence is common to all things, the distinctions between these separate things engage our attention, and if these differences consist in this that some are black, some white, some alive, others not alive, some hither and some beyond, we cannot conclude therefrom that mere existence can be imputed to all of them alike.

The unity of the universe does not consist in its existence, although its existence is a presumption of its unity, since it must first exist before it can be a unit. Existence beyond the boundary line of our horizon is an open question. The real unity of the universe consists in its materiality, and this is established, not by a pair of juggling phrases but by means of a long and difficult development of philosophy and natural science.

PHILOSOPHY

With respect to the subject in hand; the existence which Herr Duehring presents to us is "not that pure existence which is self sufficient and without any other qualities, in fact, only representing the antithesis of no-idea or absence-of-idea." Now we shall very soon see that the universe of Herr Duehring has its origin simultaneously with an existence which is without essential differentiation, progress or change, and is therefore merely in fact a contradiction of absence of thought, therefore really nothing. From this non-existence is developed the present differentiated, changeable universe which represents progressive growth; and when we grasp this idea, only by virtue of this eternal change do we arrive at "the concept of the self sufficing, universal existence." We have therefore now the concept of existence on a higher plane where it comprises within itself stability as well as change, being as well as development. Arrived at this point we find that "species and genera in fact the special and the general, are the simplest forms of differentiation, without which the constitution of things cannot be grasped."

But this is a means of distinguishing quality and after a discussion of this part of the subject we proceed "Over against the idea of species stands the idea of the whole, a homogeneity, as it were, in which no differentiation of species can longer be found," so we pass from quality to quantity and this is always "capable of measurement."

Let us compare this "clear analysis of the actual, universal scheme of things" and its "real, critical standpoint" with the fever-phantasies of a Hegel. We find that Hegel's "Logic" begins with existence as does that of Herr Duehring; that existence displays itself as nothing, as with Herr Duehring; that out of this not-be-

LANDMARKS OF SCIENTIFIC SOCIALISM

ing, a leap is made into being, and that existence is the result of this, that is a more complete and higher form of being, as with Herr Duehring. Being leads to quality, quality to quantity, just as with Herr Duehring. And in order that no essential shall be lacking Herr Duehring tells us elsewhere " from the realm of absence of sensation man leaps to that of sensation in spite of all the quantitative steps with but one qualitative leap . . . from which we can show that he is entirely differentiated from the mere gradation of one and the same quality." This is just the Hegelian standard of measurement according to which mere quantitative expansion or contraction causes a sudden qualitative change at a given point, as for example with heated or cooled water, there are points where the spring into a new set of conditions is fulfilled under normal circumstances, and where therefore quantity suddenly changes into quality.

Our investigation has likewise sought to penetrate to the deepest roots, and discovers the rooted Duehring foundations to be the " fever-phantasies " of a Hegel, the categories of the Hegelian logic, in the first place, teachings in regard to existence after the antique Hegelian method, and an ineffective cloak of plagiarism.

And not content with purloining the whole scheme of existence from his despised predecessors, Herr Duehring after giving the above example of a change of quantity into quality has the coolness to say of Marx, " Is it not comical, this appeal (of Marx) to Hegelian confusion and mistiness, that quantity changes into quality." Confused mixture, who changes his ground, who is a comical fellow Herr Duehring?

All these pretty little statements are not only not " axiomatic utterances " according to label, but are simply taken from foreign sources, that is, from Hegel's

PHILOSOPHY

"Logic." Of a truth there is not revealed in the whole chapter the shadow of any "inner connection," except so far as it is borrowed from Hegel, and the whole talk about stability and change finally runs out into mere garrulity on the subject of time and space.

From existence Hegel comes to substance, to the dialectic. Here he treats of reflex-movements, antagonisms and contradictions, positive and negative for example, and thence proceeds to causality, or the conditions of cause and effect and closes with necessity. Herr Duehring does not vary this method. What Hegel calls the "doctrines of existence" Herr Duehring has translated into "logical properties of existence." These exist, above all else in the antagonism of forces, in antithesis, Herr Duehring denies the antithesis in toto, but we shall return to this matter later. Then he proceeds to causality and thence to necessity. If Herr Duehring says of himself, "I do not philosophise from a cage," he must mean that he philosophises in a cage, the cage of the Hegelian arrangement of categories.

CHAPTER V

NATURAL PHILOSOPHY

Time and Space

We now come to natural philosophy. Here again Herr Duehring takes it upon himself to be dissatisfied with his predecessors. He says "Natural philosophy sank so low that it became barren dregs of poetry and had fallen into the degraded rubbish of the sham philosophy of a Schelling and the like, grubbing in priestcraft and mystifying the public." Disgust has rid us of these deformities, but up to the present it has been succeeded by instability, and "what is of concern to the public at large is that the disappearance of a particularly great charlatan merely gives an opportunity to a smaller but more expert successor who repeats the production in another form." Naturalists have little desire for "a flight into the kingdom of the universe-comprehending ideas," and therefore indulge too freely in speculations which "go to pieces." Thus complete salvation must be found, and, fortunately, Herr Duehring is at hand.

In order to comprehend aright the following conclusions respecting the unfolding of the universe in time and its limitation in space, we must again turn our attention to certain portions of the "scheme of the universe."

Eternity is ascribed to existence, in agreement with Hegel, what Hegel calls "tiresome (schlecht) eternity,"

NATURAL PHILOSOPHY

and this eternity is now investigated. "The plainest form of an incontrovertible idea of eternity is the piling up of numbers unlimitedly in arithmetical progression. Just as we can give a complete unity to each number without the possibility of repetition, so at every stage of its being it progresses still further and eternity consists in the unlimited manifestation of this condition. This sufficiently conceived eternity has but one single beginning with one single direction. Although it is not material to our concept to imagine a direction opposite to that in which the progression piles up, this notion of a backward moving eternity is only a hasty picture drawn by the imagination. Since it must necessarily run in a contrary direction, it would have behind it in each instance an endless succession of numbers. But this would be inadmissible as constituting the contradiction of a calculated infinity of numbers, and so it seems absurd to imagine a second direction of eternity."

The first conclusion to be drawn from this conception of eternity is that the chain of cause and effect in the universe must once have had a beginning: an endless number of causes which have followed one another endlessly is therefore unthinkable, "because innumerability is thus considered as enumerated," therefore a final cause is proved.

The second conclusion is "the law of the definite number: the accumulation of identical independent objects of an actual species is only thinkable as being made up of a definite number of these individual objects." Not only must the actual number of the heavenly bodies be definite at a given time, but the total number of all existent objects, the smallest independent particles of matter. This last necessity constitutes the real reason why no composite body is thinkable except as made up of atoms. All actual division has a fixed limit and must have it, if the contradiction of a numerated innumerability is to be avoided. On the same grounds not only must the revolutions of the sun and earth be fixed as they have occurred up to the present, even if they cannot be indicated, but all the periodical processes of nature must have had a beginning somewhere, and all the distinctions and complexities of nature which succeed each other must similarly have had an origin. This must indisputably have existed from eternity, but such an idea would be excluded if time consisted of real parts and was not arbitrarily divided to accommodate the possibilities of our understanding. It is different with time, self regarded, but the facts and phenomena of which time is made up being capable of differentiation can be enumerated. Let us conceive of a condition in which no change occurs and which undergoes no alteration in its stable identity; the time concept then becomes transformed into the general notion of existence. What is the result of piling up an empty duration of time is not discoverable. So far, Herr Duehring writes and he is not a little edified concerning the significance of these discoveries. He hopes that "it is perceived as a not insignificant truth," and later on says, "One should note the very simple phrases by which we have helped the concept of immortality and the criticism of it to a point at present unknown, through the sharpening and deepening of the simple elements of the universal conception of time and space."

We have helped! This deepening and sharpening! Who are we? In what are we manifest? Who deepens and who sharpens?

"Thesis — the world has a beginning in time and is bounded by space. Proof — If one suppose that the

NATURAL PHILOSOPHY

world has no beginning in time he is bound to grant infinity to each point of time, and so an infinite succession of things has passed away in the universe. But infinity of a series consists in the impossibility of its completion by successive syntheses. Therefore an eternal progression of the world is impossible. Hence a beginning of the world is a necessary condition of its existence, which was to be proved. Let us take the other concept. The world now appears as an eternal given whole consisting of things which have a simultaneous existence. Now we can conceive of the mass of a quantity, which can only be regarded under certain conditions, in no other way than by means of the synthesis of its parts, and we conceive the totality of the quantity by means of the completed synthesis or repeated additions of the unity to itself. Thus, in order to conceive of the universe as a whole which fills all space, the successive syntheses of the parts of an infinite universe must be regarded as being completed, that is an eternity of time must in calculating all coexisting things, be regarded as having existed, but this is impossible. Therefore an unending aggregate of actual things cannot be regarded as a given whole and therefore also not as coexistent. A world is therefore extension in space which is not unlimited and which has therefore bounds. And this was the second thing to be proved."

These statements are copied from a well-known book which made its appearance in 1781 and is entitled " The Critique of Pure Reason," by Immanuel Kant. They can be read there in Part I, Division 2, second section, second part. "First Antinomy of Pure Reason." To Herr Duehring alone remains the name and fame of having pasted the law of fixed numbers on one of the published thoughts of Kant and of having made the discovery that there was once a time when time did not exist but only a universe. For the rest, therefore, when we come across anything sensible in Herr Duehring's exposition "We" means Immanuel Kant, and the "present" is only ninety-five years old. Quite simple indeed, and unknown until now! But Kant does not establish the above statement by his proof. On the other hand, he shows the reverse, namely, that the universe has no beginning in time and no end in space, and he fixes his antinomy in this, the unsolvable contradiction that the one is just as capable of proof as the other. People of small calibre might be inclined to think that here Kant had found an insuperable difficulty, not so our bold author of fundamental results "especially his own." He copies all that he can use of Kant's antinomy and throws the rest away.

The matter solves itself very simply. Eternity in time and endlessness in space signify from the very words that there is no end in either direction, forwards or backwards, over or under, right or left. This infinity is quite different from an endless progression, since the latter always has some beginning, a first step. The inapplicability of this progression idea to our object is evident directly we apply it to space. Infinite progression translated in terms of space is a line produced continuously in a given direction. Is infinity in space expressed in this way, even remotely? On the contrary it requires six of these lines drawn from this point in three opposite directions to express the dimensions of space and we should have accordingly six of these dimensions. Kant saw this so plainly that he employed his progression merely indirectly in a round about way to express the extent of the universe. Herr Duehring on the contrary forces us to accept his six dimensions of space and at

NATURAL PHILOSOPHY

the same time has no words in which to express his contempt of the mathematical mysticism of Gauss who would not content himself with the three dimensions of space.

Applied to time, the series or row of objects, infinite at both extremities, has a certain figurative significance. But let us picture time as proceeding from unity or a line proceeding from a fixed point. We can say then that time has had a beginning. We assume just what we wanted to prove. We give a one-sided half-character to infinity of time. But a one-sided eternity split in halves is a contradiction in itself, the exact opposite of a hypothetical infinity, incapable of contradiction. We can only overcome this contradiction by assuming that the unity which we began to count the progression from, the point from which we measure the line, is a unity taken at pleasure in the series, a point taken at pleasure in the line. Hence as far as the line or series is concerned it is immaterial where we put it.

But as for the contradiction of the "counted endless progression" we shall be in a position to examine it more closely as soon as Herr Duehring has taught us the trick of reckoning it. If he has accomplished the feat of counting from minus infinity to zero, we shall be glad to hear from him again. It is clear that wherever he begins to count he leaves behind him an endless progression, and with it the problem which he had to solve. Let him only take his own infinite progression $1 + 2 + 3 + 4$ etc. and try to reckon back to 1 again from the infinite end. He evidently does not comprehend the requirements of the problem. And furthermore, if he affirms that the infinite progression of past time is capable of calculation he must affirm that time has a beginning for otherwise he could not begin to calculate:

LANDMARKS OF SCIENTIFIC SOCIALISM

Therefore he again substitutes a supposition for what he had to prove. The idea of the calculated infinite series, in other words Duehring's all-embracing law of the fixed number, is therefore a contradiction in adjecto, is a self contradiction, and an absurd one, moreover.

It is clear that an infinity which has an end but no beginning is neither more nor less than an infinity which has a beginning but no end. The least logical insight would have compelled Herr Duehring to the statement that beginning and end are mutually necessary to each other, like North Pole and South Pole, and that if one omit the end the beginning becomes the end, the one end which the series has and vice versa.

The entire fallacy would not be possible if it were not for the mathematical practice of operating with an infinite series. Because in mathematics one must proceed from the given and finite to that which is not given and infinite, all mathematical series whether positive or negative, begin with a fixed point otherwise one cannot calculate. The ideal necessities of the mathematician however are very far from being a law compulsory upon the universe.

Besides Herr Duehring will never succeed in imagining an infinity without contradiction. In the first place, infinity is a contradiction and full of contradictions. For example it is a contradiction that infinity should be made up of finite things and yet such is the case. The notion of a limited universe leads to contradictions just as much as the notion of its unlimitedness, and each attempt to abolish these contradictions leads, as we have seen, to new and worse contradictions. But just because infinity is a contradiction, it is without end, endlessly developing itself in time and space. The abolition of the contradiction would be the end of infinity.

NATURAL PHILOSOPHY

Hegel saw that very clearly, and covers the people who entered upon intricate arguments about this contradiction with merited scorn.

Let us proceed. Now, time has had a beginning. What was before this beginning? The unchangeable universe incomparable with anything else. And as no changes occur in this condition the particular concept time is transformed into the general concept existence. In the first place we have nothing to do with the transformation which goes on in the brain of Herr Duehring. We are not engaged with a concept of time, but with actual time of which Herr Duehring cannot so easily dispose. In the second place no matter how much the concept of time is transformed into the general concept existence it does not bring us one step nearer the goal. For the fundamental forms of all existence are space and time, and a thing existing outside of time is as silly an idea as that of a being outside of space. The Hegelian "past existence in which there was no time" and the neo-Schelling "being beyond the scope of thought" are rational conceptions compared with this being outside of time. For this reason Herr Duehring goes to work very cautiously " intrinsically it may be called time, but one cannot really call it time, as time does not consist in itself of real parts but is merely divided by us into parts to suit our own convenience," only a real filling up of time with distinct facts makes it capable of calculation. It is impossible to see the significance of piling up an empty duration. But it does not matter anyway. The question is whether the universe in this presupposed condition continues, that is persists, through a period of time. We have long known that it is useless to try and measure such empty space and to calculate without plan or aim and just because of the tiresomeness of such a

LANDMARKS OF SCIENTIFIC SOCIALISM

proceeding Hegel calls this infinity "miserable." According to Herr Duehring time exists only by virtue of change, not change in and through time. Because time is different from change and independent of it, we can measure it by the changes, because in order to measure we need something different from that which is to be measured. And the time in which no recognisible changes take place is very far from being no time, on the other hand since it is free from other ingredients, it is pure, that is to say, true time. Indeed if we want to contemplate time as a pure concept separated from all foreign admixture, we are obliged to eliminate all the various events which occur in time, either successively or simultaneously, and thus imagine a time in which nothing occurs. By this means we have not permitted the concept time to be overcome by the general concept of existence, but we have thereby arrived at a pure time concept. All these contradictions and impossibilities are mere child's play compared with the confusion into which he plunges the universe with its self-sufficient commencement. If the universe was in a condition in which no change occurred in it, how did it ever manage to get from that state to one of change? Moreover, an absolute condition of absence of change existing from eternity cannot possibly get out of that state unaided so as to pass over to a condition of progress and change. A first cause of motion must therefore have come from the outside, from beyond the universe, which caused the movement. This first cause of motion is clearly only another term for God, The God and the Beyond of which Herr Duehring fancied that he had so nicely settled in his scheme of the universe, return sharpened and deepened in his natural philosophy.

Further Herr Duehring says: "Where a fixed ele-

NATURAL PHILOSOPHY

ment of existence is capable of measurement, it will remain in unalterable stability. This is evident from material and mechanical force." The former quotation gives, it may be incidentally mentioned, a good example of Herr Duehring's axiomatic grandiloquence. Fixed quantities remain exactly the same, the quantity of mechanical force, once in the universe, is always the same. We will not dwell on this, so far as it is true, Descartes knew and said it three hundred years ago as regards philosophy, while in mechanical science the doctrine of the conservation of energy has been preached for the last twenty years. Herr Duehring has not improved upon it in so far as he limits it to mechanical energy. But where was mechanical energy at the period of unchangeableness? To this question Herr Duehring stubbornly refuses an answer.

Where was the unchangeable mechanical force then, Herr Duehring, and what was it busy about? Answer: " The original state of the universe, or, better, the existence of unchangeable matter, not allowing of any changes in time, is a question which no mind can pass except one which sees the acme of wisdom in the destruction of its own powers." Therefore you must either take my original condition with your eyes shut, or I, the lusty Eugene Duehring, brand you as an intellectual eunuch. Some people might be quite alarmed about this, but we who have seen a few examples of Herr Duehring's powers, can let the elegant abuse pass and reiterate the question, " But how about that mechanical energy, Herr Duehring, if you please?"

Herr Duehring is staggered at once. In fact, he stammers, " There is no proof of the actual existence of that original condition. Let us remember that this is also the case with each new step in the series with which we are acquainted. He therefore who will make difficulties in the foregoing case may see that he does not avoid them in the smaller apparent cases. Besides, the possibility exists that there are successively graduated intermediate states inserted, and thus there is a stable bridge by the means of which we can work backwards to the solution of the problem. As a matter of fact this notion of stability does not assist the main thought, but it is for us the fundamental form of regular progression, and of each transition known so far, so that we have a right to consider it as intermediate between the first original state and its disturbance. But if we consider the independent condition of equipoise from the point of view of mathematical concepts as, admittedly, without independent existence, there is no need of indicating the mode in which matter came into a dynamic condition." Outside of the mechanics of matter a change in movement of matter depends upon a change in the movement of the most insignificant particles. " Up to the present we have no universal principle of knowledge and we must therefore not be surprised if we are somewhat in the dark as to these matters."

That is all that Herr Duehring has to say, and we should seek the very pinnacle of wisdom not alone in a mutilation of the creative faculty, but in blind superstition, if we were to let the matter pass with these foolish evasions and statements. Absolute stability has no power of change in itself, Herr Duehring admits this. The absolute condition of equipoise possesses no means by which it can pass into a dynamic state. What have we then? Just three false and foolish phrases.

In the first place, Herr Duehring says that to show the transition from each most insignificant step in the chain of things with which we are acquainted to the next

NATURAL PHILOSOPHY

presents the same difficulty. He seems to think that his readers are infants. The proof of the transitions and interrelations of the most insignificant links in the chain of existence is just what constitutes the subject matter of natural science. If there is an impediment anywhere, nobody, not even Herr Duehring, thinks to explain the development as proceeding from nothing, but on the other hand as only proceeding from transition, change, and forward movement from a completed evolutionary stage. Here, however, he undertakes to show with reference to matter that it proceeds from absence of movement and therefore from nothing.

In the second place, we have the "stable bridge." This does not help us appreciably over the difficulty, but we have a right to use it as a bridge between rigid stability and motion. Unfortunately stability consists in absence of motion, and the question as to the generation of motion remains as dark a secret as before. And if Herr Duehring shifts his no-movement at all to universal movement in infinitely small particles and ascribes to this ever so long a duration of time, we are still not the thousand part of an inch further from the place whence we started. Without a creative act we can get nothing from nothing, not even anything as small as a mathematical differential. The bridge of stability is therefore not even a *pons asinorum*. Herr Duehring is the only person able to cross it.

Thirdly, as long as the present theories of mechanics prevail, this constitutes one of Herr Duehring's most reliable props, we cannot indicate how anything passes from a state of quiescence to one of motion. But the mechanical theory of heat teaches us that the movement of the mass depends upon the movements of the molecules, (so that even in this case movement proceeds from other movement and not from lack of movement) and this Herr Duehring shyly points out might serve as a bridge between the entirely static (the state of equipoise) and the dynamic (self-movement). But here Herr Duehring leaves us entirely in the dark. All his deepening and sharpening has dug a pit of folly and we are brought up necessarily in "darkness." But Herr Duehring troubles himself very little about that. He says right on the next page, with considerable audacity that he has been able to endow the self contained stability with real significance by means of the properties of matter and the mechanical forces.

In spite of all these errors and confused statements we have still an inspiring faith remaining that "The mathematics of the inhabitants of other planets cannot rest on any axioms other than our own."

Cosmogony, Physics, and Chemistry.

Proceeding we come to theories respecting the mode by which the world, as it is to-day, came into being. A universal separation of matter from one element was the notion of the Ionic philosophers, but, since Kant, the conception of an original nebulous state has played a new role and according to this gravitation and heat expansion have built up the worlds, little by little and one by one. The mechanical theory of heat of our time has fixed the origin of the earlier condition of the universe with much greater precision.

In spite of all this "the universal condition of the gaseous form can only be a point of departure for serious conclusions if one can define the mechanical system of it more precisely beforehand. If not, the idea becomes not only very cloudy, but the original nebula becomes really in the progress of those conclusions

NATURAL PHILOSOPHY

denser and more impenetrable." . . . For the present everything remains in the vagueness and formlessness of an indefinite idea, and so with regard to the gaseous universe we have only an insubstantial conception."

The theory of Kant that all existing worlds were created from a mass of rotating vapor was the greatest advance made by astronomy since the days of Copernicus. The idea that nature had no history in time was then shaken for the first time. Up to then the worlds were fixed in bounds and conditions from their very beginning, and though the individual organisms on the separate worlds were transient, the species remained unalterable. Nature was conceived as an apparently limited movement and its motion seemed to be the repetition of the same movements perpetually. It was in this conception which is entire accord with the metaphysical mode of thought that Kant made the first breach and so scientifically that most of his grounds of proof stand good today. Really the theory of Kant is a mere hypothesis even to-day. The Copernican theory of the universe has no longer any weight and since the spectroscope discovered such glowing gaseous matter in space all objections have been disposed of and scientific opposition to Kant's theory has been silenced. Even Herr Duehring cannot produce his universe without the nebulous state and he takes his revenge by asking to be shown the mechanical system of this nebulous state and because this cannot be done he inflicts all sorts of contemptuous remarks upon this nebulous state. Unfortunately modern science cannot show this system and please Herr Duehring. But there are many other questions which it cannot answer. For example regarding the question why toads have no tails it can only answer so far " Because they have lost them." But if people get angry and say that this is all vague and formless, a mere fanciful idea, incapable of being made definite and a very poor notion, such views would not carry us a step further, scientifically. Such insults and exaggerations are sufficiently numerous. What is there to hinder Herr Duehring himself from discovering the mechanical system of the original nebular state?

Fortunately we are informed that the nebular hypothesis of Kant "is far from showing a fully distinct condition of the world-medium or of explaining how matter arrived at a similar state." This is really very fortunate for Kant who is to be congratulated on having been able to trace the existing celestial bodies to the nebular condition, and who yet does not allow himself to dream of the self-contained unchanged condition of matter. It is to be remarked by the way that although the nebular condition of Kant is supposed to be the original vapor-form of matter, this is to be understood merely relatively. It is to be understood on the one hand as the original vapor form of the heavenly bodies, as they are at present, and on the other hand as the earliest form of matter to which we have been able to trace our way backwards. The fact that matter passed through an endless series of other forms before arriving at the nebular state is not excluded from this conception but is on the other hand rather included in it.

Herr Duehring is at an advantage here. Whereas science comes to a halt at the existence of the nebulous state his quack science carries him back to that "Condition of the development of the world which cannot be called actually static in the present sense of the word but most emphatically cannot be called dynamic. The unity of matter and mechanical force which we call the

NATURAL PHILOSOPHY

world is, so to speak, a formula of pure logic, to signify the self-contained condition of matter as the point of departure of all enumerable stages of material progress."

We have obviously not yet got away from the original self-contained condition of matter. Here it is explained as consisting of mechanical force and matter, and this as a formula of pure logic, etc. As soon then as the unity of matter and mechanical force is at an end evolution proceeds.

The formula of pure logic is nothing but a lame attempt to make the Hegelian categories "an Sich and fuer Sich" of use in a philosophy of realism. In "an Sich" according to Hegel the original unity of a thing consists; in "fuer Sich" begins the differentiation and movement of the concealed elements, the active antithesis. We shall therefore depict the original condition as one in which there is a unity of matter and mechanical force and the transition to movement as the separation and antithesis of these two elements. But we have not thereby established the proof of the real existence of the fantastic original condition but only this much that it exists according to the Hegelian category "an Sich" and just as fantastically disappears according to the Hegelian category "fuer Sich."

Matter, says Duehring, implies all that is real, therefore there is no mechanical force outside of matter. Mechanical force is furthermore a condition of matter. In the original condition where no change occurred matter and its mechanical force were a unity. Afterwards when the change commenced there was a differentiation from matter. Thus we are obliged to be satisfied with these mystical phrases and with the assurance that the self contained original state was neither static nor dynamic, neither in a state of rest nor of motion. We are still without information with regard to the whereabouts of mechanical force at that period and how we arrived at a condition of motion from one of rest without a push from the outside, that is without God.

Before the time of Herr Duehring materialists were wont to speak of matter and motion. He reduces motion to mechanical force as its necessary original form and so renders incomprehensible the real connection between matter and motion which was also not evident to the earlier materialists. Yet the thing is easy enough. Matter has never existed without motion, neither can it. Motion in space, the mechanical motion of smaller particles to single worlds, the motion of molecules as in the case of heat, or as electric or magnetic currents, chemical analysis or synthesis, organic life, each single each single atom of the matter of the world — they all discover themselves in one or other of the forms of motion or in several of them together at any given moment. All quiescence, all rest, is only significant in relation to this or that given form of motion. A body for example may be upon the ground in mechanical quiescence, in mechanical rest. This does not prevent its participation in the movements of the earth and of the whole solar system, just as little does it prevent its smallest component parts from completing the movements conditioned by the temperature or its atoms from going through a chemical process. Matter without motion is just as unthinkable as motion without matter. Motion is just as uncreatable or indestructible as matter itself, the older philosophy of Descartes proclaimed precisely that the quantity of motion in the world has been fixed from the beginning. Motion cannot be generated therefore it can only be transferred. If motion is transferred from one

NATURAL PHILOSOPHY

body to another, one may as far as it is regarded as transferring itself, as active, consider it as the original cause of motion, but so far as it is transferred, as passive. This active motion we call force; the passive, expression of force. It is therefore just as clear as noon that force is just as great as its expression because the same motion fulfils itself in both.

A motionless condition of matter is therefore one of the hollowest and most absurd notions, a mere delirium. In order to arrive at it one is obliged to consider the relative absence of motion in the case of a body lying on the ground, as absolute rest, and then to transfer this idea to the entire universe. This is made easier by the reduction of motion in general to mere mechanical force. By the limitation of motion to mere mechanical force we can conceive of a force as at rest, as confined, as momentarily ineffective. If for example in the transference of motion which transference is very frequently a somewhat complicated process in the carrying out of which various intermediate steps are necessary, one may stay the actual transference at a chosen point and stop the process, as for example if one loads a gun and delays the moment when the charge shall be set at liberty by the pull of the trigger, through the firing of powder. Therefore one may conceive of matter as being loaded with force in the unprogressive static period, and this Herr Duehring appears to mean by his unity of matter and force if indeed he means anything at all. This notion is absurd, since it pictures as absolute for the entire universe a condition which is by nature only relative and to which therefore only a portion of matter can be subjected at one and the same time. Let us look at it from this point of view and we do not escape the difficulty of explaining first how the universe came to be

LANDMARKS OF SCIENTIFIC SOCIALISM

loaded and in the second place, whose finger drew the trigger. We may revolve all we please but under the guidance of Herr Duehring we always come back over and over again to the finger of God.

From astronomy our realist philosopher passes on to mechanics and physics and complains that the mechanical theory of heat has brought us no further in the course of a generation than the point which Robert Mayer reached by his own efforts. Moreover the whole thing is very obscure. We must "always remember that with conditions of the movement of matter statical conditions are also given and that these last are not measured in mechanical work. If we have earlier typified nature as a great workwoman, and we still hold to the statement, we must now add that the static condition, the condition of rest, does not imply any mechanical labor. We are again without the bridge from the static to the dynamic and if latent heat, so called, is up to the present a stumbling block to the theory we can recognise a lack which may be denied in the cosmic process."

This whole oracular utterance is again merely an outpouring of bad science which very clearly perceives that it has got itself into a place from which it cannot be saved by creating motion from a state of absolute freedom from motion, and is ashamed to call upon its only saviour, the Creator of heaven and earth. If in mechanics, heat included, there is no bridge to be found from statics to dynamics, from equipoise to motion, why should Herr Duehring be obliged to find a bridge from his condition of absence of motion to motion? Thus he would have the luck to escape from his dilemma.

In ordinary mechanics the bridge from statics to dynamics is — the push from the outside. If a stone of the weight of a hundred grammes be lifted ten meters high

NATURAL PHILOSOPHY

and then flung free so that it should remain hanging in a self contained condition and in a state of rest, you would have to appeal to a public of sucking infants to declare that the existing condition of that body represents no mechanical labor and that its removal from its earlier condition has no measure in mechanical work. Any passerby would tell Herr Duehring that the stone did not come on the string by its own efforts and the first good hand book in mechanics would inform him that if he let the stone fall again, the latter in its fall does just as much mechanical work as is necessary to lift it to the height of ten meters. The very simple fact that the stone is suspended represents mechanical force in itself, since if it remain long enough, the string breaks, as soon as it, as a result of its chemical constitution, is no longer strong enough to hold the stone. All mechanical phenomena, may, we must inform Herr Duehring, be reduced to just such simple fundamental forms, and the engineer is still unborn who cannot discover the bridge from statics to dynamics as long as he has sufficient initial force at his disposal.

It is quite a hard nut and bitter pill for our metaphysician that motion should find its measure in its opposite rest. It is such a glaring contradiction, and every contradiction is an absurdity in the eyes of Herr Duehring. It is nevertheless true that the hanging stone by reason of its weight and its distance from the ground represents a means of mechanical movement sufficiently easily measured in different ways, as for example through gravity direct, through glancing on an incline or through the undulation of a wave — and it is just the same with a loaded gun. The expression of motion in terms of its opposite rest presents no difficulty at all to the dialectic philosophy. The whole contradiction in its eyes is

LANDMARKS OF SCIENTIFIC SOCIALISM

merely relative, for absolute rest, complete equipose does not exist. The movement of the particles strives towards equipose, the movement of the mass in turn destroys the equipose, so that rest and equipose where they occur are the results of arrested motion, and it is evident that this motion is capable of being measured in respect of its results, of being expressed in itself and of being restored in some form or other external to itself. But Herr Duehring would never be satisfied with such a simple explanation of the matter. Like a good metaphysician he creates a yawning gulf between motion and equipose which does not really exist and then wonders if he can find no bridge across the self-created chasm. He might just as well bestride his metaphysical Rosinante and hunt the " Ding an Sich " of Kant since it is in the last analysis nothing else than this which stands behind the undiscoverable bridge.

But what about the mechanical theory of heat and of latent heat which is a " stumbling block " in the path of the theory?

If one convert a pound of ice at freezing point under normal atmospheric pressure into a pound of water of the same temperature by means of heat there vanishes a quantity of heat which could heat the same pound of water from 0° centigrade to 79° centigrade, or seventy-nine pounds of water one degree centigrade. If one heat this pound of water to boiling point, that is, to one hundred degrees centigrade and change it into steam of the heat of one hundred degrees centigrade there vanishes up to the time when the last of the water is changed into steam a seven fold greater quantity of heat, capable of raising the temperature of 537.2 pounds of water one degree. This dissipated heat is called latent. It is transformed, by cooling the steam, into water again, and the

NATURAL PHILOSOPHY

water into ice, so the same mass of heat which was formerly latent, is again set free, that is, as heat capable of being felt and measured. This setting free of heat by the condensation of steam and the freezing of water is the reason that steam if it is cooled off at 100° transforms itself little by little into water, and that a mass of water at freezing point is but slowly transformed into ice. These are the facts. The question is what becomes of the heat while it is latent?

The mechanical theory of heat according to which the heat of a body at a certain temperature is dependent upon the greater or less vibration of the smallest physical parts (molecules) a vibration which can, under certain conditions, be transformed into some other form of motion, shows the whole thing completely, that the latent heat has performed work, has been expended in work. By the melting of the ice the close connection of the separate particles is broken asunder and changed into a loose relationship; by the conversion of water into steam at boiling point a condition is entered where the separate molecules exercise no noticeable influence upon each other, and under the influence of heat fly from one another in all directions. It is now evident that the separate molecules of a body in the gaseous state are endowed with much greater energy than in the fluid state, and in the fluid state than in the solid. Latent heat is therefore not dissipated, it is merely transformed and has taken on the form of molecular elasticity.

As soon as conditions are at an end under which the molecules can exercise this relative freedom with regard to each other as soon namely as the temperature falls below one hundred degrees to zero, this elasticity becomes released and the molecules come together with the same force with which they formerly flew apart, but

LANDMARKS OF SCIENTIFIC SOCIALISM

only to appear again as heat, as exactly the same quantity of heat as was latent before. This explanation is of course a hypothesis, as is the whole mechanical theory of heat, in so far as no one has yet seen a molecule, much less a molecule in motion. Like all recent theories, this hypothesis is full of flaws but it can at least offer an explanation which does not conflict with the uncreatability and indestructibility of motion and it is able to give an account of the whereabouts of the heat in the transformation. Latent heat is therefore by no means an obstacle in the way of the mechanical theory of heat. On the contrary this theory for the first time provides a rational explanation of the subject and an obstacle arises from the fact in particular that the physicists make use of the old and ineffective expression "latent heat" to signify the heat transformed into some other shape by molecular energy.

The static conditions of the solid, liquid and gaseous states therefore represent mechanical work in so far as mechanical work is a measure of heat. Thus the solid crust of the earth, like the water of the ocean, represents in its present form a certain quantity of heat set free which implies the same quantity of mechanical force. By the passing of the vaporous state which was the original form of the earth into the fluid state and later into a condition, for the most part solid, a certain quantity of molecular energy was set free in space, the difficulty of which Herr Duehring whispers does not therefore exist. We are frequently brought to a stop in our cosmic observations by lack of knowledge, but nowhere by insuperable theoretical difficulties. The bridge from statics to dynamics is therefore the push from the outside caused by the cooling or heating occasioned by other bodies which influence certain objects in equipoise.

NATURAL PHILOSOPHY

The further we explore Herr Duehring's philosophy, the more impossible appear all his attempts to explain rotation from absence of rotation, or to discover the bridge by which that which is purely static, self-contained, can without disturbance come to be the dynamic, in motion.

We should here be glad to get rid of the whole self-contained condition business. Herr Duehring, however, goes to chemistry and gives us three permanent natural laws established by the philosophy of realism as follows, 1. The constant amount of matter in the universe. 2. The simple chemical elements, and 3. The mechanical forces are unchangeable.

Therefore the impossibility of creating or destroying matter, the simple forms of its existence as far as they exist, and motion, these old, well known facts, inadequately expressed, that is the only positive thing which Herr Duehring is in a position to offer us as a result of his real philosophy of the inorganic world. All these things we have long known. But what we have not known is that they are permanent laws and as such natural properties of the system of things. It is just the same thing over again as in the case of Kant. Herr Duehring takes some universally known expressions, pastes the Duehring label on them and calls them " fundamentally original results and views, system shaping thoughts, profound science."

We have not long to hesitate on this account. Whatever deficiencies the most profound science and the best contrived social theories may have, for once Herr Duehring can say precisely " The quantity of gold in the universe must always remain the same and cannot be increased or diminished any more than matter in general. But unfortunately Herr Duehring does not tell us what we may buy with this gold."

LANDMARKS OF SCIENTIFIC SOCIALISM

The Organic World

"From mechanics in rest and motion to the relation of sensation and thought there is a uniform progression of interruptions." With this assurance Herr Duehring spares himself from saying anything further about the origin of life, though one might reasonably expect that a thinker who has followed the development of the world from its self-contained condition, and who is so much at home with the other heavenly bodies would be here at home also. Besides this assurance is only half true in so far as it is not yet completed by means of the log line of Hegel, of which mention has been made already. In all its gradations the transition from one form of evolution to another remains a leap, a differentiating movement. So in the transition from the mechanics of the worlds to those of the smaller amounts of matter in each single world, just so also in that from the mechanics of the mass to that of the molecule — the motion which we examine particularly in physics, so-called, heat, light, electricity, magnetism, just in the same way also the transition from the physics of the molecule to the physics of the chemical atom is completed by a differentiating leap, and it is just the same with the transition from ordinary chemical action to the chemistry of albumen which we call life. Within the sphere of life the changes become less frequent and less remarkable. Therefore Hegel must again correct Herr Duehring.

The idea of purpose furnishes Herr Duehring with his conception of the transition to the organic world. This is again borrowed from Hegel, who in his "logic"— teachings of the concept — mingled with teachings of teleology or of purpose, passes over from chemistry to life. Whichever way we look we discover Herr Duehring to

NATURAL PHILOSOPHY

be in possession of Hegelian lore which he gives forth without any embarrassment as his own fundamental philosophy. It would be too long a task to find out here just how far the application of the ideas of purpose is correctly stated and applied to the organic world. The application of the Hegelian " inner purpose " at all events is evident, that is, of a purpose which is imported into nature not through a consciously acting third party, like the wisdom of Providence, but which is inherent in matter itself, which among people who are not well versed in philosophy proceeds to the unthinking supposition of a conscious and all-wise agent; the same Herr Duehring who breaks out into unmeasured moral indignation at the least tendency towards spiritism on the part of other people, tells us that " sex sensations are certainly mainly directed towards the gratification which is bound up in their exercise." He tells us moreover that " poor Nature must always hold the objective world in order " and it has besides to perform acts which require more subtlety from Nature than we usually attribute to her. But nature knows not only why she does this and that. She has not only her housemaid's duties to perform, she has not only subtlety, which is a very pretty accomplishment, in subjective conscious thought, she has also a will, for " we must regard the additional natural desires which occur, such as feeding and propagation, not as directly but as indirectly willed." We now arrive at a consciously thinking and acting nature, and we therefore stand right at the bridge, not indeed between the static and dynamic but between pantheism and deism, or perhaps Herr Duehring is pleased to indulge himself in a little " natural-philosophical half-poetry."

Impossible. All that the realistic philosophy has to say on organic nature is limited to a war against this

LANDMARKS OF SCIENTIFIC SOCIALISM

natural philosophical half-poesy against "Charlatanism with its wanton superficialities and pseudo-scientific mysticism, against the poetic features of Darwinism."

Darwin comes in for a share of blame chiefly because he transferred the Malthusian theory of population from political economy to natural science, because he is entangled by his notions of breeding, so that his work is a sort of unscientific half-poetic attack against design in creation, and that the whole of Darwinism, after what he has borrowed from Lamark has been deducted, is a piece of brutality aimed against humanity.

Darwin had brought home with him as the result of his scientific journeys the conclusion that species of plants and animals are not fixed but are subject to variations. In order to pursue this idea he entered upon experiments in the breeding of plants and animals. Just for this reason England has become a classic land. The scientists of other countries, Germany, for example, have nothing to offer comparable with England in this respect. Moreover, most of the conclusions belong to the last century so that the establishment of the facts presented few difficulties. Darwin found that this artificial breeding produced differences in the species of plants and animals greater than occur among those which are universally recognised as belonging to different species. Therefore it was, up to a certain point, proved that species can change and furthermore there was established the possibility of a common ancestry for organisms which partake of the characteristics of different species.

Darwin now examined the question whether there were not in nature causes — which without the conscious intention of the breeder — might in the course of time, by means of heredity, produce changes in the living animal analogous to those produced by scientific breeding.

NATURAL PHILOSOPHY

These causes he found in the disproportion between the enormous number of germs made by nature and the small number of beings which actually come to maturity. But as the germ struggles for its own development there is of necessity a consequent struggle for existence, which not only shows itself directly in the wear and tear of the body, but also as a struggle for space and light, as in the case of plants. And it is evident that in this fight those individuals have the best prospect of coming to maturity and reproducing themselves which possess certain qualities, perhaps insignificant, but advantageous in their fight for existence. There is a tendency towards the inheritance of these individual properties, and if they occur in several individuals of the same species towards development in the direction once taken, by virtue of the accumulated heredity, while the individuals which are not possessed of these qualities succumb more easily and little by little disappear in the struggle for existence. Thus a species naturally changes by the survival of the fittest.

Against this theory of Darwin Herr Duehring urges that the origin of the idea of the struggle for existence is, as Darwin himself confessed, based on the views of the political economist and theorist, Malthus, on the population question, and he covers it with all the abuse appropriate to the clerical Malthusian views on keeping down the population. Now it happens that Darwin never said that the cause of the struggle for existence theory was to be sought from Malthus. He only said that his theories respecting the struggle for existence are the theories of Malthus applied to the entire vegetable and animal world. How great a blunder Darwin made when he so naively accepted the teachings of Malthus without examination may be seen from the fact that there

LANDMARKS OF SCIENTIFIC SOCIALISM

is no need to employ the spectacles of Malthus in order to detect the struggle for existence in nature,— the contradiction between the innumerable mass of germs which nature produces in such prodigality and the slight number which can manage to reach maturity, a contradiction which resolves itself into an apparently grim fight for existence. And with regard to the law of wages the Malthusian doctrines are widely advertised and Ricardo based his contentions upon them,— so the struggle for existence in nature may find a standing even without the Malthusian interpretation. Besides the organisms of nature have their law of population, the establishment of which would decide the theories of the development of species. And who gave the decisive impetus in that direction? Nobody but Darwin.

Herr Duehring is on his guard against entering upon the positive side of this question. Instead he must again find fault with the struggle for existence. There can be no argument about a struggle for existence between plants and the genial eaters of plants " in a sufficiently accurate sense the struggle for existence only occurs within the sphere of brutality, in so far as nourishment depends upon robbery and consumption." And after he has reduced the concept struggle for existence to these narrow limits he gives his wrath free play as regards the brutality of this conception which he himself has narrowed down to a brutal conception. But this moral wrath simply reacts on Herr Duehring himself, the inventor of this sort of struggle for existence. It is not Darwin therefore who seeks among the lower animals the " conditions of the operations of nature " (as a matter of fact Darwin would have included the whole of organic nature in the struggle), but one of Herr Duehring's bugaboos. The expression " struggle for exist-

NATURAL PHILOSOPHY

ence " in particular excites Herr Duehring's lofty moral scorn. That this actually exists among plants every meadow, every cornfield and every wood can show him. We need not trouble about the name, whether one call it " struggle for existence " or " lack of the conditions of existence and want of mechanical realisation," but as to how this fact operates as regards the maintenance or transformation of species. With regard to this Herr Duehring persists in a characteristically stubborn silence. We cannot trouble ourselves any more about natural selection.

But " Darwinism produces its changes and differentiations out of nothing." Darwin thoroughly understands that he is engaged with the causes which have produced changes in individuals and in the second place he is engaged with the mode in which such individual differentiations tend to mark off a race, a genus, or a species. Darwin moreover was less occupied in discovering these causes, which up to the present are either entirely unknown or on which there is only general information, than in discovering a rational form in which to establish their reality, to embrace their permanent significance. But Darwin ascribed too wide a reach to his discovery in this that he made it an exclusive means of variation in species and neglected the causes of individual differentiations from the general form. This mistake however is common to most people who make a step forwards. Next, if Darwin produces his changes in individual types out of nothing and thereby excludes the wisdom of the breeder, the breeder on his part must not only display his wisdom but he must produce out of nothing real changes in plant and animal forms. But who has given the impetus to the investigation as to whence these variations and differentiations proceed? It is again no one but Darwin.

Lately the conception of natural selection has been broadened, by Haeckel, in particular, and the variation of species has been shown to be the result of actual change owing to adaptation and inheritance, whereby adaptation is considered as the source of variations and heredity as the conserving element in the process. Even this is not correct in Herr Duehring's eyes. " Peculiar adaptation to the circumstances of life as they are offered or withheld by nature supposes impulses and facts which answer to the conception. Hence adaptation is only apparent and actual causality does not elevate itself above the lowest steps of physical, chemical and plant physiology." It is again the name which provokes Herr Duehring. But how does he deal with the matter? The question is if such changes do take place in the species of organic beings or not. And again Herr Duehring has no reply.

"If a plant in the course of its growth takes a direction by which it gets the most light the result is nothing but a combination of physical forces and chemical agents, and if we are to call it an adaptation, not metaphorically but strictly, confusion is certain to arise in the motion." This man is so exacting with other people because he is quite well acquainted with the intentions of nature and speaks of the subtlety of nature, even of its will. There is confusion, indeed, but with whom, with Haeckel or with Herr Duehring?

And the confusion is not only spiritual but logical. We have seen that Herr Duehring put forth all his efforts to make the purpose idea in nature real. " The relation of means and end does not by any means show a conscious intention." But what is adaptation without

NATURAL PHILOSOPHY

conscious intention, without any intrusion of design of which he complains so loudly, but an unconscious teleology?

If the color of tree frogs and leaf eating insects is as a rule green and that of beasts that inhabit the desert sandy-yellow, and that of polar animals white, they have certainly not come into possession of this coloring intentionally or through any kind of mental process, on the contrary the coloring can only be explained by means of the operation of physical substances and chemical agents. And yet it cannot be denied that by these colors these animals are particularly adapted to the conditions in which they are and it is certain that they are by their means rendered less visible to their enemies. Just of a similar nature are the organs by which certain plants seize and consume certain insects (the means being on their under side, suited to this purpose and adapted to this end). Now if Herr Duehring insists that the adaptation must be realised through the operation of thought, he only says that the purpose must be carried out through mental operation, must be conscious and intentional. Thus again, just as in the philosophy of realism we arrive at the Creator with a purpose, at God. Formerly this kind of declaration was called " deism " and Herr Duehring says that we had not much regard for it, but it now appears that the world has gone backwards in this respect also.

From adaptation we come to heredity and here according to Herr Duehring Darwinism is quite out. The whole organic world, Darwin explained, came from a single germ, is, so to speak, the brood of a single being. Independent similar products of nature according to Darwin do not exist without heredity and his retrogressive philosophy must come to a full stop when the end of the thread of ancestry is reached, or the original vegetable form."

The statement that Darwin traced all existing organisms from one original germ is to put it politely a piece of pure imagination on the part of Herr Duehring. Darwin says distinctly on the last page of the Origin of Species, Sixth Edition, that he regards all living beings not as separate creations but as the descendants in a direct line from some fewer beings and Haeckel makes a distinct advance on this ascribes "an entirely distinct source for plants and another for the animal kingdom" and on and between both of them "a number of original stems each of which has developed independently from one single primary monistic form." (History of Creation page 397.) This original form of life Herr Duehring discovers solely to bring it into contempt by paralleling it with the first man according to Jewish tradition, Adam. Here, unfortunately for Herr Duehring, he does not know how this original Jew turns out, according to Smith's Assyrian discoveries to have been the original Semite, and that the entire Biblical story of the Creation and the Flood has been shown to have been taken from a legendary store common to the Jews, Babylonians, Chaldeans, and Assyrians.

It is brought forward as a severe and irrefutable reproach to Darwin that he is at an end where the thread of descent fails him. Unfortunately the whole of our science deserves the same reproach. When the thread of descent fails it it is "at an end." It has not yet come to the point of creating organic beings without an ancestry, not even once has it been able to make simple protoplasm or other albuminous bodily forms out of the chemical elements. It can only say therefore with any any certainty regarding the origin of life, that it must

NATURAL PHILOSOPHY

have come about by a chemical process. But perhaps the philosophy of realism can give us some assistance here since it is engaged with independent organic natural products, without any descent one from another. How can these come into being? By original creation? But up to the present not even the most audacious advocates of spontaneous generation have claimed to create in this way anything except bacteria, fungi, or other very elementary organisms, but not insects, birds, fish or mammals. If these homogeneous products of nature — it is understood for all this discussion that they are organic — are not related through descent, they or their ancestors, then "where the thread of descent breaks" they must have been placed in the world by a separate act of creation, and this again requires a creator, what we call "deism."

Herr Duehring further explains that it was a piece of superficiality on the part of Darwin to make the mere fact of the sex-composition of qualities the foundation for the existence of these qualities." Here we have again a piece of pure imagination on the part of our profound philosopher. On the contrary Darwin says that natural selection has to do only with the maintenance of variations and not with their origin. This new supposition however of things which Darwin did not say serves to assist us to this deep idea of Duehring. "If a principle of individual variation had been sought in the inner scheme of creation it would have been an entirely rational idea. For it is natural to unite the idea of universal generation with that of sex propagation, and to regard the so-called original creation from the higher point of view, not as absolutely antagonistic to reproduction but even as reproduction itself." And the

LANDMARKS OF SCIENTIFIC SOCIALISM

man who could write this is not ashamed to reproach Hegel with writing jargon.

Let us call a halt to the vexatious and contradictory babble with which Herr Duehring proclaims his wrath against the advance given to science by the theory of Darwin. Neither Darwin nor his followers among the natural scientists have any idea of belittling Lamark's tremendous services, in fact they are the very people who first restored his fame. But we are unable to ignore the fact that in the time of Lamark science was still far from supplied with competent material to enable it to answer the question of the origin of species other than in a prophetic or, as it were anticipatory, manner. In addition to the enormous amount of material in the realm of general, as well as of that of anatomical, botany and zoology, accumulated since that time, two entirely new sciences have since come into existence — the investigation of the development of plant and animal germs (embryology), and the investigation of the organic survivals in the earth's crust which still remain. There is a distinct similarity between the steps in the development of the organic germ to mature organism, and the successive steps by which plants and animals succeed each other in the history of the world. It is just this similarity which has placed the evolution theory on its most secure foundations. The theory of evolution is however still very young and it is beyond question that upon further investigation the rigid Darwinian ideas upon the origin of species will be considerably modified.

But what has the realist philosophy of a positive nature to contribute with respect to the evolution of organic life? " The variation of species is an acceptable supposition, but there exists, in addition, the independent order of the products of nature belonging to the same species,

NATURAL PHILOSOPHY

without any intervention of descent." According to this we are to conclude that products of unlike species, that is species which vary, are descended from one another, but those of similar species not. But even this is not altogether correct, for he ventures to say of the varying species, "The part played by descent is on the contrary a very secondary activity of nature." There is heredity, then, but it is only to be reckoned as a factor of the second class. Let us be glad that heredity of which Herr Duehring has said so much that is evil and mysterious is at least let in by the back door. It is just the same with natural selection, since after all his moral indignation with respect to the struggle for existence by means of which natural selection fulfils itself he suddenly exclaims, "The most important constituent is to be found in the conditions of life and cosmic conditions, while natural selection as set forth by Darwin may be considered as secondary." Natural selection still exists, even if a factor of the second class, like the struggle for existence, and the clerical malthusian surplus-population theory. That is all, for the rest Herr Duehring refers us to Lamark.

Finally, he warns against misuse of the terms metamorphosis and evolution. Metamorphosis, he says, is a very obscure notion, and the concept of evolution is only admissible in so far as a law of evolution can be really proved. Instead of either of these expressions we should employ the term "composition" and then everything would be all right. It is the same old story over again, Herr Duehring is satisfied if we change the names. If we speak of the evolution of the chicken in the egg we give rise to confusion because we have only an incomplete knowledge of the law of evolution. But if we speak of its "composition" everything becomes clear.

LANDMARKS OF SCIENTIFIC SOCIALISM

We must therefore say no longer "this child is growing nicely" but, "he composes himself splendidly," and we congratulate Herr Duehring upon the fact that he is not only a peer of the author of the Niebelungen Ring in his opinion of himself but in his own particular capacity is also a composer of the future.

Organic World (Conclusion)

"One reflects upon our natural philosophical portion of positive knowledge in order to fix it relatively to all one's scientific hypotheses. Next in importance come all the actual acquisitions of mathematics as well as the leading principles of exact science in mechanics, physics and chemistry and particularly the scientific results in physiology, zoology, and antiquarian investigation."

Herr Duehring speaks in this confident and decided fashion with respect to the mathematical and scientific scholarship of Herr Duehring. One cannot detect in its meager shape and in its scanty and audacious results the extent of positive knowledge which lies behind. Every time the oracle is consulted for a definite statement as regards physics or chemistry we get nothing as regards physics but the equation which expresses the mechanical equivalent of heat, and concerning chemistry only this that all bodies are divisible into elements and combinations of elements. He who can speak as Duehring does about "gravitating atoms" shows at once that he is quite at a loss to understand the difference between an atom and a molecule. Atoms, of course, exist, not with respect to gravitation or any other physical or mechanical form of motion, but only as concerns chemical action. And if the last chapter on organic nature is read, the empty, self-contradictory, assertive, oracular, stupid, circuitous absolute nothingness of the final result

LANDMARKS OF SCIENTIFIC SOCIALISM

lead one to the conclusion that Herr Duehring talks about things of which he knows very little and this conclusion becomes a certainty when we come to his proposal in the course of his writing on organic life (biology) to use the term "composition" instead of evolution. He who can make such a suggestion as that gives evidence that he is not acquainted with the building up of organic bodies.

All organic bodies, the very lowest excepted, develop from small cells by the increment of visible pieces of albumen with a central cell. The cell generally develops an outer skin and the contents are more or less fluid. The lowest cell-bodies develop from one cell; the enormous majority of organic beings are many-celled and among the lower forms these take on similar, and among the higher forms greater variations of, groupings and activities. In the human body for example are bones, muscles, nerves, sinews, ligaments, cartilage, skin, all either made up of cells or originating in them. But for all organic bodies, from the amœba which is a simple and for the most part unprotected piece of albumen with a cell centre in the midst to man, and from the smallest one-celled desmidian to the highest developed plant, the mode is one and the same by which the cells propagate themselves, that is by division. The cell centre is first laced across its midst, the lacing which separates the centre into two knobs becomes stronger and stronger and at last they become separated and two cell centres are formed. The same occurrence takes place in the cell itself. Each of the cell centres becomes the middle point of a collection of cell stuff which by knitting ever closer becomes combined with the other, and finally both of them part and live on as separate cells. Through such repeated cell divisions the full sized animal gradually develops from the germ of the animal egg after fructifi-

NATURAL PHILOSOPHY

cation and the substitution of used up cells in the full grown animal is brought about similarly. To call such a process "composition" and to speak of the term "evolution" as a purely imaginary term belongs to one who does not know anything of the matter, hard as it is to imagine such ignorance at this date.

We have still somewhat to say with respect to Herr Duehring's views of life in general. Elsewhere he sets forth the following statement with respect to life. "Even the inorganic world is a self-regulated system but one may undertake to speak of life in the proper sense first when the organs and the circulation of matter through special separate channels from a central point to another germ collection of a minor formation begin."

If life begins where the separate organs begin then we must hold all Haeckel's protozoa (Protistenreich) and probably many others as dead; all organisms at least up to those composed of one cell and those included are not capable of life. If the means of circulation of matter through different channels is the distinguishing mark of life we must place outside of this definition all the upper classes of the colenterata entirely, with the exception of the medusae, and therefore all the polypi and other plant animals are also to be considered as being outside the class of living creatures. And if the circulation of matter through different canals from an inner point is the distinguishing characteristic of life we must reckon all animals as dead which either have no heart or several hearts. Besides these there belong also to this category all worms, starfish and ringed creatures (annuloids and annulous according to Huxley's definition) a portion of the shell fish, crabs, and finally a vertebrate animal, the lancelet (amphioxus) and all plants.

LANDMARKS OF SCIENTIFIC SOCIALISM

When Herr Duehring therefore undertakes to distinguish life narrowly and strictly, he gives four mutually contradictory modes of distinguishing life, one of which condemns not only the whole of plant life but about half the animal kingdom to eternal death. No one can accuse him of having deceived us when he promised us peculiar results based on individual ideas.

In another place he says "There is a simple fundamental type in nature belonging to all organisms from the lowest to the highest" and this type is to be met " in the subordinate movements of the most undeveloped plants. "This is again an absolutely false statement. The simplest type in the whole of organic nature is the cell, and it lies universally at the foundation of the highest organisms. On the other hand there is a substance among the lowest organisms lower even than the cell, the protomoeba, a single piece of undifferentiated protoplasm, without any differentiation, a complete series of monads and the entire class of siphoneae. All of these are connected with the higher organisms only by virtue of the fact that protoplasm is its substantial foundation, and that they fulfill the functions of protoplasm, that is they live and die.

Further Herr Duehring tells us "physiologically the concept of existence consists in this, that it embraces a single nerve apparatus. Sensation is therefore the characteristic of all animal organisms that is the capacity of conscious subjective recognition of circumstances. The sharp line of differentiation between plants and animals consists in the leap to sensation. This distinguishing line cannot any more be abolished by known forms of transition than it can be brought into existence by the logical necessity of externally distinguishable characteristics."

NATURAL PHILOSOPHY

And further "Plants are totally and eternally without sensation and are devoid of the faculty for it."

In the first place Hegel says that "sensation is the specific differentiation, the distinguishing mark of the animal." Thus one of Hegel's erudite statements becomes an indubitable truth of the last instance merely by being copied into Herr Duehring's book.

In the second place we now arrive for the first time at the forms of transition between animals and plants. That these intermediate forms exist, that there are organisms concerning which we are unable to say flatly whether they are plants or animals, that we are therefore unable to fix accurately the frontiers between plant and animal life, all these things make Herr Duehring logically anxious to fix a decisively distinguishing line, which in the next breath he declares cannot be thoroughly relied on. But there is no need for us to go to the doubtful region; intermediate between plants and animals are sensitive plants which at the least contact fold their leaves or close their petals. Are insect eating plants utterly without sensation? Even Herr Duehring cannot make such an assertion without indulging in "unscientific half-poetry."

In the third place Herr Duehring is again giving free rein to his imagination when he says that sensation is psychologically existent, even when the nerve apparatus is exceedingly simple. This is found regularly among reptiles yet Herr Duehring is the first to say that they have no sensation because they have no nerves. Sensation is not necessarily bound up with nerves but it is bound up with some albuminous substance the true nature of which has not yet been discovered.

In addition, the biological knowledge of Herr Duehring becomes exceedingly evident in that he is not

LANDMARKS OF SCIENTIFIC SOCIALISM

ashamed to fling at Darwin the question do animals develop from plants? so that it is a question whether he is more ignorant with regard to plants or animals.

Of life in general Herr Duehring can only tell us " The change in the form of matter which fulfills itself by plastic constructive arrangement remains a distinguishing characteristic of the individual life-process."

That is all that we learn of life and with respect to the plastic creative arrangement we sink knee deep in the nonsense of Duehring's jargon. If we want to learn what life is we shall have to look at the problem a little more closely on our own account.

That organic change in matter is the most universal and distinctive evidence of life has been declared by physiological chemists and chemical physiologists times without number during the last thirty years and their utterances are translated by Herr Duehring into his own clear and elegant language. But to define life as an organic change of matter is simply to define life as life, for organic change of matter, or change of matter with plastic creative arrangement is a statement which must itself be explained by life, and the explanation in its turn by the difference between organic and inorganic, that is between that which is alive and that which is not alive. So that with this explanation we do not get at the problem.

Organic change, as such, is frequently found where life does not exist. There are whole series of processes in chemistry, which by the proper combination of the elements, produce again their own conditions, so that thereby a certain body is the creator of a process. Thus in the manufacture of sulphuric acid by the burning of sulphur, there is created in this process sulphuric dioxide SO_2, and if one add steam and nitric acid there-

NATURAL PHILOSOPHY

to, the sulphuric dioxide takes up the water and the oxygen and becomes H_2SO_4. Nitric acid gives off oxygen and becomes nitric oxide, this nitric oxide simultaneously takes up new oxygen from the atmosphere and is transformed into a higher oxide of nitrogen and from this acid sulphuric dioxide is again given off and made by the same process, so that, theoretically, an infinitely small amount of nitric acid should be effective to transform an unlimited quantity of sulphuric dioxide, oxygen and water into sulphuric acid. Change in matter regularly occurs through the passing of fluids through dead organic and inorganic membranes as in the artificial cells of Traube. It therefore appears that there is no progress by the way of organic change for the quality of organic change which was to explain life must itself be explained by life. We must therefore seek it elsewhere.

Life is a mode of existence of protoplasm and consists essentially in the constant renewal of the chemical constituents of this substance. Protoplasm is here understood in the modern chemical sense and comprises under this name all substances analogous to the white of an egg, otherwise called protein substances. The name is not satisfactory, for the ordinary white of egg plays the least active role of all transformed substances, since it only serves as mere nourishment for the yolk, for the self-developing germ. As long however as so little is known of the chemical constituents of protoplasm the name is better than any other because more inclusive.

Whenever we discover life we also find it bound up with protoplasm, and when we find a piece of protoplasm not in solution there we find also life, without exception. Doubtless the presence of other chemical constituents is necessary to a living body, to produce the various differentiations of these elements of life. They are not necessary to life in itself, hence they enter as food and become transformed into protoplasm. The lowest forms of life with which we are acquainted are nothing but simple pieces of protoplasm and yet they have all the appearance of living objects.

But in what consist these signs of life which are common to all living objects? In this, that the protoplasm takes from its surroundings other matter suitable to itself and assimilates it while other former portions of the body become decomposed and are thrown off. Other things, not living bodies, decompose or make combinations, but cease thereby to be what they were. The rock worn by atmospheric action is no longer rock, the metal which becomes oxidised goes off in rust. But what causes the destruction of dead bodies is the essential of the existence of living protoplasm. From the very moment when the unbroken interchange in the constituents of protoplasm ceases, the continual interchange of receiving and throwing off, from that moment the protoplasmic substance itself ceases, becomes decomposed, that is, dies.

Life, the mode of existence of protoplasmic substance, therefore consists in this, that at one and the same moment it is itself and something else, and this is not the result of a process to which it is compelled by external agency, since this may happen also with objects which are dead. On the contrary life, which is change of matter, is consequent upon nourishment and throwing off, is a self-fulfilling process inherent in its medium, protoplasm, without which it cannot exist. Hence, it follows that if chemistry should ever discover how to make protoplasm artificially, this protoplasm must show some signs of life, even if very insignificant. It is, of course,

NATURAL PHILOSOPHY

doubtful if chemistry will discover the proper food for this protoplasm at the same time as the protoplasm.

Through the changes in matter produced by nourishment and throwing off, as actual functions of the protoplasm, and through its own plasticity, proceed all the other most simple factors of life, sensibility which consists in the interchange between the protoplasm and its food, contractibility which shows itself at a very low stage in the consumption of food, possibility of growth which is shown in the lowest stages of development by splitting, and internal motion without which neither the consumption nor assimilation of food is possible.

Our definition of life is, of course, very incomplete since in order to include all the widely differing manifestations of life it must confine itself to the most universal and simple. Definitions are of little scientific worth. In order to determine what life is we must examine all forms of its manifestation from the lowest to the highest. For ordinary use such definitions are very convenient and in a certain sense indispensable, and they can do no harm as long as their inevitable deficiencies are not forgotten.

(The remainder of this section simply teases Herr Duehring.)

CHAPTER VI

MORALS AND LAW

Eternal Truths

We refrain from offering examples of the hodge podge of stupidity and sham solemnity with which Herr Duehring regales his readers for fifty full pages as fundamental knowledge on the elements of consciousness. We merely quote the following: "He who merely conceives of thought through the medium of speech has never understood what is signified by abstract and true thought." Hence, animals are the most abstract and true thinkers, for their thought is never obscured by the importunate interference of speech. With regard to Herr Duehring's thought in particular, it may be perceived that they are but little suited to speech and that the German language in particular is quite inadequate to express them.

The fourth part of his book, however, possesses some redeeming features, for here and there it offers us some comprehensible notions on the subject of morals and law in spite of the tedious and involved rhetoric. Right at the beginning we are invited to take a journey to the other heavenly bodies. Thus, the elements of morality are to be found among superhuman beings among whom exist an understanding of things and a **regular** system of the harmonious conduct of life. Our share in such conclusions must then be small, but there always remains a beneficent and enlarging idea in picturing that even in other spheres individual and social life follows one pur-

MORALS AND LAW

pose which cannot be escaped or evaded by any intelligent living creature."

There is good reason for our altering the position of the statement that Herr Duehring's truth is good for all possible worlds from the close to the beginning of the chapter. When once the correctness of Herr Duehring's notions of morals and law have been established so as to apply to all world the beneficent notion may easily be extended to all time. Here again, however, we run across another final truth of last instance. The moral universe has "just as well as that of universal knowledge its general principles and simple elements." Moral principles are beyond history and the national distinctions of to-day . . . the various truths from which in the course of development the fuller moral consciousness, and, so to speak, conscience itself is derived, can, as far as their origin is investigated, claim a similar acceptation and extent to that of mathematics and its applications. Real truths are immutable and it is folly to conceive of correct knowledge as liable to the attacks of time or of change in material conditions. "Hence the certainty of sound knowledge and the sufficiency of general acceptation forbid to doubt the absolute correctness of the fundamental principles of knowledge. . . . Continual doubt is in itself an evidence of weakness and is merely the expression of a barren condition of confusion, which although conscious of possessing nothing still seeks to maintain the appearance of holding on to something. Regarding morals, it denies universal principles with respect to the manifold variations in moral ideas owing to geographical and historical conditions, and thinks that with the admission of the unavoidable necessity of evil and wickedness there is no need for it to acknowledge the truth and efficiency

LANDMARKS OF SCIENTIFIC SOCIALISM

of moral impulses. This mordant scepticism which is not directed against any false doctrine in particular, but against human capacity to recognise morality resolves itself finally into nothingness, it is no more than mere nihilism. It flatters itself that it can attain supremacy and give free rein to unprincipled pleasures by destroying moral ideas and creating chaos. It is greatly deceived, however, if merely pointing at the inevitable fate of the intellect with respect to error and truth is sufficient to show by analogy that natural liability to error does not exclude the arriving at a correct decision but rather tends to that end."

Up to now we have not commented upon Herr Duehring's pompous opinions on final truths of the last instance, sovereignty of the will, absolute certainty of knowledge, and so forth, until the matter could first be brought to an issue. Up to this point the investigation has been useful to show how far the separate assertions of the philosophy of realism had "sovereign validity" and "unrestricted claim to truth" but we now come to the question if any and what product of human knowledge can have in particular "sovereign validity" and "unrestricted claims to truth." If I speak of human knowledge I do not do so as an affront to the dwellers in other worlds whom I have not the honor to know, but only because animals have knowledge also, not sovereign, however. The dog recognises a divinity in his master, who may, however, be a great fool.

"Is human thought sovereign?" Before we can answer "yes" or "no" we must first examine what human thought is. Is it the thought of an individual man? No. It exists only as the individual thoughts of many millions of men, past, present and to come. If I now say, having comprehended the thought of all men

MORALS AND LAW

in the future also under my concept, that it is able to understand the entire universe, if man only lasts long enough, and the organs of perception are unlimited, and the objects to be comprehended have no limits upon their comprehensibility, my statement is banal and barren. The most valuable result of such a conclusion would be to cause in us a tremendous distrust of present day knowledge. Because, to all appearance, we are just standing at the threshold of human history and the generations which will correct us will be much more numerous than those whose knowledge — often with little enough regard,— we ourselves correct. Herr Duehring himself explains the necessity of consciousness, knowledge and perception only becoming apparent in a collection of separate individuals. We can only apply the word sovereignty to the thought of these individuals in so far as we do not know of any force which can defeat thought. But we all know that there is no significance to nor power of interpretation of the sovereign power of the knowledge of the thought of each individual, and, according to our experience, there is much more that requires improvement and correction in it than not.

In other words, the sovereignty of thought is realised in a number of highly unsovereign men capable of thinking, the knowledge which has unlimited pretensions to truth is realised in a number of relative blunders; neither the one nor the other can be fully realised except through an endless eternity of human existence.

We have here again the same contradiction as above between the necessary, as an absolute conceived characteristic of human thought, and its reality in the very limited thinking single individual, a contradiction which can only be solved in the endless progression of the

LANDMARKS OF SCIENTIFIC SOCIALISM

human race, that is endless as far as we are concerned. In this sense human thought is just as sovereign as not — sovereign, and its possibility of knowledge just as unlimited as limited. It is sovereign and unlimited as regards its nature, its significance, its possibilities, its historical end, it is not sovereign and limited with respect to individual expression and its actuality at any particular time.

It is just the same with eternal truths. If mankind only operated with eternal truths and with thought which possessed a sovereign significance and unlimited claims to truth, mankind would have arrived at a point where the eternity of thought becomes realised in actuality and possibility. Thus the famous miracle of the enumerated innumerable would be realised.

But what about those truths which are so well established that to doubt them is to be, as it were, crazy? That twice two is four, that the three angles of a triangle are equal to two right angles, that Paris is in France, that a man will die of hunger if he does not receive food, etc? Do we not perceive then that there are eternal truths, final truths of last instance? Quite so. We can divide the entire field of knowledge in the old-fashioned way into three great divisions. The first includes all the sciences which are concerned with inanimate nature and which can be treated mathematically, more or less — mathematics, astronomy, mechanics, physics and chemistry. If one like to use big words to express simple things, it may be said that certain results of these sciences are eternal truths, final truths of last instance, whence they are called the exact sciences. But all the results are by no means of this character. With the introduction of variable quantities and the extension of the variability to the infinitely small and the infinitely

MORALS AND LAW

large, mathematics, otherwise erect, meets with its fall, it has eaten of the apple of knowledge and there has been opened up to it the path of limitless progress as well as that of error. The virgin condition of absolute purity, the undisturbable certainty of all mathematics has vanished forever, a period of controversy has intervened, and we have now arrived at the state of affairs in which most people carry on the operations of multiplication and division not because they really understand what they are engaged in, but from mere belief because the operation has so far always given correct results. Astronomy and mechanics, physics and chemistry are in a still more confused state, and hypotheses crowd one another thick as a swarm of bees. It cannot be otherwise. In physics we investigate the movements of molecules, in chemistry the development of molecules from atoms, and if the theory of light waves should not be correct we have no absolute knowledge that we even see these interesting things. The lapse of time produces a very thin crop of final truths of last instance. In geology we are in a still more embarrassing situation for we are here involved in the study of preceding epochs in which, as a matter of fact, neither we ourselves nor any other human being ever existed. Here there is much labor spent in the harvesting of truths of last instance, and they are a scanty crop withal.

The second division of knowledge is occupied in the investigation of living organisms. In this field the changes and causalities are so complex that not only does the solution of each question bring about the rise of an unlimited number of new questions, but the solution of each of these separate new questions depends upon years, frequently centuries, of investigation, and can then be only partially completed. So that the need of sys-

LANDMARKS OF SCIENTIFIC SOCIALISM

tematic arrangement of the various interrelations continually surrounds the final truths of the last instance with a prolific and spreading growth of hypotheses. Look at the long succession of progressive steps from Galen to Malpighi necessary to establish correctly so simple a thing as the circulation of the blood of mammals, yet how little we know of the origin of blood corpuscles and how many mistakes we make in, for example, rationally connecting the symptoms and cause of a disease. Besides there are frequently discoveries like those of the cell which compel us to entirely revise all hitherto firmly established truth of the last instance in biology, and to lay numbers of such truths aside for good and all. He who would therefore in this science undertake the proclamation of absolute and immutable truths must be content with such platitudes as the following: " All men must die; all female mammals have mammary glands, etc." He will not even be able to say that the greater animals digest their food by means of the stomach and bowels and not with the head because the centralised system of nerves in the head is not adapted to digestion.

But things are worse with regard to final truths of last instance in the third group of sciences — the historical. These are concerned with the conditions of human life, social conditions, forms of law and the state with their idealistic superstructure of philosophy, religion, art, etc., in their historic succession and in their present day manifestations. In organic nature we have at least to do with a succession of regular phenomena which regularly repeat themselves as far as our immediate observation goes, within very wide limits. Organic species have remained on the whole unaltered since the time of Aristotle. In social history, on the other hand, repetitions of conditions are the exception, not the rule,

MORALS AND LAW

directly we leave behind the prehistoric conditions of humanity, the stone-age, so-called. Where such repetitions do occur, moreover, they never recur under precisely similar conditions, as for example the occurrence of early tribal communism among all peoples anterior to civilisation and the form of its break up. As regards human history, then, as far as science is concerned, we are at a greater disadvantage than in biology. Furthermore, when the intimate relations existing between a social and political phenomenon come to be recognised it is not, as a rule, perceived until the conditions are actually on the way to decay. Knowledge is therefore entirely relative, since it is limited to a given people and a given epoch, and their nature under transitory social and political forms, when it examines relations and forms conclusions. He who therefore is after final truths of last instance, pure and immutable, will only manage to catch flat phrases and the most arrant commonplaces, like these — man cannot, generally speaking, live without working; up to the present men have for the most part been divided into masters and servants; Napoleon died on May 5th, 1821, and things of that sort.

It is worth noting that in this department of knowledge pretended final truths of last instance are met with most frequently. Only the person who wishes to show that there are eternal truth, eternal morality, and eternal justice in human history, and that these are similar in scope and application to those of mathematics, will proclaim that twice two is four and that birds have beaks and the like to be eternal truths. We can also certainly rely upon the same friend of humanity taking the opportunity to explain that all former inventors of eternal truths have been more or less asses or charlatans, that they have been circumscribed by error and have made mistakes. The fact of their error, however, is natural and proves the existence of the truth, and that it can be reached, and the newly arisen prophet has a ready-to-hand stock of final truths of last instance, eternal law and eternal justice. This has happened hundreds, nay, thousands of times, so that it is a wonder that men are still sufficiently credulous to believe it not only of others, but even of themselves. Here we find a prophet clad in the armour of righteousness who proclaims in the old-fashioned way that whoever else may deny there is still one left to declare final truths of last instance. Denial, nay, doubt even, is a weakness, barren confusion, mole-like scepticism, worse than blank nihilism, confusion worse confounded and other little amiabilities of this sort. As with all prophets, there is no scientific investigation, but merely off-hand condemnation.

We might have made mention of the sciences which investigate the laws of human thought, logic and dialectics. Here we are, however, no better off as regards eternal truths. Herr Duehring explains that the dialectic proper is pure nonsense, and the many books which have been and are still being written on logic prove clearly that final truths of last instance are more sparsely distributed than many believe.

Moreover, we are not at all alarmed because the step of science upon which we to-day stand is not a bit more final than any of the preceding steps. Already it includes an immense amount of material for investigation and offers a great chance for specialisation and study to anyone who desires to become expert in any particular branch. Whoever expects to find final and immutable truths in observations which in the very nature of things must remain relative for successive generations, and can only be completed piecemeal, as in cosmogony, geology

MORALS AND LAW

and human history, which must always be incomplete owing to the complexity of the historical material, shows perverse ignorance even where he does not, as in the present case, set up claims of personal infallibility.

Truth and error, like all such mutually antagonistic concepts, have only an absolute reality under very limited conditions, as we have seen, and as even Herr Duehring should know by a slight acquaintance with the first elements of dialectics, which show the insufficiency of all polar antagonisms. As soon as we bring the antagonism of truth and error out of this limited field it becomes relative and is not serviceable for new scientific statements. If we should seek to establish its reality beyond those limits we are at once confronted by a dilemma, both poles of the antagonism come into conflict with their opposite; truth becomes error and error becomes truth. Let us take, for example, the well-known Boyle's law, according to which, the temperature remaining the same, the volume of the gas varies as the pressure to which it is subjected. Regnault discovered that this law does not apply in certain cases. If he had been a realist-philosopher he would have been obliged to say, " Boyle's law is mutable, therefore it does not possess absolute truth, therefore it is untrue, therefore it is false." He would thus have made a greater error than that which was latent in Boyle's law, his little particle of truth would have been drowned in a flood of error; he would in this way have elaborated his correct result into an error compared with which Boyle's law with its particle of error fastened to it would have appeared as the truth. Regnault, scientist as he was, did not trouble himself with such childish performances. He investigated further and found that Boyle's law is only approximately correct, having no validity in the case of gases which can be made liquid by pressure when the pressure approaches the point where liquefaction sets in. Boyles law therefore is shown only to be true within specific bounds. But is it absolute, a final truth of last instance within specific bounds? No physicist would say so. He would say that it is correct for certain gases and within certain limits of pressure and temperature, and even then within these somewhat narrow limits he would not exclude the possibility of a still narrower limitation or change in application as the result of further investigation. This is how final truths of last instance stand in physics, for example. Really scientific works as a rule avoid such dogmatic expressions as truth and error, but they are constantly cropping up in works like the Philosophy of Reality, where mere loose talking vaunts itself the supreme result of sovereign thought.

But a naïve reader may say, " Where has Herr Duehring expressly stated that the content of his philosophy of reality is final truth of the last instance?" Well, for example, in his dithyramb on his system which we quoted above, and again where he says " Moral truths as far as they are known are as sound as those of mathematics." Does not Herr Duehring explain that by reason of his powers of criticism and searching investigations, the fundamental philosophy has been brought to light and that he has thus bestowed upon us final truths of last instance? But if Herr Duehring does not set up such a claim either on his own behalf or that of his time, if he says that some time in the misty future final truths of last instance will be established, and that therefore his own statements are merely accidental and confused, a kind of " mole-like scepticism " and " barren confusion," what is all the fuss about, and what useful purpose is served by Herr Duehring?

MORALS AND LAW

If we gain no ground in the matter of truth and error we gain less in respect of good and evil. Here we have an antagonism of ethical significance, and ethics is a department of human history in which final truths are but slight and few. From people to people, from age to age, there have been such changes in the ideas of good and evil that these concepts are contradictory in different periods and among different peoples. But some one may remark, " Good is still not evil and evil is not good; if good and evil are confused all morality is abolished, and each may do what he will." When the rhetoric is stripped away this is the opinion of Herr Duehring. But the matter is not to be disposed of so easily. If things were as easy as that there would be no dispute about good and evil. Everybody would know what was good and what was evil. How is it to-day, however? What system of ethics is preached to us to-day? There is first the Christian-feudal, a survival of the early days of faith, which is as a matter of fact subdivided into Catholic and Protestant, of which there are still further subdivisions, from the Jesuit-Catholic and orthodox Protestant to loosely drawn ethical systems. There figure also the modern or bourgeois, and still further the proletarian future system of morality, so that the progressive European countries alone present three contemporaneous and coexistent actual theories of ethics. Which is the true one? No single one of them, regarded as a finality, but that system assuredly possesses the most elements of truth which promises the longest duration, which existent in the present is also involved in the revolution of the future, the proletarian.

But if we now see that the three classes of modern society, the feudal aristocracy, the bourgeoisie and the proletarian, have their distinctive ethical systems, we can

LANDMARKS OF SCIENTIFIC SOCIALISM

only conclude therefrom that mankind consciously or unconsciously shapes its moral views in accordance with the material facts upon which in the last instance the class existence is based — upon the economic conditions under which production and exchange are carried on.

But in the three above mentioned systems of ethics there is much which is common to all three of them, and might not this at least constitute a portion of an eternally stable system of ethics? These ethical theories pass through three distinct steps in their historical development, they have therefore a common historical basis and hence necessarily much in common. Further, for approximately similar economic stages there must, necessarily be a coincidence of similar stages of economic development, and ethical theories must of necessity coincide with a greater or less degree of closeness. From the very moment when private property in movables developed there had to be ethical sanctions of general effect in all communities in which private property prevailed, thus: Thou shalt not steal. Is this commandment, then, an eternal commandment? By no means. In a society in which the motive for theft did not exist stealing would only be the practice of the weak-minded, and the preacher of morals who proclaimed "Thou shalt not steal" as an eternal commandment would only be laughed at for his pains.

We here call attention to the attempt to force a sort of moral dogmatism upon us as eternal, final, immutable moral law, upon the pretext that the moral law is possessed of fixed principles which transcend history and the variations of individual peoples. We state, on the contrary, that up to the present time all ethical theory is in the last instance a testimony to the existence of certain economic conditions prevailng in any community

MORALS AND LAW

at any particular time. And in proportion as society developed class-antagonisms, morality became a class morality and either justified the interests and domination of the ruling class, or as soon as a subject class became strong enough justified revolt against the domination of the ruling class and the interests of the subject class. That, by this means, there is an advance made in morals as a whole, just as there is in all other branches of human knowledge, there can be no doubt. But we have not yet advanced beyond class morals. Real human morality superior to class morality and its traditions will not be possible until a stage in human history has been reached in which class antagonisms have not only been overcome but have been forgotten as regards the conduct of life. Now the colossal egotism of Herr Duehring may be understood when it is seen that, on the eve of a revolution which will bring about a state of society devoid of classes, he claims from the midst of an old and class divided society to proclaim an eternal system of morals independent of time and material change. He himself declares what up to the present has been hid from the rest of us that he understands the structure of this future society at least as regards its salient features.

In conclusion he makes a revelation which is essentially original but none the less " fundamental respecting the origin of evil." We have the fact that the type of the cat with its inherent treachery is pictured as the representative animal type, and this also displays a form of character to be found also in man. There is no mystery then about evil if one can detect a mysticism in the cat or any other beast of prey. Evil is — the cat. Goethe was evidently wrong when he introduced Mephistopheles as a black dog instead of a cat similarly colored. This is ethics suited not only to all worlds but to cats also.

Equality

By dint of experience we have come to learn Herr Duehring's "method." It consists in separating each department of knowledge into what are assumed to be its most simple elements, then of making so called self evident axioms with regard to these simple elements, and thereupon operating with the results obtained in this way. Thus a sociological question is to be "decided on simple axiomatic principles just as if it were a matter of elementary mathematics." Thus the application of the mathematical method to history, ethics and law gives mathematical certainty to the final results which appear as pure and immutable truths.

This is only another form of the old ideological, *a priori* method so called, which learned the properties of an object not from the object itself but derived them by proof from the concept of the object. First you derive a concept of the object from the actual object, then you turn the spit and measure the object in terms of its derivative the concept. The concept is not shaped after the pattern of the object but the object after the pattern of the concept. In Herr Duehring's method, the simplest elements, the last abstractions to which he can attain do duty for the concept which is unchangeable, the simplest elements are under the best conditions purely imaginary in their nature. The philosophy of realism hence appears to be mere ideology, and has no derivation

MORALS AND LAW

from real life but is absolutely dependent upon the imagination. When such an ideologist proceeds to construct a system of morals and law from his concept of the so-called simplest elements of society instead of from the real social conditions of the men about him, where does he get his material for construction? The material evidently consists of two kinds — firstly, the slim vestiges of reality which are still present in every fundamental abstraction, and secondly in the actual content which our ideologist evolves from his own consciousness. And what does he discover in his consciousness? For the most part moral and ethical philosophic ideas and these constitute an expression corresponding more or less closely, whether positive or negative, harmonious or hostile, with the social and political conditions which environ him. Besides he probably has notions derived from literature pertaining to these conditions, and finally he has possibly personal idiosyncrasies. Let our ideologist dodge all that he can, the historical reality which he has thrown out of doors comes in again at the window and although he may fancy that he is employed in the manufacture of moral and legal doctrines good for all worlds and all ages he is actually making a distorted, counterfeit of the conservation or revolutionary tendencies of his time, because torn from its real place, as things seen in a concave mirror are upside down.

Herr Duehring therefore resolves society into its simplest elements and discovers accordingly that the most elementary society consists of at least two human beings. He thereupon operates with these two human beings to produce his axiom. Then he delivers himself of the fundamental maxim of morals, " Two human wills, as such, are entirely identical, and the one can in consequence make no positive demands upon the other."

LANDMARKS OF SCIENTIFIC SOCIALISM

Here the " foundation of moral law " is apparent, so " in order to develop the principal concepts of justice we require two human beings under absolutely simple and elementary conditions."

That two human wills or two human beings are just alike is not only no axiom, it is a glaring exaggeration. In the first place two human beings may differ as regards sex, and this simple fact shows us, if we look at childhood for a moment, that the elements of society are not two men, but a little man and a little woman, which constitute a family, the simplest and earliest form of association for productive purposes. But Herr Duehring cannot by any means agree to this. On the one hand the two constituents of society might very possibly be made alike and on the other Herr Duehring would not be able to construct the moral and legal equality of man and woman from the original family. Therefore one of two things must take place. Either the molecules of Herr Duehring's society from the multiplication of which all society is built up is merely *a priori* and destined to fail, since two men cannot produce a child, or we must consider them as two heads of families. In this case the entire foundation is made its very opposite. Instead of the equality of man we have at the most the equality of two heads of families, and since women are not comprehended we have the consequent subjection of women.

We are sorry to warn the reader that these two notorious men cannot be got rid of, for a long time. They take up in the realm of social conditions the role heretofore played by the dwellers in the other world with whom it is to be hoped we have now finished. Should any question of political economy, of politics or any other such matter require solution, out come the two men and

MORALS AND LAW

make the thing axiomatic forthwith. This is a remarkable, clever, and system-shaping discovery of our system-shaping philosopher. But to give the truth its due we are regretfully bound to say that he did not discover the two men. They are common to the whole of the eighteenth century. They appear in Rousseau's Treatise on Equality, 1754, where, by the way, they serve to prove axiomatically the direct opposite of Herr Duehring's contentions. They play an important part in political economy from Adam Smith to Ricardo, but here they are so far unequal that they follow different trades, principally hunting and fishing, and they exchange their mutual products. They serve through the entire eighteenth century principally as mere illustrative examples, and the originality of Herr Duehring consists in the fact that he elevates this method of illustration to a fundamental method for all social science and to a measure of all historical instruction. There is no easier way to arrive at "a really scientific philosophy of things and men."

In order to create the fundamental axiom the two men and their wills are mutually equal and neither has any right to lord it over the other. We cannot find two suitable men. They must be two men who are so free from all national, economic, political and religious conditions, from sex and personal peculiarities that nothing remains of either of them but the mere concept "man" and then they are entirely equal. They are therefore two fully-equipped ghosts conjured up by that very Herr Duehring who particularly ridicules and denounces "spiritistic" movements. These two phantoms must of course do all that their wizard wants of them and so their united productions are a matter of complete indifference to the rest of the world.

LANDMARKS OF SCIENTIFIC SOCIALISM

Now let us follow Herr Duehring's axiomatic utterances a little further. These two men cannot make positive demands upon each other. The one who does so and enforces his demand thereupon performs an unjust act, and with this idea as a foundation Herr Duehring explains the injustice, the tyranny, the servitude, in short all the evil happenings of history up to the present time. Now Rousseau has in the work above mentioned proved the contrary just as axiomatically, by means of two men. A. cannot forcibly enslave B. except by putting B. in a place where he cannot do without A. This is far too materialistic an idea for Herr Duehring. He has accordingly put the same matter somewhat differently. Two shipwrecked men being by themselves on an island form a society. Their wills are, theoretically speaking, entirely equal and this is acknowledged by both. But in reality the inequality is tremendous. A. is resolute and energetic, B. inert, irresolute and slack. A. is sharp, B. is stpuid. How long will it be before A. imposes his will upon B., first by taking the upper hand, and keeping it habitually, under the pretence that B.'s submission is voluntary. Whether the form of voluntariness continues or force is resorted to slavery still is slavery. Voluntary entering into a state of slavery lasted all through the Middle Ages in Germany up to the Thirty Years War. When serfdom was abolished in Prussia after the defeats of 1806 and 1807 and with it the duty of the nobility to take care of their subjects in need, sickness and old age the peasants thereupon petitioned to be allowed to remain in slavery — for who would care for them when they were in trouble? The concept of the two men is just as applicable to inequality and slavery as it is to equality and mutual aid, and since, under the penalty of extinction, men must as-

MORALS AND LAW

sume the headship of a family, hereditary slavery may be foreseen in it.

Let us put this view of the case on one side for a moment. We assume that we are convinced by Herr Duehring's maxim and that we are zealous for the full equalisation of the two wills, for the "universal sovereignty of man" for the "sovereignty of the individual," magnificent expressions, in comparison with which Stirner's "individual" with his private property is a mere bungler though he might claim his modest part therein. Then we are all free and independent. All? No, not even now. There are still "occasional dependent relations" but these are to be explained "on grounds which must be sought not in the action of two wills as such but in a third consideration, in the case of children, for example, in the inadequateness of their self-assertion."

Indeed, the foundations of independence are not to be sought in the realisation of the two wills as such. Naturally not, since the realisation of one of the wills is thus interfered with. But they must be sought in a third direction. And what is the third direction? The actual fixing of a subjected will as an inadequate one. So far has our realistic philosopher departed from reality that will, the real content, the characteristic determination of this will serves him as a third ground, for abstract and indefinite speech. However this may be we must agree that equality has its exceptions. It does not apply to a will which is infected with inadequateness of self expression.

Further, "Where the animal and the human are intermingled in one person can one in the name of a second fully developed human being demand the same actions as in the case of a single human being . . . our supposition is here of two morally unequal persons of which

LANDMARKS OF SCIENTIFIC SOCIALISM

one has a share of purely animal characteristics in a certain sense the typical fundamental conception which characterises the differences in and between groups of men." Now the reader may see by these modest excuses in which Herr Duehring turns and winds like a Jesuit priest to establish a casuistical position, how far the human human can prevail over the bestial human, how far he can employ deceit, warlike, keen terrorising means of deceit against the latter without overstepping immutable ethical bounds.

Therefore, if two persons are "morally unequal" there is an end of equality. It was therefore not worth while to conjure up two fully equal men, since there are no two individuals who are morally equal. But inequality consists in this that one is a human being and the other has some part of the animal in his composition. It is evident that since man is descended from the animal creation he is not free from animality. So that as regards man degrees of animality can only be differentiated to a greater or less degree. A division of men into two sharply differentiated groups, into humans and human beasts, into good and bad, into sheep and goats, even Christianity, let alone the realist philosophy, is aware, implies a judge who makes the distinction. But who shall be judge as regards the realist philosophy? We must follow the practice of Christians according to which the pious little sheep undertake to act as judges of the universe against their unworthy neighbors the goats, with results which are too well known. The sect of the realist philosophers supposing it ever comes into existence will certainly not give up anything quietly. This is indeed a matter of small concern to us but we are interested in the confession that as a conclusion of the moral inequality between men equality no longer exists.

MORALS AND LAW

Again "If the one acted in accordance with truth and science but the other in accordance with a superstition or prejudice a mutual disagreement would generally occur. At a certain stage of incapacity barbarism or an evil tendency of character must in all circumstances produce an antagonism. Force is the last resort not alone with children and incapables. The peculiar characteristics of whole classes of men, whether in a state of nature or civilised, may render necessary the subjection of their inimical will, due to their own impotency, in order to bring them into harmony with social arrangements. But such a man has challenged his own equality by the perversity of his inimical and hurtful actions, and if he suffers at the hands of a superior force he only reaps the recoil of his own actions.'

Thus not only moral but spiritual inequality is sufficiently potent to do away with the "full equality" of two wills and to furnish an ethical rule by which all the shameful acts of civilised plundering states against backward peoples down to the atrocities of the Russians in Turkestan may be justified. When General Kaufmann, in the summer of 1873, fell upon the Tartar tribes of the Jomuden, burnt their tents, mowed down their wives and families, as the command ran, he explained that the destruction was due to the perversity, the inimical minds of the people of the Jomuden, and was employed for the purpose of bringing them back to the social order, and the means used by him had been the most efficient.

But he who wills the end wills also the means. But he was not so cruel as to insult the Jomuden people in addition and to say that he massacred them in the name of equality, that he considered their wills equal to his own. And again in this conflict the select, those who pose as champions of truth and science, the realist philos-

LANDMARKS OF SCIENTIFIC SOCIALISM

ophers in the last instance must be able to distinguish superstition, prejudice, barbarism, evil tendencies of character, and when force and subjection are necessary to bring about equality. So that equality now means equalisation by means of force, and the will of one recognises the will of the other as equal by overthrowing it.

The phrase that an external will in its bringing about equalisation by force is only to be regarded as producing equality is nothing but a distortion of the Hegelian theory that punishment is a right of the criminal. "That punishment is to be regarded as implying a right to it in accordance with which the criminal is respected as a rational being." (Rechtsphil, 100.)

We may pause here. It would be superfluous to follow Herr Duehring any further in the piecemeal destruction of his axiomatically established equality, universal human sovereignty, etc., to observe how he brings society into existence with two men and produces yet a third in order to establish the state, because to put the matter briefly, no majority can be had without the third, and without him, that is, without the domination of the majority over the minority, no state can exist. There is no need either for us to observe how he launches his future social state on the more peaceful waters of construction, where we may have the honor some fine morning of beholding it. We have seen so far that the complete equality of two wills only exists as long as they do not will anything. That as soon as they cease to become human wills as such and to be converted into real individual wills, into wills of real persons, that is, equality ceases; that childhood, idiocy, animality so called, superstition, prejudice, supposed lack of power on the one hand and supposed humanity and insight into truth and science on the other hand, that therefore every difference

MORALS AND LAW

in the quality of the two wills and in the degree of intelligence accompanying it justifies an inequality which may go as far as subjection. Why should we seek further since Herr Duehring has brought his own edifice of equality which he so laboriously constructed tumbling to the ground?

But if we are now prepared to meet Herr Duehring's silly and incompetent consideration of equality of rights we are not yet ready to take issue with the idea itself which through the influence of Rousseau has played a theatrical part, and since the days of the great Revolution a practical and political part, and now plays no insignificant role in the agitation carried on by the socialist movement of all countries. The establishment of its scientific soundness has a value for the proletarian agitation.

The idea that all men have something in common as men and that they are equal with respect to that common quality is naturally older than history. But the modern doctrine of equality is something quite different than that. This derives from the property of humanity, common to man, the equality of man, as man, or at least of all citizens of a given state or of all members of a given society. Until the conclusion of equality of rights in the state and society was deduced from the original notion of relative equality, and until this conclusion was to be stated as something natural and self evident, many thousands of years had to pass and indeed have passed. In the oldest and most elementary communities it may be said that equality of rights among the members existed in the highest degree, women, slaves, and foreigners, however, being excluded. Among the Greeks and Romans inequality existed to a greater degree. Greeks and barbarians, freemen and slaves, citizens and subjects, Roman citizens and Roman subjects (to employ

LANDMARKS OF SCIENTIFIC SOCIALISM

a comprehensive expression) that these should have any claim to equality of political rights would have been regarded by the ancients necessarily as madness. Under the Roman Empire there was a complete elimination of all these distinctions with the excepiton of those of freemen and slaves. There arose therefore as far as the freemen were concerned that equality of private individuals upon which Roman law was founded and developed as the most perfect system of jurisprudence based on private property with which we are acquainted. But while the contradiction of freemen and slaves existed there could be no statement based upon the universal equality of man as such, as was recently shown in the slave states of the Northern American Union.

Christianity recognised one equality on the part of all men, that of an equal taint of original sin, which entirely corresponded with its character as a religion of slaves and the oppressed. In the next place it recognised completely the equality of the elect but it only declared this at the beginning of its teaching. The traces of common property in possessions which may be found occasionally in the earliest days of the religion was based rather upon the mutual assistance which persecuted people hold out to each other, than upon any real concepts of human equality. Very soon the establishment of the antithesis between the priesthood and the laity put an end to even this expression of Christian equality. The inundation of Western Europe by the Germans abolished for centuries all concepts of equality by the creation of a universal, social and political gradation of rank of a much more complicated nature than had existed up to that time. Contemporaneously with this Western and Middle Europe entered upon a historical development, shaped for the first time a compact civilisation, and a

MORALS AND LAW

system which was on the one hand dynamic and on the other conservative, the leading national states. Thereupon a soil was prepared for the declaration of the equality of human rights so recently made.

The feudal middle ages moreover developed the class in its womb destined to be the apostle of the modern agitation for equality, the bourgeois class. In the beginning even under the feudal system the bourgeois class had developed the prevalent hand-industry and the exchange of products even within feudal society to a high degree considering the circumstances, until with the close of the fifteenth century the great discoveries of lands beyond the seas opened before it a new and individual course. The trade beyond Europe which up to that time had been carried on between the Italians and the Levant was now extended to America and the Indies and soon exceeded in amount the reciprocal trade of the European countries as well as the internal commerce of any particular land. American gold and silver flooded Europe and like a decomposing element penetrated all the fissures, crevices and pores of feudal society. The system of hand-labor was no longer sufficient for the growing demand, it was replaced by manufacture in the leading industries of the most highly developed peoples.

A corresponding change in the political structure followed this powerful revolution in the economic conditions of society but by no means immediately. The organisation of the State remained feudal in form while society became more and more bourgeois. Trade, particularly international, and to a greater degree world-commerce demanded for its development the free and unrestricted possessors of commodities, who have equality of right to exchange commodities at least in one and the same place. The transition from hand labor to man-

LANDMARKS OF SCIENTIFIC SOCIALISM

ufacture presupposes the existence of a number of free laborers, free on the one hand from the fetters of the gild and on the other free to employ their labor force in their own behalf, who could make contracts for the hire of their labor force to the manufacturers and therefore face him as if endowed with equal rights as contracting parties. At last then there arose equality of rights and actual equality of all human labor, for labor force finds its unconscious but strongest expression in the law of value of modern bourgeois economy according to which the value of a commodity finds its measure in the socially necessary labor incorporated in it. But where the economic circumstances render freedom and equality of rights necessary, the political code, gild restrictions and peculiar privileges oppose them at every step. Local provisions of a legal character, differential taxation, exceptional laws of every description, interfere not only with foreigners or colonials but frequently enough also with whole categories of citizens in the nation itself. Gild privileges in particular constituted a continual impediment to the development of manufacture. The course was nowhere open and the chances of the bourgeois victory were by no means equal, but to make the course open was the first and ever more pressing necessity.

As soon as the demand for the abolition of feudalism and for the equality of rights was set on the order of the day it had necessarily to take an ever widening scope. As soon as the claim was made in behalf of commerce and industry it had also to be made in behalf of the peasants who, being in every stage of slavery from serfdom labored for the most part without any return for the feudal lords and were obliged in addition to perform innumerable services for them and for the State. Also

MORALS AND LAW

it became desirable to abolish feudal privileges, the immunity of the nobility from taxation, and the superiority which attached to a certain status. And as men no longer lived in a world empire like the Roman, but in an independent system with states which approximated to a similar degree of bourgeois development and which had intercourse with one another on an equal footing, the demand took on necessarily a universal character reaching beyond the individual state, and freedom and equality were thus proclaimed as human rights. But as regards the special bourgeois character of these human rights, it is significant that the American Constitution which was the first to recognise these rights of man in the same breath established slavery among the colored people: class privileges were cursed, race privileges were blessed.

As is well known, the bourgeois class as soon as it escaped from the domination of the ruling class in the cities, by which process the medieval stage passes into the modern, has been steadily and inevitably dogged by a shadow, the proletariat. So also the bourgeois demands for equality are accompanied by the proletarian demands for equality. Directly the demand for the abolition of class privileges was made by the bourgeois there succeeded the proletarian demand for the abolition of classes themselves. This was first made in a religious form and was based upon early Christianity, but later derived its support from the bourgeois theories of equality. The proletarians take the bourgeois at their word, they demand the realisation of equality not merely apparently, not merely in the sphere of government but actually in the sphere of society and economics. Since the French bourgeoisie of the great Revolution placed equality in the foreground of their movement, the French

LANDMARKS OF SCIENTIFIC SOCIALISM

proletariat has answered it blow for blow with the demand for social and economic equality, and equality has become the special battle cry of the French proletariat.

The demand for equality as made by the proletariat has a double significance. Either it is, as was particularly the case at first, in the Peasants' War, for example, a natural reaction against social inequalities which were obvious, against the contrast between rich and poor, masters and slaves, luxurious and hungry, and as such it is simply an expression of revolutionary instinct finding its justification in that fact and in that fact alone. On the other hand it may arise from reaction against the bourgeois claims of equality from which it deduces more or less just and far reaching claims, serves as a means of agitation to stir the workers, by means of a cry adopted by the capitalists themselves, against the capitalists, and in this case stands or falls with bourgeois equality itself. In both cases the real content of the proletarian claims of equality is the abolition of classes. Every demand for equality transcending this is of necessity absurd. We have already given examples and can furnish many more when we come to consider Herr Duehring's prophecies of the future.

So the notion of equality, in its proletarian as well as in its bourgeois form, is itself a historic product. Certain circumstances were required to produce it and these in their turn proceeded from a long anterior history. It is therefore anything but an eternal truth. And if the public regards it as self-evident in one sense or another if it, as Marx remarks "already occupies the position of a popular prejudice" it is not due to its being an axiomatic truth but to the universal broadening of conception in accordance with the spirit of the eighteenth century. If Herr Duehring then can set up his two

MORALS AND LAW

famous men in housekeeping on the grounds of equality, it is apparent that the prejudices of the mass of men in its favor is an antecedent condition. In fact Herr Duehring calls his philosophy the "natural" because it proceeds from generally recognised things, which appear to him to be entirely natural. But why they seem to him to be natural he does not take the trouble to enquire.

Freedom and Necessity

(The former part of this section is taken up with a criticism of Herr Duehring's knowledge of law of which he had boasted. It is a purely technical discussion and is of merely local interest. Having disposed of Duehring's juristic claims Engels proceeds to discuss "Freedom and Necessity" as follows.)

One cannot deal properly with the question of morals and law without a discussion of free will, human responsibility, and the limits of necessity and freedom. The realistic philosophy has not only one but two solutions of these questions.

"One must substitute for false theories of freedom the actual conditions in which reason on the one hand and instinct on the other unite upon a middle ground. The fundamental facts of this sort of dynamics are to be learned from observation and as regards the calculation in advance of phenomena which have not yet occurred, we must judge of them in general terms according to their special qualities. In this way the silly speculations with respect to the freedom of the will which have wasted thousands of years are not only entirely removed but are replaced by something positive, something useful for practical life." So freedom of the will consists in this that reason impels men to the right and irrationality to the left and according to this parallelogram of forces the true direction is that of the diagonal.

MORALS AND LAW

Freedom would therefore be the average between insight and impulse, between understanding and lack of understanding, and its degree would to use an astronomical expression be empirically established by the "personal equation." But a few pages later we read "We establish moral responsibility upon freedom by which we only mean susceptibility to known motives according to the measure of natural and acquired reason. All such motives in spite of antagonism realise themselves in action with the inevitability of natural law, but we count upon this inevitable necessity when we deal with morals."

This second definition of freedom which is quite opposed to the first is nothing but a very weak paraphrase of Hegel's notions on the subject. Hegel was the first man to make a proper explanation of the relations of freedom and necessity. In his eyes freedom is the recognition of necessity. "Necessity is blind only in so far as it is not understood. Freedom does not consist in an imaginary independence of natural laws but in a knowledge of these laws and in the possibility thence derived of applying them intelligently to given ends. This is true both as regards the laws of nature and of those which control the spiritual and physical existence of man himself,— two classes of laws which we can distinguish as an abstraction but not in reality. Freedom of the will consists in nothing but the ability to come to a decision when one is in possession of a knowledge of the facts. The freer the judgment of a man then in relation to a given subject of discussion so much the more necessity is there for his arrival at a positive decision. On the other hand lack of certainty arising from ignorance which apparently chooses voluntarily between many different and contradictory possibilities of decision shows thereby its want of freedom, its control by things which it should

LANDMARKS OF SCIENTIFIC SOCIALISM

in reality control. Freedom, therefore, consists in mastery over ourselves and external nature founded upon knowledge of the necessities of nature, it is, therefore, necessarily a product of historical development. The first human beings to become differentiated from the lower animals were in all essentials as devoid of freedom as these animals themselves but each step in human development was a step towards freedom. At the threshold of human history stands the discovery of the transformation of mechanical motion in heat, the generation of fire by friction; at the close of development up to the present stands the discovery of the transformation of heat into mechanical motion, the steam engine. In spite of the tremendous revolution in the direction of freedom which the steam engine has produced in society it is not yet half complete. There is no question that the production of fire by friction still surpasses it as an agent in the liberation of humanity. Because the production of fire by friction for the first time gave man power over the forces of nature and separated him for ever from the lower animals. The steam engine can never bridge so wide a chasm. It appears however as the representative of all those productive forces by the help of which alone a state of society is rendered possible in which no class subjection or pain will be produced by reason of the lack of means for the sustenance of the individual, in which moreover it will be possible to speak of real human freedom as arising from living in accordance with the recognised laws of nature. But considering the youth of humanity it would be absurd to wish to impute any universal absolute validity to our present philosophical views, and it follows from the mere facts that the whole of history up to the present time is to be regarded as the history of the period extending from the time of

MORALS AND LAW

the practical discovery of the transformation of mechanical movement into heat to that of the transformation of heat into mechanical movement.

(The above constitutes a reply to the view which regards history simply as the record of human error and is followed by a discussion of Duehring's opinions in that regard.)

CHAPTER VII

THE DIALECTIC

Quantity and Quality

(Here Herr Duehring contends "The first and most important statement with respect to the foundation logical properties of existence points to the exclusion of contradiction. Contradiction is a category which can belong to thought alone but which can pertain to nothing real. There are no contradictions in things; in other words the law of contradiction is itself the crowning point of absurdity." To which Engels replies as follows):

The thought content of the foregoing passages is contained in the statement that contradiction is an absurdity and cannot occur in the actual world. This statement will have for people of average common sense the same self-evident truth as to say that straight cannot be crooked nor crooked straight. But the differential calculus shows in spite of all the protests of common sense that under certain conditions straight and crooked are identical, and reaches thereby a conclusion which is not in harmony with the common sense view of the absurdity of there being any identity between straight and crooked. Considering moreover the significant role which the so called Dialectic of the Contradiction played in the ancient Greek philosophy, a stronger opponent than Herr Duehring would be obliged to meet it with better arguments than a mere affirmation and a number of epithets.

As long as we regard things as static and without life,

THE DIALECTIC

each by itself, separately, we do not run against any contradictions in them. We find certain qualities sometimes common, sometimes distinctive, occasionally contradictory, but in this last case they belong to different objects and are hence not self contradictory. While we follow this method we pursue the ordinary metaphysical method of thought. But it is quite different when we consider things in their movement, in their change, their life and their mutually reciprocal relations. Then we come at once upon contradictions. Motion is itself a contradiction since simple mechanical movement from place to place can only accomplish itself by a body being at one and the same moment in one place and simultaneously in another place by being in one and the same place and yet not there. And motion is just the continuous establishing and dissolving the contradiction.

Here we have a contradiction which is " objective, and so to speak corporeal in things and events." And what does Herr Duehring say about it? He affirms that " in rational mechanics there is no bridge between the strictly static and the dynamic." Finally the reader is able to see that there is behind this pretty little phrase of Herr Duehring nothing more than this — that the metaphysical mode of thought can absolutely not pass from the idea of rest to that of motion because the aforesaid contradiction intervenes. Motion is absolutely inconceivable to the metaphysician, because a contradiction. And as he affirms the inconceivability of motion he admits the existence of this contradiction against his will and therefore admits that it constitutes an objective contradiction in actual facts and events, and is moreover an actual fact.

But if simple mechanical motion contains a contradiction in itself still more so do the higher forms of motion

LANDMARKS OF SCIENTIFIC SOCIALISM

of matter and to a high degree organic life and its development. We saw above that life consists chiefly in this that a being is at one and the same time itself and something different. Life itself then is likewise a contradiction contained in things and events, always establishing and dissolving itself, and as soon as the contradiction ceases life also ceases, death comes on the scene. Thus we saw also that we cannot put an end to the Contradictions in the realm of thought, and how for example the contradiction between the intrinsically unlimited possibilities of human knowledge and its actual existence in the persons of human beings with limited faculties and powers of knowledge, is dissolved in the, for us at least, practically endless progression of the race, in unending progress.

We stated just now that higher mathematics holds as one of its basic principles that straight and crooked may be identical under certain circumstances. It shows another contradiction, that lines which apparently intersect yet are parallel from five to six centimeters from the point of intersection, should be such as should never intersect although indefinitely produced, and yet, notwithstanding these and even greater contradictions, it produces not only correct results but results which are unattainable by lower mathematics.

But even in the latter there is a host of contradictions. It is a contradiction, for example, that a root of A should be and actually is a power of A. A to the power of one-half equals the square root of A. It is contradiction that a negative magnitude should be the square of anything, since every negative magnitude multiplied by itself gives a positive square. The square root of minus one is therefore not only a contradiction but an absurd contradiction, a veritable absurdity. And yet the square

THE DIALECTIC

root of minus one is in many instances the necessary result of correct mathematical operations, nay further, where would mathematics higher or lower be if one were forbidden to operate with the square root of minus one.

Mathematics itself enters the realm of the dialectic and significantly enough it was a dialectic philosopher, Descartes, who introduced this progressiveness into mathematics. As is the relation of the mathematics of variable magnitudes to that of invariable quantities, so is the relation of the dialectic method of thought to the metaphysical. This does not prevent the great majority of mathematicians from only recognising the dialectic in the realms of mathematics, a condition of things satisfactory to those who operate in the antiquated, limited, metaphysical fashion by methods attained by means of the dialectic.

. . . .

(Duehring having made an attack upon Marx's " Capital " because of its reliance upon the dialectic, and having indulged in the epithets to which he is too prone with respect to this work, Engels takes up its defence in that respect as follows) :

It is not our business to concern ourselves at this point with the correctness or incorrectness of the investigations of Marx as regards economics, but only with the application which he makes of the dialectic method. So much is certain, that it is only now that the readers of " Capital " will by the aid of Herr Duehring understand what they have read properly, and among them Herr Duehring himself, who in the year 1867 was still in a position, as far as possible to a man of his calibre, to review the book rationally. He did not then, it may be noted, first translate the arguments of Marx into Duehringese, as now seems indispensable to him. Even if he at that time made the blunder of identifying the Marxian dialectic with that of Hegel he had not altogether lost the ability to distinguish methods from the results attained by them and to comprehend that an abuse of the former is no contradiction of the latter.

Herr Duehring's most astonishing observation is that from the Marxian standpoint, " in the last analysis everything is identical," that therefore in the eyes of Marx, for example, capitalists and wage workers, feudal, capitalistic and social methods of production are " all one." In order to show the possibility of such sheer stupidity it only remains to point out that the mere word " dialectic " makes Herr Duehring mentally irresponsible and makes what he says and does so inaccurrate and confused as to be in the last analysis " all one."

· · · · · · · · · · ·

(Herr Duehring remarks, " How comical for example is the declaration based upon Hegel's confused notions that quantity becomes lost in quality and that money advanced [i. e. for productive purposes. Ed.] becomes capital when it reaches a certain limit merely through quantitative increase." To which Engels replies thus):

This seems peculiar when presented in this washed out fashion by Herr Duehring. On page 313 (2nd ed. " Capital ") Marx, after an investigation of fixed and variable capital and surplus value, derives from his investigations the conclusion that " not every amount of gold or value capable of being transformed into capital is so transformed; rather a certain minimum of gold or of exchange value is presupposed to be in the possession of the individual owner of gold or goods." He thereupon gives an example, thus, in a branch of industry the worker works eight hours per day for himself, i. e. in order to produce the value of his wages, and the follow-

THE DIALECTIC

ing four hours for the capitalist in producing surplus value to go into their pockets. One must have sufficient values to permit of the setting up of two workmen with raw material, means of labor and wages, in order to live as well as a workman. But since capitalistic production is not undertaken for mere livelihood but for increase of wealth, our individual with his two workmen would still be no capitalist. If he lives twice as well as an ordinary workman and transforms half of the surplus value produced into capital he will have to employ eight workmen and possess four times the aforementioned amount of value, and only after this and other examples for the purpose of illustrating and establishing the fact that not every small amount of value can effect a transformation of itself into capital, but that each period of industrial development and each branch of industry has its own minimum, fixed, Marx remarks " Here, as in nature, the correctness of the law of logic, as discovered by Hegel, is established — that mere quantitative changes at a certain point suddenly take on qualitative differences."

One may remark the elevated and dignified fashion in which Duehring makes Marx say the exact opposite of what he did say. Marx says " The fact that a given amount of value can only transform itself into capital as soon as it has attained a definite minimum, varying with circumstances, in each individual case, — this fact is proof of the correctness of the law of Hegel. Herr Duehring makes him say " Because, according to the law of Hegel, quantity is transformed into quality therefore ' a sum of money when it has reached a certain amount becomes capital.' He says just the opposite.

We have seen above in the Scheme of the Universe that Herr Duehring had the misfortune to acknowledge

LANDMARKS OF SCIENTIFIC SOCIALISM

and apply, in a weak moment, this Hegelian system of calculation, according to which at a given point quantitative changes suddenly become qualitative. We then gave one of the best known examples, that of the transformation of the form of water which at 0° C. changes from a liquid to solid and at 100° C. from liquid to gaseous, where thus at both these points of departure a mere quantitative change in temperature produces a qualitative change in the water.

We might have cited from nature and human society a hundred more such facts in proof of this law, thus the whole fourth section of Marx's "Capital" entitled "Production of Relative Surplus Value in the realm of coöperative industry, the Division of Labor, and Manufacture, Machinery and the Great Industry," goes to show innumerable instances in which qualitative change alters the quantity of the thing, and where also, to use Herr Duehring's exceedingly odious expression, quantity is converted and transformed into quality. So also the mere coöperation of large numbers, the melting of several diverse crafts into one united craft, to use Marx's expression, produces a new "industrial power" which is substantially different from the sum of the individual crafts.

Marx, in the interest of the entire truth, has remarked, in complete contrast to the perverted style of Herr Duehring "The molecular theory employed in modern chemistry, first scientifically developed by Laurent and Gerhardt, rests upon no other law. But what does Herr Duehring care for that? He knows that "the eminently modern constructive elements of scientific thought make just the same mistake as was made by Marx and his rival Lassalle; half-knowledge and a touch of pseudo-philosophy furnish the tools necessary for a display of

THE DIALECTIC

learning." While with Herr Duehring "elevated notions of exact knowledge in mechanics, physics and chemistry" are, as we have seen, the foundations. But that the public may be in a position to decide we shall examine somewhat more closely the example cited by Marx in his note.

Here we have, for example, the homologous series of compounds of carbon of which many are known and each has its own algebraic formula. If we, for example, according to the practice of chemistry, represent an atom of carbon by C, an atom of hydrogen by H, an atom of oxygen by O and the number of atoms contained in each combination of carbon by n, we can express the molecular formula of each one of this series thus,

$C_nH_{2n} + 2$ — Series of normal paraffin.

$C_nH_{2n} + 2O$ — Series of primary alcohol.

$C_nH_{2n}O_2$ — Series of the monobasic oleic acids.

Let us take, for example, the last of this series and set one after the other $n=1$, $n=2$, etc., we get the following results omitting the compounds.

CH_2O_2 — Formic Acid — boiling point 100°— melting point 1°.

$C_2H_4O_2$ — Acetic Acid — boiling point 118°— melting point 17°.

$C_3H_6O_2$ — Propionic Acid — boiling point 140°— melting point —.

$C_4H_8O_2$ — Butyric Acid — boiling point 162°— melting point —.

$C_5H_{10}O_2$ — Valerianic Acid — boiling point 175°— melting point —.

And so on to $C_{30}H_{60}O_2$, Melissic Acid, which melts first at 180°, and which has no boiling point, because it does not evaporate without splitting up.

Here we see therefore a whole series of qualitatively

LANDMARKS OF SCIENTIFIC SOCIALISM

different bodies, produced by single quantitative additions of the elements and always in the same proportions. This occurs absolutely where all elements of the combinations change their quantity in the same proportions, so with normal paraffin, C_nH_{2n+2}: the lowest is CH_4 a gas, the highest known is $C_{16}H_{34}$, a body forming a hard colorless crystal which melts at 21° and boils at 278°. In both the series each new step is reached through the introduction of CH_2, an atom of carbon and two atoms of hydrogen, to the molecular form of the preceding step, and this quantitative change in the molecular form brings about a qualitatively different body.

These series are merely obvious examples. Almost universally in chemistry, particularly in the different oxides of nitrogen, in the oxi-acids of phosphorus or sulphur, one can see how "quantity suddenly changes into quality" and how this so called "confused Hegelianism" is, so to speak, inherent in things and events, and no one is ever confused or beclouded by it, except Herr Duehring. If Marx is the first to observe this, and if Herr Duehring points this out, without understanding it (since he could not let so unheard of a crime pass), he should explain which of the two, Marx or Duehring, is without elementary conceptions of natural science and the established principles of chemistry, and do it without boasting about his own ideas on natural philosophy.

In conclusion, let us call attention to a witness on the change of quantity into quality, namely Napoleon. He describes the conflicts between the French cavalry, bad riders but disciplined, with the Mamelukes who, as regards single combat were better horsemen but undisciplined, as follows — Two Mamelukes were a match for three Frenchmen, one hundred Mamelukes were equal to one hundred Frenchmen, three hundred Frenchmen

THE DIALECTIC

could beat three hundred Mamelukes and a thousand Frenchmen invariably defeated fifteen hundred Mamelukes." Just as in the statement of Marx, that a certain amount of money, variable in amount, is necessary as a minimum, to make its transformation into capital possible, so, according to Napoleon, a certain minimum number of cavalrymen is required to bring into being the force of discipline inherent in military organisation, to make them evidently superior to greater numbers of individually better riders and fighters, cavalry at least as brave, though irregular. But what effect has this argument on Herr Duehring? Was not Napoleon utterly defeated in his conflict with Europe? Did he not suffer defeat after defeat? And why? Simply as a result of his introduction of confused Hegelian ideas into cavalry tactics.

Negation of the Negation

"The historical sketch (of the so called original accumulation of capital in England) is comparatively the best part of Marx's book and it would be even better if it had been developed scientifically and not by means of the Dialectic. The Hegelian negation of the negation is called upon to serve here as a midwife, in default of anything better and clearer, and by means of it the future is brought into existence from the present. The abolition of private property which is shown to have been going on since the sixteenth century is the first negation. Another negation must follow which is characterised as the negation of the negation and therefore the restoration of individual private property, but in a higher form, founded on the common ownership of land and instruments of labor. If this new 'individual private property' is called also 'social property' by Herr

LANDMARKS OF SCIENTIFIC SOCIALISM

Marx, the higher Hegelian unity is here manifested in which the contradiction will be destroyed, that is, in accordance with this juggling of words, be destroyed and preserved. . . . The dispossession of the dispossessor is, as it were, in this case the automatic product of historical reality in its material external form. . . . It would be difficult for a cautious man to convince himself of the necessity of communism in land and property on the credit of Hegel's shiftiness, of which the negation of the negation is an example. . . . The confusion of the Marxian philosophic notions will not be strange to him who knows what can be done by means of the Hegelian dialectic or rather what cannot be done. For those who do not know the trick, it must be noted that the first negation of Hegel is the teaching of the catechism with respect to the Fall, and the second is a higher unity leading to the Redemption. On these analogies, which pertain to religion no logic of facts can be established. . . . Herr Marx consoles himself in the midst of his simultaneously individual and social property and leaves his disciples to solve his profound dialectic puzzle." Thus far Herr Duehring is quoted.)

So Marx cannot prove the necessity of the social revolution, the restoration of a common property in land and the means of production, except by a reliance upon Hegel's negation of the negation. And, since he founds his socialistic theories upon analogies pertaining to religion, he comes to the conclusion that in future society a simultaneously individual and social property will prevail, as the Hegelian higher unity of the contradiction destroyed.

Let us leave the negation of the negation for a little and look at "the coexistent individual and social property." This will be called by Herr Duehring a "cloud

THE DIALECTIC

realm," and, strange to say he is really right in this regard. But sad to say it is not Marx who is found to be in the cloud realm but on the contrary Herr Duehring himself. Since by virtue of his wonderful versatility in the vagaries of Hegel he does not experience any difficulty in telling us the necessary contents of the as yet unpublished volume of "Capital," so, after setting Hegel right, he is able to correct Marx without any trouble in that he ascribes to him a higher unity of a private property of which Marx has not said a word.

Marx says "It is the negation of the negation. This reestablishes private property but on the basis of the acquisitions of the capitalistic era, of the cooperation of free laborers and their common ownership of the land and the means of production. The transformation of the private property of individuals, depending upon the labor of individuals, into capitalistic property is naturally a process much more tedious, hard and difficult than the transformation of capitalistic private property, as it now exists, resting upon social production, into social property." That is all. The condition attained by the dispossession of the dispossessor is here shown as the restoration of individual private property resting however on a basis of social property in the land and means of production. For people who can understand English, the meaning of this is that social property extends to the land and means of production, and private property to the products, therefore to consumption. And that the matter should be evident even to infants Marx shows on page 56. "A society of free men who labor with social means of production, and consciously expend their individual labor power as social labor power," therefore a socialistically organised society, and he says further "The total product of the society is a social product.

LANDMARKS OF SCIENTIFIC SOCIALISM

A portion of this product serves again as a means of production. It remains social. But another portion is consumed by the members of the society. It must therefore be distributed among them." And that ought to be clear, even to Herr Duehring, in spite of his having Hegel on the brain. The coexistent individual and social property, this confused and indefinite thing, this nonsense proceeding from the Hegelian dialectic, this misty world, this deep dialectic puzzle which Marx leaves his pupils to solve is merely a creation of Herr Duehring's imagination. Marx, as a so-called Hegelian, is obliged, as a result of the negation of the negation, to furnish a correct higher unity, and since he does not do this in accordance with the taste of Herr Duehring, the latter has to take a lofty stand and to smite Marx in the interests of the full truth of things upon which Herr Duehring holds a patent.

What attitude did Marx take to the negation of the negation? On page 761 and following he states the conclusion with respect to his economic and historical investigations into the so-called accumulation of original capital, extending over the fifty preceding pages. Before the capitalistic era in England, at least, small production existed, based upon the private property of the worker in his tools. The so called accumulation of capital consists in the expropriation of these immediate producers, that is in the abolition of private property resting on the labor of individuals. This was possible because the aforesaid small production is only compatible with a narrow and primitive stage of production and of society and at a certain grade of development furnishes the means of its own suicide. This suicide, the transformation of individual and divided modes of production into social production, constitutes the early history

THE DIALECTIC

of capitalism. As soon as the workers are transformed into proletarians and their means of labor into capital, as soon as the capitalistic methods of production are firmly established, the growing association of labor and the further transformation of the land and other means of production and hence the further expropriation of the owners of private property takes on a new form, " there is no longer the self-employing worker to expropriate, but the capitalist who expropriates many workers. This expropriation fulfils itself through the play of laws immanent in capitalistic production itself, through the concentration of capital. One capitalist kills many. Hand in hand with this concentration, or the expropriation of many capitalists by a few, there develop continually the conscious technical application of science, the deliberate organised exploitation of the soil, the transformation of the instruments of labor into instruments of labor which can only be employed collectively, and the economising of all means of production through their employment as the common means of production of combined social labor. With the constantly diminishing numbers of capitalist magnates who usurp and monopolise all the advantages of this process of transformation, grows the mass of misery, pressure, slavery, degradation and robbery but there grows also revolt and the constant progress in union and organisation of the working class brought about through the mechanism of the capitalistic process of production. Capitalism becomes an impediment to the methods of production developed with and under it. The concentration of the means of production and the organisation of labor reach a point where it comes into collision with its capitalistic covering. It is broken. The hour of capitalistic private property strikes. The expropriators are expropriated."

LANDMARKS OF SCIENTIFIC SOCIALISM

And now I ask the reader, where are the dialectic twists and twirls, the intellectual arabesques, where the confused thought the result of which is the identity of everything, where the dialectic mystery for the faithful, where the dialectic hocus pocus, and the Hegelian intricacies, without which, Marx, according to Herr Duehring, cannot develop his own ideas? Marx simply pointed to history and showed briefly that just as the small industry necessarily produced the conditions of its own downfall, by its own development, that is to say by the expropriation of the small holders of private property so now the capitalistic method of production has itself developed likewise the material circumstances which must cause its downfall. The process is a historical one and, if it is at the same time dialectic, it is not to the discredit of Marx, that it happens to be so fatal to Herr Duehring.

In the first place, since Marx is ready with his historical economic proof, he proceeds " The capitalistic method of production and method of appropriation, that is to say capitalistic private property is the first negation of individual private property founded on labor of individuals, the negation of capitalistic production will be self-produced with the necessity of a natural process, etc. (as quoted above).

Although Marx therefore shows the occurrence of this event as negation of the negation, he has no intention of proving by this means that it is a historical necessity. On the contrary "After he has shown that the actual fact has partially declared itself, and has, as yet partially to declare itself, he shows it also as a fact which fulfils itself in accordance with a certain dialectic law. That is all. It is therefore again merely supposition on Herr Duehring's part to assert that the negation of the

THE DIALECTIC

negation must act as a midwife by whose means the future is brought out of the womb of the present, or that Marx wants to convince anyone of the necessity of social ownership of land and capital upon the credit of the negation of the negation.

It shows a complete lack of comprehension of the nature of the dialectic to regard it as Herr Duehring does, as an instrument of mere proof, just as one can after a limited fashion employ formal logic or elementary mathematics. Formal logic is itself more than anything else a method for the discovery of new results, for advancing from the known to the unknown, and so, but in a much more distinguished sense, is the dialectic, which, since it transcends the narrow limits of formal logic, attains a more comprehensive philosophical position. It is the same with mathematics. Elementary mathematics, the mathematics of constant quantities, proceeds within the limits of formal logic, at least as a rule: the mathematics of variable quantities which is peculiarly concerned with calculations running to the infinite, is substantially nothing but the application of the dialectic in mathematics. Mere proof becomes secondary before the manifold application of the method to new fields of investigation. But nearly all the proofs of higher mathematics from the first of the differential calculus, are, strictly speaking, false from the standpoint of elementary mathematics. This cannot be otherwise, if one, as is here the case, wishes to establish results won in the realm of dialectics by means of formal logic. For a crass metaphysician like Herr Duehring to want to prove anything by means of the dialectic would be the same wasted labor as Leibnitz and his pupils went through when they tried to establish the thesis of calculation to infinity by means

LANDMARKS OF SCIENTIFIC SOCIALISM

of the mathematics of their time. The differential gave them the same spasms as the negation of the negation gives Herr Duehring and it played a role in it as we shall see. They admitted it at last, at least as many as did not die first, not because they were convinced but because it always worked out right. Herr Duehring, is, as he says, just in his forties, and if he attains old age, as we hope he will, he may also experience the same.

But what is this dreadful negation of the negation which makes life so bitter to Herr Duehring and which is to him what the unpardonable sin, the sin against the Holy Ghost, is to Christianity? It is a very simple process, and one, moreover, which fulfils itself every day, which any child can understand when it is deprived of mystery, under which the old idealistic philosophy found a refuge, and beneath which it will pay unprotected metaphysicians to take refuge from the stroke of Herr Duehring. Let us take a grain of barley. Millions of such grains of barley will be ground, cooked and brewed and then consumed. But let such a grain of barley fall on suitable soil under normal conditions; a complete individual change at once takes place in it under the influence of heat and moisture, it germinates. The grain, as such disappears, is negated, in its place arises the plant, the negation of the grain. But what is the normal course of life of this plant? It grows, blossoms, bears fruit and finally produces other grains of barley and as soon as these are ripe the stalk dies, and becomes negated in its turn. As the result of this negation of the negation, we have the original grains of barley again, not singly, however, but ten, twenty or thirty fold. Forms of grain change very slowly and so the grain of barley remains practically the same as a hundred years ago. But let us take a cultivated ornamental plant, like the dahlia or

THE DIALECTIC

orchid. Let us consider the seed and the plants developed from it by the skill of the gardener, and we have in testimony of this negation of the negation, no longer the same seeds but qualitatively improved seed which produces more beautiful flowers, and every repetition of this process, every new negation of the negation, increases the tendency to perfection. Similarly this process is gone through by most insects, butterflies, for example. They come out of the egg by a negation of the egg, they go through certain transformations till they reach sex maturity, they copulate and are again negated, since they die as soon as the process of copulation is completed, and the female has laid her innumerable eggs. That the matter is not so plainly obvious in the case of other plants and animals, seeing that they produce seeds, plants, and animals not once but oftener, does not affect us in this case, we are now only concerned in showing that the negation of the negation actually does occur in both kingdoms of the organic world. Besides, all geology is a series of negated negations, one layer after another following the destruction of old and the establishment of new rock foundations. First, the original crust of the earth, through the cooling of the fluid mass, and through oceanic, meteorological, and chemical atmospheric action, being broken up into small parts, these broken masses form layers in the seas. Local elevations of the seas, through the ebb and flow of the waters, bring portions of these layers afresh under the influence of rain, the warmth of the seasons, and the oxygen and carbon in the atmosphere: melted and almost cooled masses of rock from the interior of the earth underlie these and break through the layers. Through millions of centuries new layers are continually being formed, always to a large extent destroyed and serving again as

LANDMARKS OF SCIENTIFIC SOCIALISM

building materials for new layers. But the result of the process is always positive, the restoration of a piece of ground made up of exceedingly diverse chemical elements to a condition of mechanical pulverisation, which is the cause of a most abundant and diverse vegetation.

It is the same also in mathematics. Let us take an ordinary algebraic quantity a. Let us negate it, then we have — a (minus a). Let us negate this negation, that is let us multiply — a by — a and we have $+ a^2$, that is the original positive quantity but in a higher form that is to the second power. It does not matter that we can attain the same a^2 by the multiplication of a positive by itself. The negated negation is established so completely in a^2 that under all circumstances it has two square roots a and — a. And this impossibility, the negated negation, the getting rid of the negative root in the square has much significance in quadratic equations. The negation of the negation is more evident in the higher analyses, in those "unlimited summations of small quantities," which Herr Duehring himself explains as being the highest operations of mathematics and which are usually called the differential and integral calculus. How do these forms of calculation fulfil themselves? I have for example in a given problem two variable quantities x and y, of which one cannot vary without causing the other to vary also under fixed conditions. I differentiate x and y, that is I consider x and y as being so infinitesimally small that they do not represent any real quantities, even the smallest, so that, of x and y nothing remains, except their reciprocal relations, a quantitative relation without any quantity; therefore $\dfrac{dx}{dy}$, the relation

THE DIALECTIC

of the two differentials of x and y, is $\frac{0}{0}$ but $\frac{0}{0}$ is fixed as the expression of $\frac{y}{x}$. That this relation between two vanished quantities, the fixed moment of their vanishing, is a contradiction I merely mention in passing, it should give us as little uneasiness as it has given mathematics for the two hundred or so years past. What have I done except to negate x and y; not as in metaphysics so as not to trouble myself any further about them, but in a manner demanded by the problem? Instead of x and y, I have therefore their negation dx and dy in the formulæ or equations before me. I now calculate further with these formulæ. I treat dx and dy as real quantities, as quantities subject to certain exceptional laws, and at a certain point I negate the negation, that is, I integrate the differential formula. I get instead of dx and dy the real quantities x and y again, and am thereby no further forward than at the beginning, but I have thereby solved the problem over which ordinary geometry and algebra would probably have gnashed their teeth in vain.

It is not otherwise in history. All civilised peoples began with common property in land. Among all peoples which pass beyond a certain primitive stage the common property in land becomes a fetter upon production in the process of agricultural development. It is cast aside, negated, and, after shorter or longer intervening periods, is transformed into private property. But at a higher stage, through the development still further of agriculture, private property becomes in its turn a bar to production, as is to-day the case with both large and small land proprietorship. The next step, to negate it in turn,

LANDMARKS OF SCIENTIFIC SOCIALISM

to transform it into social property, necessarily follows. This advance however does not signify the restoration of the old primitive common property, but the establishment of a far higher better developed form of communal proprietorship, which, far from being an impediment to production, rather, for the first time is bound to put an end to its limitations and to give it the full benefit of modern discoveries in chemistry and mechanical inventions.

But again; ancient philosophy was primitive naturalistic materialism. In the state of thought at that period it was, as such, incapable of clear conceptions of matter. But the necessity of clearness on this point led to the doctrine of a soul which could leave the body, then to the idea of the immortality of the soul, finally, to monotheism. The old materialism was therefore negated by idealism. But in the further development of philosophy idealism became untenable, and is negated by modern materialism. This, the negation of negation, is not the mere reestablishment of the old, but unites, with the surviving foundations, the whole thought content of a two thousand years' development of philosophy and science, as well as the history of these two thousand years. It is in a special sense no philosophy but a single concept of the universe which has to prove and realise itself not in a science of sciences apart, but in actual science. Philosophy is here also cast aside, that is " destroyed and preserved," destroyed as to its form, preserved as to its real content. Where Herr Duehring only sees word-jugglery a more real content is brought to light by the newer point of view.

Finally, even the Rousseau doctrine of equality, of which that of Herr Duehring is only a feeble and false plagiarism, has no existence unless the Hegelian nega-

THE DIALECTIC

tion of the negation serve it is a midwife, although it originated twenty years prior to the birth of Hegel. Far from being ashamed of this it bears in plain sight the stamp of its dialectic derivation in its earliest manifestation. In a state of nature and savagery men were equal, and, since Rousseau regards speech as a falsifying of natural conditions, he is quite right in predicating equality of animals of one species as far as this reaches, and the same also with regard to those speechless animal-men, recently hypothetically classified by Haeckel as Alali. But these equal animal men had one quality beyond the other animals,— perfectibility, the power of further development and this was the reason of inequality. Rousseau sees therefore in the existence of equality a step forward. But this advance was self contradictory, it was at the same time a retrogression. "All further advances (beyond the primitive stage) were so many steps, seemingly in the development of individual men, but actually in the decay of the species. Working in metals and agriculture were the two arts whose discovery brought about this great revolution" (the transformation of the primitive forests into cultivated lands, but also the introduction of poverty and slavery together with private property). "The poets hold that gold and silver, the philosophers that iron and corn have civilised men and ruined the human race." Each new advance of civilisation is at the same time an advance of inequality. All contrivances with which society endows itself by means of civilisation are in direct opposition to their original purpose. "It is beyond question and a foundation principle of the entire public law that people made rulers to defend their liberties, not to destroy them." And yet these rulers become of necessity the oppressors of the people and they carry the oppression to the point

LANDMARKS OF SCIENTIFIC SOCIALISM

where inequality is brought to a climax and, then, transformed into its opposite, again becomes the reason of equality, for to despots all are equal, that is equally of no account. Here is the extreme of inequality, the crowning point which closes the circle, and touches the point from which we have proceeded; here all private individuals are equal, since they are of no account, and subjects have no law other than the will of their master. " But the despot is master only as long as he has the power, and for this reason he cannot complain of the use of force if he is banished. . . . Force upholds him, force throws him down, everything goes according to a straight and naturally appointed path." And thus again inequality is transformed into equality, but not into the old materialistic equality of speechless, primitive men, but into the higher equality of organised society. The oppressor is oppressed, it is negation of the negation.

We have then, as regards Rousseau, not merely a method of thought which is quite analogous to that pursued in Marx's " Capital," but also a whole series of single dialectic turns of which Marx avails himself: Processes, which are antagonistic in their nature, containing a contradiction in themselves, are transformed from one extreme to its opposite, finally, as the quintessence of the whole, negation of the negation. Although Rousseau in 1754 could not speak the jargon of Hegel, he was then, at a period twenty-three years before the birth of Hegel, deeply infected with the Hegel contagion, the dialectic of contradiction, doctrine of logic, theology, etc. And if Duehring in his misapplication of Rousseau's theory of equality, operates with his two victorious men, he having lost his feet, falls, of necessity into the arms of the negation of the negation.

The conditions under which the equality of the two

THE DIALECTIC

men flourishes and which is set forth as an ideal condition is shown on page 271 of the Philosophy as the original condition. This original condition on page 279 is of necessity destroyed by the "robber system"— first negation. But we have now, thanks to the philosophy of reality, arrived at the point of abolishing the "robber system" and substituting for it the economic commune discovered by Herr Duehring — negation of the negation, equality on a higher plane.

What is the negation of the negation, therefore? It is a very far reaching, and, just, for this reason, a very important law of development of nature, human history and thought, a law which we see realised in the animal and vegetable kingdoms, in geology, in mathematics, in history, and philosophy, and which Herr Duehring himself, in spite of his opposition and resistance, must follow, after his own fashion. It is evident that I say nothing of the special development of the grain of barley from the germ to the crop bearing plant, if I say it is negation of the negation. Since the integral calculus is likewise negation of the negation, with the other assertion I should only affirm that the life process of a grain of barley is integral calculus or even socialism. But that is just the kind of thing which the metaphysicians push off on the dialectic. If I say that all these processes constitute negation of the negation, I embrace them all under this one law of progress, and leave the distinctive features of each special process without particular notice. The dialectic is, as a matter of fact, nothing but the science of the universal laws of motion, and evolution in nature, human society and thought.

At this point, however, the objection may be urged that the final negation is no true negation, I negate a grain or barley also when I grind it, an insect when I crush it, a

LANDMARKS OF SCIENTIFIC SOCIALISM

positive quantity when I eliminate it, etc. Or I negate the statement "the rose is a rose" if I say "the rose is no rose" and what happens if I negate this negation again and say "but the rose is a rose"? These objection are, in fact, the chief arguments of the metaphysicians against the dialectic and are quite worthy of this idiotic method of reasoning. To negate in the dialectic is not simply to say "No," or to describe a thing as non-existent, or to destroy it after any fashion that you may choose. Spinoza says "omnis determinatio est negatio," every limitation or determination is at the same time a negation. Furthermore, the sort of negation here is shown first by means of the universal and in the second place by means of the distinctive nature of the process. I must not only negate but I must also restore the negation again. I must therefore so direct the first negation that the second remains possible or shall be so. How? Just according to the peculiar nature of each particular case. I grind a grain of barley, I crush an insect, I have certainly fulfilled the first act but have made the second impossible. Every species of things has therefore its own peculiar properties to be negated in order that a progression may proceed, and every species of properties and ideas is precisely the same in this regard. In infinitesimal calculations the negation is brought about after a different fashion than in the restoration of positive powers from negative roots. That has to be learnt like everything else. With the mere knowledge that the stalk of barley and infinitesimal calculation fall under the principle of the negation of the negation, I cannot cultivate more barley nor can I differentiate and integrate, just as I cannot play the violin by virtue of a mere knowledge of the laws of harmony. But it is evident that a merely childish negation of the negation

172

THE DIALECTIC

such as writing down a and erasing it, or by affirming that a rose is a rose and that it is not a rose leads to no conclusion other than to show the silliness of the people who undertake processes so tedious. And yet metaphysicians would inform us that that is the right way to carry out the negation of the negation.

Herr Duehring is therefore a mystifier when he asserts that the negation of the negation was an analogy made by Hegel derived from religion and built up on the story of the Fall and the Redemption. Men thought dialectically a long time before they knew what the dialectic really was, just as they spoke prose a long time before the term " prose " was used. The law of the negation of the negation which operates in history and which until it is once learned goes on in our brains unconsciously to ourselves, was first clearly formulated by Hegel, and if Herr Duehring desires to employ it in secret but cannot stand the name, he should discover a better name. But if he insist on expelling it from the processes of thought, he must first be good enough to expel it from nature and from history, and find a system of mathematics in which, $-a$ multiplied by $-a$ does not give us $+a^2$ and where the differential and integral calculus are both forbidden by law.

Conclusion

In this short section Engels leaves the general discusion in order to again pay his respects to the shortcomings and deficiencies of Herr Duehring. The matter possesses no general interest for Engels merely teases his opponent upon the magnificence of his claims and the slightness of his performances.

PART II

CHAPTER VIII

POLITICAL ECONOMY

I. Objects and Methods

Political economy is, in the widest sense, the science of the laws controlling the production and exchange of the material necessities of life in human society. Production and exchange are two entirely different functions. Production may exist without exchange, exchange — since there can only be exchange of products — cannot exist without production. Each of the two social functions is controlled by entirely different external influences and thus has, generally speaking, its own peculiar laws. But on the other hand they become so mutually involved at a given time and react one upon the other that they might be designated the abscisses and ordinates of the economic curve.

The conditions under which men produce and exchange develop from land to land, and in the same land from generation to generation. Political economy cannot be the same for all lands and for all historical epochs. From the bow and arrow, from the stone knife and the exceptional and occasional trading intercourse of the barbarian to the steam engine with its thousands of horse-power, to the mechanical weaving machine, to the railway and the Bank of England is a tremendous leap. The Patagonians do not have production on a large scale and world-commerce any more than they have swindling

POLITICAL ECONOMY

or bankruptcy. Anyone who should attempt to apply the same laws of political economy to Patagonia as to present-day England would only succeed in producing stupid commonplaces. Political economy is thus really a historical science. It is engaged with historical material, that is, material which is always in course of development. At the close of this investigation it can, for the first time, show the few (especially as regards production and exchange) general laws which apply universally. In this way it is made evident that the laws which are common to certain methods of production or forms of exchange are common to all historical periods in which these methods of production and forms of exchange are the same. Thus for example with the introduction of specie, there came into being a series of laws which holds good for all lands and historical epochs in which specie is a means of exchange.

The method of distributing the product is in accordance with the method of production and exchange of a given society at a given time. In the tribal or village community with communal ownership of land, of which there are obvious survivals in the history of all civilized peoples, there is practically an equal distribution; where a greater inequality of distribution of the product has been introduced among the members of a society, it is a sign of the coming dissolution of the community — large and small farming have very different modes of distribution according to the historical circumstances from which they have developed. But it is apparent that large farming requires a different mode of distribution than small farming; that the large farming shows the existence of class antagonism — slave-holders and slaves, landlords and tenants, capitalists and wage workers,— but that, on the contrary, in small farming, class distinction does not

LANDMARKS OF SCIENTIFIC SOCIALISM

arise from the farming operations of separate individuals but from the mere beginnings of farming on a large scale. The introduction and development of the use of gold into a country where formerly exchange of actual goods was the exclusive or general practice, is closely associated with a slow or rapid revolution of the mode of distribution hitherto prevailing, and to such an extent that inequality of distribution among individuals and, so, antagonism between rich and poor becomes more and more apparent. Local gild hand-production as it prevailed in the Middle Ages made great capitalists and life-long wage-workers just as impossible as the great modern industry, the credit system of to-day, and form of exchange, corresponding with the development of these, free competition, render them inevitable.

With the difference in distribution however class differences are introduced. Society becomes divided into upper and lower classes, into plunderers and plundered, into master and servant classes, and the state which the original groups composed of societies claiming the same ancestry only regarded as a means of protection of the common interests (remnants of which remain in the Orient, e. g.) and against foreign force, takes upon itself the duty of maintaining the economic and political supremacy of the dominant class against the dominated class by means of force.

So distribution is not a mere passive witness of production and exchange; it has an immediate influence on both. Every new method of production and form of exchange is impeded, not only through the old forms and their particular forms of political development, but also through the old methods of distribution. It can only bring about its own method of distribution as the result of long conflict. But just in proportion as a given

POLITICAL ECONOMY

method of production and exchange is built up and develops, distribution all the more rapidly reaches a point where it outstrips its predecessor and where it comes into collision with the system of production and exchange existing up to that time. The old tribal communistic forms of which we have already spoken may last thousands of years, as is seen in the case of the Indians and Slavs of to-day, until intercourse with the outside world develops causes of disruption within them as a conclusion of which their dissolution comes about. Modern capitalistic production on the other hand which is hardly three hundred years old and which first became dominant with the introduction of the greater industry about one hundred years ago, has, in this short time, developed antagonisms in distribution — concentration of capital on the one hand in the possession of a few persons and, on the other, concentration of propertyless masses in the great cities — which must of necessity bring it to an end.

The connection between the form of distribution and the material economic conditions of a society is so much in the nature of things that it is generally reflected in the popular instinct. As long as a method of production is in the course of development, even those whose interests are against it, who are getting the worst of the particular method of production, are highly satisfied. It was just so with the English working class at the introduction of the greater industry. As long as this method of production remained the normal social method, satisfaction with the methods of distribution was, on the whole, prevalent; and when a protest against it rose even in the bosom of the dominant class itself (Saint-Simon, Fourier, Owen) it found at first practically no sympathy among the masses of the exploited. But directly the method of production has travelled a good portion of its upward progress, when half of its life was over, when its destiny was in a great measure accomplished and its successor was knocking at the door — then, for the first time the ever increasingly unequal distribution appeared as unjust. Then was the first appeal made from actual facts to so-called eternal justice. This appeal to morality and justice does not bring us a step further scientifically. Economic science can find no grounds of proof in moral indignation, however justifiable, but merely a symptom. Its task is to show the newly developing social wrongs as the necessary results of existing methods of production and, at the same time, as signs of its approaching dissolution, and to point out, amid the break up of the existing economic system, the elements of the new organization of production and exchange which will abolish those social wrongs. The feeling stirred up by the poets whether in the picturing of these social wrongs or by attack upon them or, on the other hand, by denial of them and the glorification of harmony in the interests of the dominant class, is quite timely, but its slight value as furnishing proof for a given period is shown by the fact that one finds an abundance of it in every epoch.

Political economy, as the science of the conditions and forms under which various human societies have produced and exchanged and according to which they have distributed the products of their labor,— political economy, in this broad sense, has yet to be planned for the first time. All that we have so far of political economic science is almost entirely limited to the beginning and development of the capitalistic mode of production. It begins with the genesis and growth of the capitalistic mode of production, and exchange, recognises the necessity of the disappearance of these by means of the capitalistic forms, then develops the laws of the capitalistic

POLITICAL ECONOMY

methods of production and their corresponding forms of exchange on the positive side, that is on the side on which they further the objects of society, as a whole and closes with the socialist criticism of the capitalistic methods of production, that is, with the exhibition of its laws on the negative side, with the proof that this method of production arrives at the point, by its own development, where it is no longer possible. This criticism proves that the capitalistic methods of production and exchange constitute more and more an insufferable fetter upon production itself. The mode of distribution which is necessarily associated with this form of production has brought about a class condition which grows daily more unberable. It has produced the daily sharpening antagonism between the continually less numerous but constantly richer capitalists and the more numerous, but on the whole, continually poorer propertyless wage-workers. Finally the tremendous productive forces of the capitalistic methods of production, which are practically unlimited, are only awaiting their seizure at the hands of an organized co-operative society to secure for all the members of that society the means of existence and the fuller development of their faculties in an ever increasing degree.

In order to fully accomplish this criticism of the bourgeois economy acquaintance with the capitalistic form of production of exchange and of distribution was not enough. Preceding forms and others, existing side by side with the capitalistic mode in a few highly developed countries, had to be examined and compared at least in their chief features. Such an investigation and comparision has been undertaken as a whole by Max alone and we consider that this investigation practically sums up all that has been established respecting theoretical economy prior to that of the bourgeois.

LANDMARKS OF SCIENTIFIC SOCIALISM

While political economy in a narrow sense arose in the minds of a few geniuses of the seventeenth century, it is, in its positive formulation by the physiocrats and Adam Smith, substantially a child of the eighteenth century, and expresses itself in the acquisitions of the great contemporary French philosophers with all the excellencies and defects of that time. What we have said of the French philosophers applies also to the economists of that day. The new science was with them not the expression of the condition and needs of the time but the expression of eternal reason; the laws of production and exchange discovered by them were not the laws of a given historical form of those facts but were eternal natural laws; they derived them from the nature of man. But this man, seen clearly, was a burgher of the Middle Ages on the high road to becoming a modern bourgeois, and his nature consisted in this that he had to manufacture commodities and carry on his trade according to the given historical conditions of that period.

(Herr Duehring having applied the two man theory to political economic conditions and having decided that such conditions are unjust, upon which conclusion he bases his revolutionary attitude, Engels remarks as follows):

" If we have no better security for the revolution in the present methods of distribution of the products of labor with all their crying antagonisms of misery and luxury, of poverty and ostentation, than the consciousness that this method of distribution is unjust and that justice must finally prevail, we should be in evil plight and would have to stay there a long time. The mystics of the Middle Ages who dreamed of an approaching thousand years kingdom of righteousness had the consciousness of the injustice of class antagonisms. At the beginning of mod-

POLITICAL ECONOMY

ern history three hundred years ago, Thomas Muenzer shouted it aloud to all the world. In the English and French bourgeois revolutions the same cry was heard and died away ineffectually. And if the same cry, after the formation of class antagonisms and class distinctions left the working, suffering classes cold until 1830, if it now takes hold of one land after another with the same results and the same intensity, in proportion as the greater industry has developed in the individual countries if, in one generation, it has acquired a force which defies all the powers opposed to it and can be sure of victory in the near future — how comes it about? From this, that the greater industry has created the modern proletariat, a class, which for the first time in history can set about the abolition not of this or that particular class organization or of this or that particular class privilege but of classes in general, and it is in the position that it must carry out this line of action on the penalty of sinking to the Chinese coolie level. And that the same greater industry has on the other hand produced a class which is in possession of all the tools of production and the means of life but in every period of prosperity (Schwindelperiode) and in each succeeding panic shows that it is incapable of controlling in the future the growing productive forces; a class under whose leadership society runs headlong to ruin like a locomotive whose closed safety valve the engine driver is too weak to open. In other words it has come about that the productive forces of the modern capitalistic mode of production as well as the system of distribution based upon it are in glaring contradiction to the mode of production itself and to such a degree that a revolution in the modes of production and distribution must take place which will abolish all class differences or the whole of modern society will fall. It is in these actual material facts, which are necessarily becoming more and more evident to the exploited proletariat, that the confidence in the victory of modern socialism finds its foundation and not in this or that bookworm's notions of justice and injustice.

II. The Force Theory.

(Herr Duehring argues that the causes of class subjection are to be sought in political conditions and that political force is the primary, and economic conditions merely the secondary, cause of class distinctions Engels makes the following reply to these arguments):

This is Herr Duehring's theory. It is set out, decreed so to say, here and in several other places. But we cannot find the slightest attempt to prove it or to disprove the opposite theory in the three thick volumes. Moreover if there was an abundance of proof we should get none from Herr Duehring, for the matter is proven by the famous fall of man in that Robinson Crusoe made Friday his slave. That was an act of force and so a political act. And this slavery constitutes the point of departure and fundamental fact of history up to the present time and inoculates the heirs of sin with injustice so certainly that only lately it has become milder and "transformed into the more indirect forms of economic dependency." Since the whole of the remaining actual "force-possession" rests upon this original enslavement, it is clear that all economic phenomena can be explained from original political causes, that is from force. And whoever is not satisfied with this is a secret reactionary.

Let us first remark that one has to be as much in love with himself as Herr Duehring is to consider this idea as "original" since it is not so by any means. The idea

POLITICAL ECONOMY

that the political doings of monarch and states are decisive events in history is as old as the writing of history itself and is the reason why we are so little aware of the real and quietly developing progress of the peoples which goes on behind these noisy and spectacular activities. This idea has dominated the whole of history in the past and got its first shock at the hands of the French bourgeois historians of the Restoration period.

To proceed, let us grant for the present that Herr Duehring is correct when he says that all history up to now has been the slavery of man by men, and we are still a long way from the root of the matter. Let us ask now how it was that Robinson came to enslave Friday. Was it merely for the pleasure of doing so? Surely not. On the contrary we are informed that Friday " was subjugated as a slave or mere tool for economic service and was kept in subjection merely as a tool." Robinson only enslaved Friday that he might work for the benefit of Robinson. And how could Robinson derive benefit from the labor of Friday? Only by virtue of the fact that Friday produced more means of livelihood by his labor than Robinson had to give him to keep him able to work. Robinson has therefore, contrary to Herr Duehring's pretty prescription, made, by the enslavement of Friday, a political organization, not just because he wanted to, but simply as a means of providing himself with food, and he ought to see how little he has in common with his lord and master Herr Duehring.

The childish example therefore which Herr Duehring has discovered in order to show that force is the "historical fundamental" proves that force is only a means to further an economic interest, and in history the economic side is likewise more fundamental than the political. The example therefore proves just the opposite of what it ought to prove. And, as with Robinson and Friday, so it is also with all the examples of lordship and slavery up to now. Slavery, to use Duehring's own elegant expression, always implies a means for supplying sustenance (using the term in its broadest sense) and never merely implies a political organization which has been developed by its own will. One would have to be a Herr Duehring to venture to call taxes only a secondary feature of government, or, to say that the political groupings of the dominant bourgeois of to-day and the subjugated proletariat are purely voluntary and not made to serve the material interests of the bourgeois, namely profit making and the accumulation of capital.

Let us give our attention again to our two men. Robinson "sword in hand" makes Friday his slave. But to do this Robinson uses something else besides his sword. A slave is not made by that means solely. In order to be able to keep a slave one has to be superior to him in two respects, one must first have control over the tools and objects of labor of the slave and over his means of subsistence also. Therefore, before slavery is possible, a certain point in production has to be reached and a certain degree of inequality in distribution attained. And when slave labor becomes the dominant mode of production of an entire society a higher development of the powers of production, of trade and of wealth, accumulation occurs. In early tribal communities which had common ownership of the soil, slavery is either nonexistent or its role is very subordinate. So it was at first in Rome, as a state of farmers, but when Rome became the capital city of the world and the soil of Italy came more and more to be owned by a numerically small class of enormously wealthy property owners, the population of framers perished in front of the slave population. When at the

POLITICAL ECONOMY

time of the Persian War, the number of slaves in Corinth was 460,000, and in Ægina 470,000, and there were ten slaves to every freeman in the population, the explanation must be sought in something other than force; there were a highly developed art and handicraft and foreign commerce. Slavery in the United States of America was much less due to force than to the English cotton industry; where there was not cotton grown or where slaves were not raised, as in the border states, for the cotton producing states, it perished of its own accord and without any employment of force simply because it did not pay.

When Herr Duehring therefore calls the property of the present day property resting on force and designates it as "that form of domination which does not merely signify the exclusion of one's fellow beings from the use of the natural means of sustenance, but implies in addition that the subjection of man has lain at the foundation of human slavery" he puts the matter upside down. The subjection of humanity to slavery in all its forms means the control by the master of the means of labor by virtue of which alone he can employ his slaves upon them and the disposal of the means of livelihood by which he can keep his slaves alive. In all cases therefore it implies a certain power of possession which transcends the ordinary? How did this arise? Occasionally it is clear that it was seized and can therefore be said to rest upon force but this is by no means essential. It can be got by labor, be robbed, be obtained by trade, or taken by fraud. It must be worked for generally before it can be stolen.

Private property does not historically come into existence by any means as a rule as the product of robbery and violence. On the contrary. It arises from the limitation of certain things in the early tribal communes. It develops in the first place within the tribe and afterwards in exchange with peoples outside of the tribe in the form of wares. In proportion as the products of the tribe assume the form of commodities, i. e., the less they are produced for the use of the producer and the more for the purpose of exchange, the exchange destroys the original form of distribution in the commune itself, and the more unequal become the shares of the individual members of the community with respect to material possessions. So the old communal ownership of land becomes more and more invaded, the communal property is rapidly converted into a village of farmers, each tilling his own piece of ground. Oriental despotism and the changing government of conquering nomads had no power to alter the old form of communal ownership for a thousand years. But the continual destruction of the primitive domestic industry through the competition of the products of the great industry is bringing about its dissolution. The thing has little to do with force as has lately appeared in the matter of the division of the communal property of the feudal societies on the Moselle and in Hochwald. The peasants are finding the substitution of individual for communal holdings to their interests. Even the growth of a primitive aristocracy as among the Celts, the Germans, and in Mesopotamia, is a result of the communal ownership of landed property, and does not depend upon force in the slightest degree but upon free will and custom. Especially where private property arises it appears as the result of a change in the methods of production and exchange in the interests of the increase of production and the development of commerce and therefore arises from economic causes. Force plays no role in this. It is clear that the institution of private

POLITICAL ECONOMY

property must have already existed before the robber is able to possess himself of other people's goods and that force may change the possession but cannot alter private property as such.

But to explain the "subjection of men to slavery" in its modern form, in wage-labor, we can make no use of either force or property acquired by force. We have already mentioned the part which the transformation of the products of labor into commodities, their production not for use alone, but for exchange, plays in the destruction of the primitive communal property and therefore in the bringing into existence directly or indirectly the universality of private property. But Marx has proved in his "Capital"— and Herr Duehring does not venture to intrude upon the matter — that at a certain stage in economic development the production of commodities is transformed into capitalistic production and that at this point "the law of appropriation resting upon the production and circulation of commodities, the law of private property, by its own inevitable dialectic becomes changed into its opposite, the exchange of equivalents, which appeared as its original mode of operation, but has now become so twisted that there is only an appearance of exchange since. In the first place, the portion of capital exchanged for labor-force is itself only a portion of the product of another's labor taken without an equivalent, and in the second place, it is not only supplied by its producers, the workers, but it must be supplied also with a new surplus. Originally property seemed to us to be established on labor only — property now appears (as a conclusion of the Marxian argument), on the side of the capitalist, as the right to unpaid labor and, on the side of the workingman, as an impossibility, the ownership of his own product. The difference be-

LANDMARKS OF SCIENTIFIC SOCIALISM

tween property and labor is the result of a law which apparently proceeded from their identity." In other words if we exclude the possibility of force, robbery, and cheating absolutely, if we take the position that all private property originally depended upon the personal labor of its possessor and that equivalents are always exchanged we nevertheless come, in the course of the development of production and exchange, of necessity, to the modern capitalistic methods of production, to the monopolisation of the means of production and livelihood in the hands of a single class few in numbers, to the degradation of the other consisting of the immense majority of producers to the position of propertyless proletarians, to the periodical alternations of swindling operations and trade crises and to the whole of the present anarchy in production. The entire result rests on purely economic grounds without robbery, force, or any intervention of politics or the government being necessary. Property resting on force becomes a mere phrase which merely serves to obscure the understanding of the real development of things.

This course, historically expressed, is the story of the development of the bourgeoisie. If "political conditions are the decisive causes of economic conditions the modern bourgeoisie would necessarily not have progressed as the result of a fight with feudalism, but would be the darling child of its womb. Everybody knows that the opposite is the case. The bourgeoisie, originally bound to pay feudal dues to the dominant feudal nobility, recruited from bond slaves and thralls, in a subject state, has, in the course of its conflict with the nobility captured position after position, and finally has come into possession of the power in civilized countries. In France it directly attacked the nobility, in England it made the aristocracy

POLITICAL ECONOMY

more and more bourgeois and finally incorporated it with itself as a sort of ornament. And how did this come about? Entirely through the transformation of economic conditions which was sooner or later followed either by the voluntary or compulsory transformation of political conditions. The fight of the bourgeoisie against the feudal nobility is the fight of the city against the country, of industry against landlordism, of economy based on money against economy based on natural products. The distinctive weapons of the bourgeois in this fight were those which came into existence through the development of increasing economic force by reason of the growth at first of hand manufacture and afterwards machine-manufacture and through the extension of trade. During the whole of this conflict the political power was in the hands of the nobility, with the exception of a period when the king employed the bourgeoisie against the nobility in order to hold one in check by means of the other. From the very moment, however, in which the bourgeoisie still deprived of political power began to be dangerous because of the development of its economic power the monarchy again turned to the nobility and thereby brought about the revolution of the bourgeois first in England and then in France. The political conditions in France remained unaltered until the economic conditions outgrew them. In politics the noble was everything, the bourgeois nothing. As a social factor the bourgeoisie was of the highest importance while the nobility had abandoned all its social functions and yet pocketed revenues, social services which it did not any longer perform. Even this is not sufficient. Bourgeois society was, as far as the whole matter of production is concerned, tied and bound in the political feudal forms of the Middle Ages, which this production, not

LANDMARKS OF SCIENTIFIC SOCIALISM

only as regards manufacture but as regards handwork also had long transcended amid all the thousandfold gild-privileges and local and provincial tax impositions which had become mere obstacles and fetters to production. The bourgeois revolution put an end to them. But the economic condition did not, as Herr Duehring would imply, forthwith adapt itself to the political circumstances,— that the king and the nobility spent a long time in trying to effect — but it threw all the mouldy old political rubbish aside and shaped new political conditions in which the new economic conditions might come into existence and develop. And it has developed splendidly in this suitable political and legal atmosphere, so so splendidly that the bourgeoisie is now not very far from the position which the nobility occupied in 1789. It is becoming more and more not alone a social superfluity but a social impediment. It takes an ever diminishing part in the work of production and becomes more and more, as the noble did, a mere revenue consuming class. And this revolution in its position and the creation of a new class, that of the proletariat, came about without any force-nonsense but by purely economic means. Further more, it has by no means accomplished it by its own willful act. On the other hand it has accomplished itself irresistibly against the wish and intentions of the bourgeoisie. Its own productive forces have taken the management of affairs and are driving modern bourgeois society to the necessity of revolution or destruction. And if the bourgeoise now appeals to force to ward off the ruin arising from the decrepit economic condition it proves thereby that it suffers from the same error as Herr Duehring, in that it thinks that "political conditions are the distinctive causes of economic condition" and that by the use of the prime factor of mere

POLITICAL ECONOMY

political force it can maunfacture the secondary factor of economic conditions. It thinks that it can shape economic conditions and their inevitable development, and therefore eliminate the economic effects of the steam engine, and the modern industry which has proceeded from it. It thinks that it can abolish the world commerce and the bank credit development of to-day from the universe by means of Krupp guns and Mauser rifles.

III. Force Theory (Continued).

Let us look at this omnipotent "force" of Herr Duehring a little more closely. Robinson enslaved Friday "sword in hand." How did he get the sword? Robinson's imaginary island never grew swords on trees and some answer to this question is due from Herr Duehring. We might just as well assume that as Robinson became possessed of a sword so, one fine morning, Friday appeared with a loaded revolver in his hand. Thereupon the "force" is entirely reversed. Friday takes command and Robinson must submit. We beg pardon of the reader for returning to the story of Robinson Crusoe, which is more appropriate to the nursery than to an economic discussion, but what can we do about it? We are compelled to pursue Herr Duehring's axiomatic scientific methods and it is not our fault if we always find ourselves in the realms of childishness. The revolver then triumphs over the sword and it should be apparent even to the maker of childish axioms that superior force is no mere act of the will but requires very real preliminary conditions for the carrying out of its purposes, especially mechanical instruments, the more highly developed of which have the superiority over the less highly developed. Furthermore these tools must be produced, whence it appears that the producer of the more highly developed tool of force, commonly called weapon, triumphs over the producer of the less highly developed tool. In a word, the triumph of force depends upon the production of weapons, therefore upon economic power, on economic conditions, on the ability to organize actual material instruments.

Force at the present day implies the army and the navy, and the two of them cost, to our sorrow, a heap of money. But force cannot make money, on the contrary it gets away very fast with what is made, and it does not make good use of it as we have just discovered painfully with respect to the French indemnity. Money must therefore finally be provided by means of economic production, force is thus again limited by the economic conditions which shape the means of making and maintaining the instruments of production. But that is not all by any means. Nothing is more dependent upon economic conditions than armies and fleets. Arming, concentration, organization, tactics, strategy, depend before anything else upon the degree of development in production and transportation. In the trade of war the free inventivness of liberal-minded generals has never worked a revolution, but the discovery of better weapons and the change in military equipment have never failed to do so. The inventiveness of the general under the most favorable conditions finds its limitations in the adaptation of methods of warfare to the new weapons and the new soldiers.

At the beginning of the fourteenth century gunpowder was brought from the Arabs to Western Europe and, as every schoolboy knows, entirely revolutionized warfare. The introduction of gunpowder and firearms was however by no means an act of force but an industrial and therefore economic advance. Industry is

POLITICAL ECONOMY

still industry whether its object in the creation or the destruction of material things. The introduction of firearms not only produced a revolution in the methods of warfare but also in the relations of master and subject. Trade and money are concomitants of gunpowder and firearms and these former imply the bourgeoisie. Firearms from the first were bourgeois instruments of warfare employed on behalf of the rising monarchy against the feudal nobility. The hitherto unassailable stone castles of the nobles submitted to the cannon of the burghers, the fire of their guns pierced the mail armor of the knights. The supremacy of the nobility fell with the heavily armed cavalry of the nobility. With the development of the bourgeoisie, infantry and artillery became more and more the important arms of the service and because of artillery the trade of war had to create another industrial subdivision, to-wit, engineering.

The development of firearms proceeded very slowly. Shooting remained clumsy and small arms were ineffective in spite of many individual inventions. Three hundred years elapsed before a musket was produced which sufficed for the arming of a complete infantry. First at the beginning of the eighteenth century, a musket with a bayonet attached, which discharged a stone superseded the pike as an infantry weapon. The infantry of that day was exceedingly unreliable, only kept together by physical force, composed of the basest elements of society, frequently made up of men picked up by the press gang and prisoners of war intermingled with soldiers recruited by the various princes. The only fighting formation in which these soldiers could be made to use the new weapon was the linear tactic, which reached its highest development under Frederick II. The whole infantry of an army was drawn up in a very long hollow square three files deep and advanced in battle array en masse. It was usually permitted to one of the two wings to be a little in advance or a little in the rear. This helpless body could only advance and keep its formation on perfectly level ground and then only at a slow marching time (seventy-five steps to the minute) a change of formation during the fight was impossible and victory or defeat was determined rapidly at a stroke as soon as the infantry came under fire.

These helpless lines in the American Revolutionary War came into collision with the rebel troops, which certainly could not drill but could shoot so much the better in that they were fighting for their own interests and therefore did not desert like the enlisted soldiers. These did not, like the English, deploy in massed bodies on the open field, but in rapidly moving bodies of sharpshooters in the thick woods. The organised lines were here powerless and had to contend against invisible and unapproachable foes. The sharpshooters thereupon were brought into existence as a part of the army organization — a new method of fighting arising from a change in the military material.

What the American Revolution began the French completed in the military realm. To the drilled troops of the Coalition the French Revolution opposed soldiers who were badly drilled but who constituted large masses, the product of the whole nation. Some means had to be discovered of protecting Paris with these masses. That could not be done without victory in the open field. A mere musketry engagement would not suffice, a form would have to be discovered by which the masses could be utilized and this was found in the column. The column formation allowed slightly drilled troops to keep better order and by means of a better

POLITICAL ECONOMY

marching speed (one hundred steps to the minute) allowed it to break through the stiff old-fashioned line arrangement. It was possible by this formation to fight in country unsuitable to the line formation, to mass troops in places suitable, to associate scattered sharpshooters with the columns, to keep back, occupy and wear the lines of the enemy, until the decisive movement came when a charge could be made by the troops held in reserve. This new method of combining riflemen and columns and making a complete army corps consisting of all arms, which was fully developed on its tactical and strategic side by Napoleon, was only rendered possible by the change in military material brought about by the French Revolution. There were still two very important technical preliminaries, first the making of light carriages for field pieces which were constructed by Gribevaul by means of which alone the required quick advance was rendered possible, and making the army rifle a more precise weapon by adapting to it some of the features of the hunting rifle. Without these improvements military sharpshooting would have been impossible.

The revolutionary method of arming the entire population was subjected to certain limitations and chiefly as regards the excusing of the well to do, and in this form became common to most of the great continental countries. Prussia alone sought by its militia system to make the entire force of its people available for military purposes. Prussia was the first state to provide its entire infantry with the latest weapons, and to place officers in the rear, since between 1830 and 1860 trained officers leading their troops had played an unimportant part. The results of 1866 were largely due to these innovations.

In the Franco Prussian War two armies came into contact both of which had their officers in the rear and

LANDMARKS OF SCIENTIFIC SOCIALISM

which both used substantially the same tactics as in the time of the old smooth bore flintlocks. The Prussians however by the introduction of company columns had made an attempt to discover a method of fighting more suitable to the new system of arming. But on the 18th of August at St. Privat the Prussian guard which employed the company column formation lost the most part of five regiments, over a third of its strength in two hours (176 officers and 5114 men) after which the company column form of battle order came in for no less criticism than the battalion column form and the line formation. Every attempt to oppose a solid formation to the fire of the enemy was thereafter abandoned. The battle was thereafter, on the German side, carried on by dense swarms of riflemen into which the columns dissolved under the fire of the enemy spontaneously, without orders from the superior officers, and this was, in fact, the only possible method of advance under fire. The private soldier was again cleverer than his officer; he had discovered the only form of fighting formation, and set himself to follow it in spite of the resistance of his leaders.

In the Franco-German war there is a point of departure of entirely different significance from all preceding wars. In the first place the weapons are now so complete that a new revolutionary departure in this respect is no longer possible. When you have cannon with which you can decimate a battalion as far as your eye can make it out, and when you have rifles by which you can aim at individuals, and which take less time to load than to aim, all further advances as far as battle in the field goes are immaterial. The era of progress on this side is substantially closed. In the second place, however, this war has induced all the great states of the

POLITICAL ECONOMY

continent to adopt the highly developed Prussian militia system and thus to take up a military burden which will ruin them in a few years. The army has become the main object of the state, it has become an object in itself. The people only exist to furnish and maintain soldiers. Militarism dominates and devours Europe. But this militarism has in it the seeds of its own destruction. The competition of the various states with each other necessitates the spending of more money every year on the army, the fleet, weapons of destruction, etc., and thus accelerates financial breakdown. On the other hand, with the increasingly rigid military service, the whole people becomes familiar with the use of military weapons. It therefore becomes able at some time to impose its will upon the dominating military authority. And this time arrives as soon as the mass of the people — country and city workers and farmers — has the will. At this point the army of the classes becomes the army of the masses, the machine refuses to do the work, militarism goes under in the dialectic of its own development. What the bourgeois democrats of 1848 could not accomplish, just because they were bourgeois and not proletarian, namely the endowment of the laboring masses with a will, the content of which corresponded with their class condition, socialism will certainly accomplish. And that means the destruction of militarism and with it of all standing armies absolutely and entirely.

That is the moral of our history of modern infantry. The second moral which brings us back to Herr Duehring is that the entire organization and methods of warfare of modern armies and, with them, victory and defeat, are dependent upon material things, that is upon economic conditions, upon soldier material and upon weapon material and therefore upon the quality of a population

LANDMARKS OF SCIENTIFIC SOCIALISM

and upon technique. Only a hunting people like the Americans could rediscover the sharpshooter. Now the Yankees of the old States have, from purely economic causes, become transformed into farmers, industrialists, sailors and merchants, who no longer shoot in the primeval forests and on that account have become all the more successful in the field of speculation where they have developed into colossal appropriators. Only a Revolution like the French which emancipated the burghers and still more the peasants could discover the simultaneously massed armies and free advance by which they overcame the stiff old line formation, the military product of the absolutism against which they fought. And as for the advances in technique as soon as they were applicable and were applied, forthwith changes, nay revolutions, in the methods of warfare were at once made, often against the will of the military leaders as we have seen over and over again to be the case. A diligent subaltern could explain to Herr Duehring how at the present day the making of war is dependent upon the productivity and means of communication of the back country as well as of the theatre of war. In short, economic conditions and means of power are always the things which help " force " to victory, and without them " force " comes to an end. So that he who would reform the art of war according to the axioms of Herr Duehring would only get a flogging for his pains.

If we go from the land to the sea we shall discover a complete revolution, even within the last twenty years. The warship of the Crimean War was the wooden three decker, with from sixty to a hundred guns, which depended upon its sailing power and had only a weak auxiliary steam engine. It carried in general thirty-two pounders of about sixty hundred weight and only a few

POLITICAL ECONOMY

sixty-eight pounders of ninety-five hundred weight. At the end of the war ironclad floating batteries were used, clumsy and slow but impregnable to the artillery of that time. Very soon iron plates were placed on the warships, at first thin, four inches thickness of iron was then considered to constitute a remarkably great thickness. But the progress in artillery soon discounted the thickness of armour, for every addition to the armour there was a new and more powerful artillery which pierced it with the greatest ease. So now we have warships with ten twelve, fourteen twenty-four inches of armour plate (the Italians are going to build a warship with armour-plate three feet thick) on the one hand and on the other hand guns which reach to a hundred tons and which hurl projectiles amounting to two thousand pounds in weight to unheard of distances. The modern war vessel is a rapid travelling armoured screw steamer of eight to ten thousand tons and of from six to eight thousand horse power provided with turrets and four or six very powerful big guns, together with a ram at the bow below the water line for the purpose of destroying the ship of the enemy. It is a colossal machine in which steam not only furnishes the driving power but also steers, raises the anchor, moves the towers, aims and loads the guns, works the pumps, takes in and lowers the boats, which are frequently steamers, and so forth. And the contest between the armour plate and the projectile is so far from having been settled that a ship is to-day practically obsolete as soon as it has left the ways. The modern warship is not only a product of modern industry but a masterpiece, a product of the dissipation of wealth. The country in which the greater industry has developed the most completely has a monopoly of shipbuilding. All the Turkish, almost all the Russian and the greater

LANDMARKS OF SCIENTIFIC SOCIALISM

part of the German warships are built in England. Armour plate of the best type is made almost exclusively in Germany. Of the three iron foundries which are alone in the position to turn out the heaviest artillery, two of them, Woolwich and Elswick, are in England, the third Krupp's is in Germany. Here it may be seen that the pure political power which Herr Duehring maintains to be the original reason for economic conditions is on the contrary inseparable from economic conditions and that not only the existence but the very management of the tool of force on the sea, the warship, is in itself a branch of modern industry. And that this is so gives nobody more trouble than just that force, the state, which has now to pay more for one ship than it had formerly for a small fleet and sees that these expensive ships are obsolete as soon as they are launched. And the state is just as much upset as Herr Duehring would be over the fact that the controller of the economic force of the ship, the engineer, is a much more important person than the man of pure force, the captain. On the other hand we have no further grounds for annoyance when we see that how as a result of this contest between armour plate and projectile the battle ship has arrived at the point when it is as expensive as it is unfit for fighting and that this contest shows the dialectic law of progress at work in naval warfare according to which militarism like every other historical phenomenon must come to an end as a result of its own development.

We can thus see as plain as noonday that it is not true that " the original reason must be sought in pure political force and not in indirect economic force." Quite the contrary. Economic force is the control of the power of the great industry. Political force in naval matters which is dependent upon modern ships of war is by no

POLITICAL ECONOMY

means "pure force" but is involved in economic force, in the advanced development of metallurgy, in the mastery of historical technique and the possession of rich coal-fields.

IV. Force Theory (Conclusion)

(Herr Duehring makes an argument which is briefly summarised by Engels as follows and which may be said to involve the notion that the monopolization of land is the cause of human slavery and is the product of force. Engels proceeds):

Thesis — The domination of nature by man is the reason of the domination of man by man.

Proof — The existence of landlordism on a large scale cannot be carried on anywhere except by means of slavery.

Proof of proof — Landlordism on a large scale cannot exist without slavery because the great landlord with his own family without the help of slaves can only cultivate a small piece of his property.

Therefore, in order to show that man cannot subdue nature without the subjugation of his fellowman, Herr Duehring transforms "nature" forthwith into "private ownership of large tracts of land" and this indefinite private ownership into the ownership exercised by a great landlord, who naturally cannot cultivate his land without slaves.

In the first place the domination of nature and the cultivation of private landed property do not imply the same thing. The domination of nature in industrial affairs is displayed in a manner altogether different from that in agricultural affairs, for these latter are always at the mercy of the climate instead of being supreme over the climate.

LANDMARKS OF SCIENTIFIC SOCIALISM

In the second place if we limit ourselves to the exploitation of private property in land in large amounts we come to the question as to whom the land belongs. We find that in the beginnings of civilised peoples the land was not owned by great landlords but was held in common by tribal and village communities. From India to Ireland the exploitation of land property in large tracts has proceeded from the tribal and village communal ownership which was the original form. Sometimes the land was cultivated in common for the benefit of the common members, sometimes in separate pieces, parcelled by the community to separate families from time to time with wood and willow land retained for communal use.

It is pure imagination on the part of Herr Duehring to declare that the exploitation of landed property is responsible for the existence of master and servant. Who is the owner of private landed property in the entire Orient where the land is possessed by the community or the State and the word landlord is not to be found in the language? The Turks first introduced a species of feudalism into the lands which they conquered. The Greeks in heroic times had a classified system of rank which itself bore witness to a long unknown preceding history, but the land was then cultivated by an independent peasantry. The large possessions of the nobles and leaders of the tribes were the exception and had no permanence. Italy was originally cultivated by small peasant farmers; when in the latter days of the Roman Republic the great holdings, the *latifundia* destroyed the small farmer-holdings, cattle raising was substituted for agriculture, and as Pliny points out Italy was ruined (*latifundia Italiam perdidere*). In the whole of Europe during the Middle Ages small farming was the rule and

POLITICAL ECONOMY

it is very appropriate to the above discussion to note what tasks these peasant were obliged to perform for the feudal lords. The Frisians, lower Saxons, Flemings and people from the lower Rhine who invaded the lands of the Slavs to the east of the Elbe and cultivated them did so under very favorable terms of rent but by no means under a species of slavery. In North America, by far the greatest amount of the land is cultivated by the labor of free small farmers, while the great landed proprietors of the South with their slaves and extravagant farming methods destroyed the soil until the land ceased to be productive and the cultivation of cotton travelled ever Westward. In Australia and New Zealand the attempts to artificially establish an agrarian aristocracy by the British government have failed. In short, if we except the tropical and sub-tropical colonies, in which the climate is prohibitive of agriculture by Europeans, it seems that the idea of a great land holding class originally dominating nature by means of the employment of slaves and serfs is a pure product of the imagination. Things are quite otherwise. If one goes to the older countries like Italy the land was not waste originally but the transformation of the agricultural land cultivated by the small farmers into cattle-land utterly ruined the country.

Latterly, for the first time since the growth in the intensity of the population has increased the value of land and especially since the progress in agriculture has made possible the reclamation of poor lands, the greater landlordism has begun to obtain possession of waste and pasture lands and has stolen the old communal lands of the peasants in this country, as well in England as in Germany. And this has not happened without a counterpoise. For every acre of common land which the great

LANDMARKS OF SCIENTIFIC SOCIALISM

landlords in England converted into arable land they have made at least three acres of arable land in Scotland into shooting preserves and mere places for the hunting of wild animals.

We have to consider the declaration of Herr Duehring to the effect that the cultivation of large parcels of land has not come into existence otherwise than through great landlords and their slaves, a declaration which we have seen implies an entire ignorance of history. We have now to see how far at different epochs the cultivation of the soil has been carried on by means of slaves, as in the palmy days of Greece, or by means of tenants, like the socage tenure, since the Middle Ages, and then what has been the social function of the greater landlordism at different periods of history.

If Herr Duehring means that the mastery of man by men as a preliminary to the mastery of nature by man is a universal law, that our present economic condition, the stage attained to-day in agriculture and industry, is the result of a society which has developed itself in class antagonisms, in mastership on the one hand and in slavery on the other hand, he says something which is a mere commonplace since the publication of the Communist Manifesto. We have thus to explain the existence of these classes and when Herr Duehring has no further explanation to give than " force " we are right back at the beginning again. The mere fact that the subject and the plundered have always been more numerous and that therefore the actual force has rested with them is enough to show the stupidity of the entire force theory. We have therefore still to explain the origin of master and subject classes. They have come into being in two ways.

When men originally sprang from the lower animals

POLITICAL ECONOMY

they came into history, still half-wild animals, elementary, with no power over the forces of nature, still unacquainted with their own powers, as poor as the animals and hardly more productive than they. There prevailed a certain equality in the conditions of life and as far as the heads of families were concerned an equality of social condition — there was at least an absence of those class distinctions which developed later in the agricultural communities. In such a social state there were certain common interests which overrode the interests of the individual in certain respects, the settlement of disputes, the repression of individuals who exceeded their rights, the looking after the water supply, particularly in hot countries, and finally under the conditions of life in the primeval forests, religious functions. We find analogous communal duties exercised by communal officials at all periods as well in the oldest German mark communities as in India to-day. These are contemporaneous with a sort of beginning of authority and state power in a rudimentary form. The productive forces develop; a denser population produces common and then conflicting interests between members of the society, the grouping of which in accordance with a new division of labor causes the creation of new organs for the purpose of maintaining the society on the one hand and repressing the antagonistic interests on the other. These organs which act for the entire group have different forms according to the varying circumstances of the individual groups, partly through the natural growth of a hereditary leadership in a world where everything proceeds naturally and partly through a growing need owing to the development of conflicts with other groups. How these social functions which were subsidiary to society came in the course of time to triumph over society; how the original servant, under favorable conditions became transformed into the master, how, according to circumstances, this master made his appearance as Oriental despot or satrap, as Greek chieftain, as Celtic clan chief, etc., how far he relied on force for this transformation and finally how the individual leaders associated themselves into a dominant class we have here no opportunity to consider. We can only state that real social duties lay at the base of the political domination and that the political supremacy has only existed as long as the politically supreme fulfilled these social functions. How many despotisms have risen and fallen among the Persians and Hindoos, and everybody knows quite well that the public management of the irrigation was the prime necessity of agriculture in those places. The "educated" English were the first to observe this among the Hindoos; they let the canals and locks fall into disuse and they have now discovered by the regular recurrence of famine that they have neglected the only opportunity to make their rule at least as righteous as that of their predecessors.

But there is another form of class distinction besides the one described. The natural division of labor in the agricultural families permitted at a certain point of prosperity the introduction of foreign labor power. This was particularly the case in countries where the old common ownership of the soil had disappeared or where at least the old system of common cultivation had become supplanted by the cultivation of separate plots by individual families. Production had so far developed that the human labor force was able to produce more than was necessary for the support of the individual laborer. The time was ripe for the employment of more labor-power, labor-power had become a value. But the

POLITICAL ECONOMY

limitations of the communal system did not afford any attainable surplus labor power. Yet war did give such an opportunity for getting surplus labor power and war was as old as the simultaneous existence of groups of communal groups in close juxtaposition. Up to this time men did not take prisoners of war, they killed them right off, and, at a still earlier date, they ate them. But at the stage of economic development of which we speak they had a value and they were not only allowed to live but were set to work. So force instead of being the master of economic conditions was pressed into the service of those conditions. Slavery was discovered. It soon became the dominant form of production among all people who had developed beyond the tribal communal stage and as a matter of fact was at the end one of the main reasons for the break up of the communal system. Slavery first made the division of labor between agriculture and industry completely possible and brought into existence the flower of the old world, Greece. Without slavery there would have been no Grecian state, no Grecian art and science and no Roman Empire. There would have been no modern Europe without the foundation of Greece and Rome. We must not forget that our entire economic, political and intellectual development has its foundation in a state of society in which slavery was regarded universally as necessary. In this sense we may say that without the ancient slavery there would have been no modern socialism.

It is very easy to make preachments about slavery and to express our moral indignation at such a scandalous institution. Unfortunately the whole significance of this is that it merely says that these old institutions do not correspond with our present conditions and the sentiments engendered by these conditions. We do not how-

LANDMARKS OF SCIENTIFIC SOCIALISM

ever in this way explain how these institutions came into existence, why they came into existence and the role which they have played in history. And when we enter upon this matter we are obliged to say in spite of all contradiction and accusations of heresy that the introduction of slavery under the conditions of that time was a great step forwards. It is a fact that man sprang from the lower animals and has had to employ barbaric and really bestial methods in order to rid himself of barbarism. The old communal system where it persisted built up the most elementary form of the state, Oriental despotism, from India to Russia. Only where it has been dissolved has the people progressed and the next economic step lay in the development of production by means of slave labor. It is evident that as long as human labor was so little productive that it afforded only a small surplus over the necessary means of life, the development of the productive forces, the institution of commerce, the development of the State and of law and the foundation of art and science were only possible through an increase in the subdivision of labor. This implied the broad division between the mass of the workers and the directors of labor, trade, state, state-business, and later the occupation of a few privileged persons in art and science. The simplest and most natural form of this subdivision of labor was slavery. In the conditions of the ancient, and especially the Greek world, the advance to a society founded on class distinction could only be for the slaves, the prisoners of war from whom the majority of slaves were recruited instead of being murdered as they would have been at an earlier date or instead of being eaten as they would have been at a stage still earlier.

Here we add that all the historical antitheses of rob-

POLITICAL ECONOMY

bers and robbed of master and subject classes find their explanation in the relatively undeveloped productivity of human labor. As long as the actual working people claim that they have no time left at the close of their necessary labors to attend to the common business of society — the organization of labor, the business of the government, the administration of justice, art, science, etc., just so long will distinct classes exist which are free from actual labor to carry on these functions. Naturally these classes do not hesitate to lean more and more and more upon the shoulders of the working class for their own advantage. The development of the great industry with its enormous increase in the forces of production for the first time permitted of the subdivision of labor in all social grades and thus allowed of the reduction of the time necessary for labor so that enough leisure remains for all to take part in the actual public business — theoretical as well as practical. So that now for the first time the dominant and exploiting classes have become superfluous and even an obstacle to social progress, and so now for the first time they will be unceremoniously brushed aside in spite of their " pure force."

When Herr Duehring then shows his scorn of the Greek civilisation because it was founded on slavery he might just as reasonably reproach the Greeks for not having steam engines and electric telegraphs. And when he explains that our modern wage slavery is only a somewhat transformed and ameliorated inheritance of chattel slavery and not to be explained from itself (that is from the economic laws of modern society) it only signifies that wage slavery, like chattel slavery, is a form of class domination and class subjection as every child knows, or it is false. So we might with the same right maintain that wage slavery is only a milder form of cannibalism, the established original method of disposing of conquered enemies.

The role which force has played in history with respect to economic development is therefore clear. In the first place, all political force rests originally on an economic social function, and developed in proportion as the old tribal communistic society was dissolved and transformed into various grades of private producers, and the administrators of the communal functions therefore became more widely separated from the rest of the community. In the second place, when political force, independent of society, has transformed itself from the position of servant to that of master, it may work in two directions. In the first place, it may work sensibly and in the direction of general economic development. In this case there is no quarrel between the two; economic development is advanced. Or it may work against it and then with few exceptions it succumbs to the economic development. These few exceptions consist of individual cases of tyranny where barbaric conquerors have overcome a country and have destroyed the economic forces which they did not know how to handle. Thus the Christians in Spain destroyed the irrigation works upon which the highly developed agriculture and horticulture of that country depended. Every conquest by a more barbarous people interferes with economic development and destroys numerous productive forces. But in the great majority of instances of the permanent conquest of a country, the more barbaric conquerors are obliged to adopt the higher economic conditions into which their conquest has brought them. They are assimilated into the conquered people and are compelled to adopt their language. But where — apart from instances of conquest — the inner political forces of a country comes in

POLITICAL ECONOMY

conflict with its economic development, which at the present day is practically true of all political force, the battle has always ended with the destruction of the political force. Without exception and inexorably, economic development has attained its goal. The last most striking example of which we have already called attention to, the French Revolution. If, as according to Herr Duehring's teachings, the economic development and the economic conditions of a certain country are altogether dependent upon political forces there is no explanation of the fact that Frederick William IV after 1848 could not succeed, in spite of his army, in attaching the guilds of the Middle Ages and other romantic tomfooleries to the steam-engines, railroads and the newly developing greater industry, or why the Czar who is still much more powerful could not only not pay his debts but could not collect his forces without drawing on the credit of the economic conditions of Western Europe.

According to Herr Duehring force is the absolute evil. The first act of force is to him the first fall into sin. His whole conception is a preachment over the infection of all history up to the present time with the original sin. He talks about the disgraceful falsifying of all natural and social laws by the invention of the devil, force. That force plays another role in history, a revolutionary role, that it is in the words of Marx, the midwife of the old society which is pregnant with the new, that it is the tool by the means of which social progress is forwarded, and foolish, dead political forms destroyed,— of that Herr Duehring has no word to say, only with sighs and groans does he admit the possibility that force may be necessary for the overthrow of a thievish economic system. He simply declares that every application of force demoralizes him who uses it. And this in spite of the moral and intellectual uplift which has followed every victorious revolution. He says this in Germany, too, where a powerful and necessary uprising would at least have the advantage of abolishing the slavish snobbery of the national mind which has prevailed since the humiliation of the Thirty Years War. And this foolish and senseless sort of preaching is set up in opposition to the most revolutionary party known to history.

V. Theory of Value

It is now about a hundred years since a book appeared in Leipsic which by the beginning of this century had gone through thirty-one editions and which was distributed throughout the towns and the country districts by officials, preachers and humanitarians, of all sorts, and which was universally adopted in the schools as a reader. This book was called, " The Children's Friend " by Rochow. It had the object of teaching the children of the peasant and laboring classes their vocation in life and their duties to their social and political superiors, and making them satisfied with their lot in life, with black bread and potatoes, compulsory servitude, low wages, fatherly beatings and other similar agreeable things. In pursuit of this end, the youth in town and country was informed what a wise provision of nature it was that man was obliged to get his food and enjoyment by means of his labor, and how fortunate the peasant and handworker ought to feel that they were able to spice their food with hard labor while the spendthrift and the picture suffered the pangs of indigestion or lack of appetite. These commonplaces which old Rochow thought good enough for the peasant children of his

POLITICAL ECONOMY

day have been elevated into the "absolute fundamental" of the newest political economy by Herr Duehring.

Value is defined as follows by Herr Duehring "Value is what economic goods and activities will fetch in exchange." What they will fetch is shown "by the price or some other equivalent, wages for example." In other words Value is price. Or not to do Herr Duehring an injury and to show the absolute absurdity of his definition in his own language, "Value is prices." On page 19 he says "Value and its prices expressed in money" and he also affirms that the same value has very different prices and therefore has different values. If Hegel had not died long ago he would hang himself out of pure jealousy, for, with all his theology, he could not have produced this value which has as many different values as it has prices. One would have to possess the confidence of Herr Duehring to begin a new and more profound treatment of political economy with the declaration that there is no difference between value and price except that one is expressed in terms of money and the other is not.

(After gentle raillery of Duehring's statements Engels proceeds.)

The actual, practical value of an object according to Herr Duehring consists in two things, first in the amount of human labor contained in it and secondly in a forcibly imposed tax. In other words value as it exists to-day is a monopoly price. If all wares have this monopoly price, as according to this theory, only two things are possible. Either every buyer, as buyer, loses what he made as seller, for prices have only changed their names, they are really the same, everything remains as it was and the much talked of exchange value is merely imaginary, or the imposed cost represents real values, values produced

LANDMARKS OF SCIENTIFIC SOCIALISM

by the working value-making class, but taken by the monopolising class, and this sum of values is simply unpaid labor. In this latter case we come, in spite of the force theory, and the compulsory taxation theory and the special exchange value theory back again to the Marxian theory of value.

The fixing of the value of a commodity by wages which is frequently confused by Adam Smith with the fixing of value by the time expended in labor has been, since the time of Ricardo, denounced by political economists and only to-day persists in popular economics. It is now the sycophants of the existing capitalistic system who declare that value is fixed by wages and therefore declare the profits of the capitalists to be higher kind of wages, wages of abstinence, in that the capitalist has not dissipated his capital, wages of superintendence, premiums on risks, etc. Herr Duehring only differs from them in that he calls profits robbery. In other words Herr Duehring founds his socialism on the worst teachings of the popular economists. His popular economics and his socialism stand or fall together.

It is clear that what a workman accomplishes and what he costs are different matters from what a machine makes and what it costs. The value which a workman makes in a day of twelve hours has nothing in common with the value of the means of life which he consumes in this working day and the periods of rest in connection with it. There may be one, three, four or seven hours of labor time incorporated in these means of livelihood according to the stage of the productivity of labor. Let us take seven hours as the necessary time for the production of them. Then Herr Duehring and the vulgar economists declare that the product of twelve hours labor has the value of the product of seven hours

POLITICAL ECONOMY

labor or in other words twelve is equal to seven. To make the matter more explicit, a peasant produces say twenty hectolitres of wheat in a year. During this time he consumes a sum of values which may be expressed by fifteen hectolitres. Then the twenty hectolitres have the same value as the fifteen in the same market under identical conditions. In other words 20 equals 15. And this is called political economy!

The entire development of human society from the position of savagery began from the day when the labor of a family resulted in the production of more than was necessity for its support, from the day when a part of the labor was no longer expended on mere means of living but was transformed into means of production. A surplus of labor product over and above the cost of the maintenance of labor, and the creation and increase of a social production and reserve fund out of this surplus was and is the foundation of all social, political and intellectual development. In history up to the present time this fund has been the property of a certain superior class which has, with its possession, also the political mastery and the spiritual supremacy. The approaching social revolution will make this social production and reserve fund that is the entire mass of raw material, instruments of production, and means of life for the first time really social property, in that it will put an end to its monopolisation by the superior class and make it the common possession of the entire society.

It is one of two things. Suppose value shows itself in the cost of maintenance of the necessary labor, that is in present society in wages. If such is the case every worker gets the value of his product in wages and the robbery of the working class by the capitalistic class is an impossiblity. Let it be granted that the cost of main-

LANDMARKS OF SCIENTIFIC SOCIALISM

taining a worker in a given society is three marks. Then the daily product of the worker is, according to the popular economist, of the value of three marks. Now let us consider that the capitalist who employs this worker takes a profit on this product and sells it for four marks. Other capitalists do the same thing. But thereupon the worker can no longer maintain himself with three marks a day, it will cost him four marks. Other conditions remaining the same, wages expressed in terms of the means of life must remain the same and wages expressed in gold will rise therefore from three to four marks daily. What the capitalists gain in the form of profit on the working class they have to return in the form of wages. So we are just where we were at the beginning. If wages signify value, no plunder of the working class by the capitalist is possible. But the creation of a surplus is impossible if, according to our hypothesis the workers consume as much as they produce. And since the capitalists produce no value it is impossible to see how they can live. And if such a surplus of production over consumption does exist, if such a production and reserve fund exists in the hands of the capitalists there is no other explanation possible than that the working class uses only enough values for its own maintenance and turns over the rest of the goods which it produces to the capitalist.

On the other hand, if this production and reserve fund actually exists in the hands of the capitalist class, if it has really come into existence through the piling up of profits, (we will leave rent out of the question for the present); it necessarily comes from the accumulated profits of the capitalist class taken from the working class over and above the sums paid by the capitalist class to the working class in the form of wages. **Value**

POLITICAL ECONOMY

therefore does not depend upon wages, but upon amount of labor. The working class renders to the capitalist class a greater amount of value than it receives in wages and thus the profit of capital as of all other forms of the appropriation of unpaid for products of labor is to be explained on the simple ground of the surplus value discovered by Marx.

VI. *Simple and Compound Labor*

(The argument of Duehring against which Engels here directs his efforts may be best summed up in Duehring's concluding words " Marx in his utterances on value cannot escape the lurking ghost of highly skilled labor. The prevalent notion of the intellectual classes has been a hindrance to him in this matter, for according to this idea it is an enormity to reckon the labor time of a barrow pusher and an architect as economic equivalents.")

Engels thereupon says " the passage in the works of Marx which caused this outbreak on the part of Duehring is very short. Marx is examining the question as to the basis of the value of commodities and answers it by the statement that it is the amount of human labor contained in them. " This " he goes on " is the expression of that simple labor force which belongs to the average human being without any special devolpment. Skilled labor is a power or rather a multiple of simple labor, so that a small amount of skilled labor is equivalent to a larger amount of unskilled labor. Practice shows that this reduction to the terms of unskilled labor takes place. A commodity may be the product of skilled labor, its value may be equivalent to a product of unskilled labor skilled labor. The proportion in which different forms of labor are reduced to their general standard in un-

LANDMARKS OF SCIENTIFIC SOCIALISM

skilled labor is established by a social process going on behind the backs of the producers, and appears to them merely customary."

Here Marx is only dealing with the value of commodities, that is of objects produced and exchanged by private producers in a society consisting of private producers producing for their own profit. He is therefore not concerned here with " absolute value " whatever that may be but only with the value which is realised in a given form of society. This value under the given social conditions is shaped and measured by the human labor incorporated in the commodities and this human labor shows itself as the expression of simple human energy. But every piece of work is not merely an expression of simple labor force. Very many labor products require the expenditure of more or less time, money, trouble, and acquired skill or knowledge. Do these kinds of compound labor show at the same period of time the same commodity values as simple labor, are they the expression of merely simple labor force? Evidently not. The product of an hour of compound labor is a commodity of higher, double or three times the value of a product of an hour of simple labor. The value of the product of compound labor can in this comparison be expressed through the measure of simple labor; and this reduction of compound labor is carried on by means of a social progress behind the back of the producer, by means of which can here be established according to the theory of value but not explained.

The thing which Marx states here is a simple fact which happens every day before our eyes in the present capitalistic society.

(After some invective and satire hurled at Duehring Engels proceeds:)

POLITICAL ECONOMY

Let us examine with regard to equality of value a little more closely. All labor time is of equal value, that of the barrow pusher and that of the architect. Therefore labor time and consequently labor itself has a value. But labor is the creator of all values. It is the only thing which gives the original products of nature a value in the economic sense. Value in itself is nothing but the expression in a given object of necessary, social, human labor. One might just as well speak of and fix a value to labor as speak of the value of value, of the weight, not of a specific body, but of gravity itself. Herr Duehring calls people like Owen, St. Simon and Fourier, social alchemists. When he invents a value for labor time, that is for labor, he shows that he is far below these same alchemists.

For Socialism, which will emancipate human labor force from its place as a commodity, the understanding that labor has no value and can have none is a matter of the greatest importance. With an understanding of it, all attempts made by Herr Duehring by means of his crude worker-socialism (Arbeitersozialismus) to regulate the division of the means of existence, as a kind of higher wages, fall to the ground. From it there follows the broader view, since it is controlled by purely economic motives, that distribution regulates itself in the interests of production, and production is advanced in the greatest degree by a method of distribution which permits all the social departments to develop, maintain, and express their capacities to the fullest possible extent. To the ideas of the intellectuals which have come into Herr Duehring's possession, it must always seem to be an enormity that it will abolish barrow pushing and architecture simultaneously as professions, and that the man who has given half an hour

LANDMARKS OF SCIENTIFIC SOCIALISM

to architecture will also push the cart a little until his work as architect is again in demand. It would be a pretty sort of socialism which perpetuated the business of barrow-pushing.

If the equality of value of labor time has the significance that workers produce equal products in equal periods of time it is evidently false, unless an average is first taken. Of two workmen at the same branch of industry the value of the product of their labor time will differ according to the intensity of labor and their respective ability. No scheme of economic equality, at least on our planet, can remedy this unfortunate state of affairs. What then is left of the equality of all and every sort of labor? Nothing but high sounding phrases which have no economic value, nothing but the evident inability of Herr Duehring to distinguish between the fixing of value by labor and the fixing of value by the wages of labor, only the ukase, which is the foundation of the new social economy, that wages shall be equal for equal amounts of labor time. Really the old French communists and Weitling had much better grounds for their equality of wages theories.

How then do we solve the whole weighty question of the higher wages of compound labor? In a society of private producers, private individuals or their families have to bear the cost of creating intellectual workers. An intellectual slave always commanded a better price, an intellectual wage worker gets higher wages. In an organized socialist society, society bears the cost and to it therefore belong the fruits, the greater value produced by intellectual labor. The laborer himself has no further claim. Whence it follows that there are many difficulties connected with the beloved claim of the worker for the full product of his toil.

POLITICAL ECONOMY

VII. *Capital and Surplus Value*

("Marx does not have the usual economic idea of capital that it is means of production already produced, but he seeks to endow it with a special dialectic history in the metamorphosis of a historical idea. Capital is expressed in gold, it creates an historical period which has its beginning in the sixteenth century and the establishment of a world-market. Any keen economic analysis is impossible with such a notion. Such barren conceptions which are half historical and half logical destroys the possibility of any proper discrimination with respect to the matter." These remarks of Duehring are answered as follows by Engels:)

According to Marx, then, capital manifested itself as gold at the beginning of the sixteenth century. It is just as if anybody were to say that specie had expressed itself as cattle for three thousand years, because formerly cattle had performed the gold functions along with others. Only Herr Duehring could be guilty of such a crude and distorted expression. Marx in his analysis of the economic forms in which the process of the circulation of commodities takes places simply declares gold to be the last form. "This last product of the circulation of commodities is the form in which capital first appears. Historically capital comes with the possession of property in the form of money, as hoards of money, merchant-capital, and usury-capital. . . . This history is going on every day before our eyes. New capital comes on the scene, that is the market,—the market for commodities, the labor market or the money market, simply as money, money which is transformed into capital by a definite process." Again Marx states the fact. It is useless for you to struggle against

LANDMARKS OF SCIENTIFIC SOCIALISM

it, Herr Duehring, Capital must express itself in gold.

Marx further examines the process by which money is transformed into capital and discovers that the form in which money circulates as capital is the inversion of the form in which it circulates as the universal equivalent. The individual owner of commodities sells to buy, he sells what he does not need, and buys with the money thus obtained what he does need. The budding capitalist buys on the contrary what he does not want himself, he buys to sell, and to sell for a higher money value than he put into the business, he makes a money profit, and this profit Marx calls surplus value.

What is the origin of this surplus value? Either the buyer buys goods below their value or the seller sells them above their value. In both cases gain and loss would balance one another, since every buyer is also a seller. It can also not arise from extortion, for extortion might enrich one at the expense of the other but it could not increase the total sum of money neither could it increase the amount of commodities in circulation. " The entire capitalist class of a country cannot overreach itself."

Now, we find that the totality of the capitalist class in every country grows richer before our very eyes, by the process of selling dearer than it bought, by appropriating surplus value. So we are just at the beginning of the discussion. Where does this surplus value come from? This question has to be answered on purely economic grounds to the exclusion of all cheating, and all invasion of force. How is it possible to keep selling dearer than one buys under the assumption that equal values are always exchanged for equal values?

The solution of this problem is the crowning glory of the work of Marx. He sheds clear daylight in economic

POLITICAL ECONOMY

places where the earlier socialists no less than the bourgeois economists have groped in utter darkness. From his work dates the origin of scientific socialism.

The solution is as follows. The power of increase in money which is transformed into capital cannot proceed from the money neither does it depend upon trade, since the money only realizes the price of the commodities and this price is, since we hold that only equal values are exchanged, no different from its value. On the same grounds the power of increase cannot come from the exchange of commodities. The change therefore depends upon the commodities which are exchanged, but not upon their value, since they are bought and sold at their value. It arises from their consumption-value as such; that is the change must arise out of the consumption of commodities. " In order for a commodity to derive value from consumption our possessor of money must be fortunate enough to discover a commodity whose use-value has the peculiar property of being a source of value, whose consumption would imply the expenditure of labor and thus be value-producing. And the possessor of money finds such a specific commodity on the market in the shape of labor-power." If, as we have seen, labor has no value this is by no means the case with labor-force. This has a value, as it is a commodity, and, as a matter of fact, it is a commodity to-day and this value is fixed " like that of every other commodity by the amount of labor time necessary for the production and reproduction of this specific commodity." It is fixed by the labor time which is necessary for the procuring of the means of livelihood required to maintain the laborer in a condition to continue laboring and reproduce his kind. Let us suppose that these means of livelihood represent, taking one day with another, six

LANDMARKS OF SCIENTIFIC SOCIALISM

hours labor-time a day. Our budding capitalist who buys labor force for his business, that is hires a laborer, pays this laborer the full daily value of his labor force, if he pays him a sum of money which represents six hours of labor. If the laborer has only expended six hours in the service of the capitalist he has got the full return of his expenditure, the day's value of his labor-force has been paid. But money could not be transformed into capital in this fashion, it would have produced no surplus value. The buyer of labor-power has quite another view of the nature of his business. Since only six hours' work is necessary to maintain the laborer for twenty-four hours, it does not follow that the laborer cannot work twelve hours out of the twenty-four. The value of labor force and its realization in the labor-process are two different magnitudes. The owner of money pays out a day's value of labor-force but there belongs to him its use for the day, the whole day's labor. That the value which it produces in the course of a day is double its own value for the day is fortunate for the buyer but according to the laws of exchange no injustice to the seller. The laborer then costs the owner of money according to our calculation the value product of six hours' labor, but he gives him daily the value product of twelve hours' labor. The difference to the credit of the owner of the money is six hours' unpaid extra labor, an unpaid for surplus product, in which the labor of six hours is incorporated. The trick is done. Surplus value is produced, money is transformed into capital.

While Marx, in this way, proved how surplus value exists and the only possible way in which it can exist, under the laws which regulate the exchange of commodities he also exposed the present capitalistic methods of production and the methods of appropriation resting

POLITICAL ECONOMY

upon them and unveiled the secret upon which the whole arrangement of the society of to-day depends.

There is a necessary presupposition to this origin and birth of capital. "For the transformation of money into capital the money owner must first find free laborers in the market, free in the double sense that as a free person the laborer can use his labor power as a commodity, that he has no other wares to sell, that he is unemployed and that he is free of everything necessary to the realisation of his labor power." But this condition of a possessor of money or commodities on the one hand, and, on the other, of the possessor of nothing, except his own labor force, is no natural condition of affairs nor is it common to all periods of history; "it is clearly the result of a historical development, the product of a whole series of older forms of social production." And this free laborer first strikes our notice as a historical phenomenon at the end of the fifteenth and the beginning of the sixteenth century as a result of the dissolution of feudal society. Thereupon with the creation of the world trade and the world market which dates from the same period the foundation was laid for the mass of moveable wealth to become more and more transformed into capital and for the capitalistic system, directed more and more to the production of surplus value, to become the dominant system.

VIII. *Capital and Surplus Value (Conclusion)*

(Duehring having said that the term surplus value merely signifies in ordinary language, rent, profit and interest, Engels still further explains)

We have already seen that Marx does not say that the surplus product of the industrial capitalist, of which

LANDMARKS OF SCIENTIFIC SOCIALISM

he is the first owner, is always exchanged for its value, as Herr Duehring points out. Marx plainly says that trade profit only constitutes a portion of the surplus value and under the foregoing conditions this is only possible if the factory proprietor sells his product under value to the trader and thus parts with a portion of the booty. Marx' contention rationally put is How is surplus value transformed into its subordinate forms, profit, interest, trade-profits, ground rents etc.? and this question Marx undertakes to answer in the third volume of Capital. But since Herr Duehring cannot wait long enough for the second volume to appear he has in the meantime to take a close look at the first volume. He thereupon reads that the immanent laws of capitalistic production, the course of the development of capitalism, realise themselves as the necessary laws of competition and thus are brought to the consciousness of the individual capitalists as dominant motives. That therefore a scientific analysis of competition is only possible when the real nature of capital is grasped, just as the apparent movement of heavenly bodies can only be understood by apprehending their real movement, and not merely those movements which are perceptible to the senses. So Marx shows how a certain law, the law of value, appears under given conditions in the competitive system and makes evident its impelling force. Herr Duehring might have understood that competition plays an important role in the distribution of surplus values, and, after sufficient thought, might have grasped at least the outlines of the transformation of surplus value into its subordinate forms from the examples given in the first volume.

Herr Duehring finds competition to be the stumbling block in the way of his comprehension. He cannot un-

POLITICAL ECONOMY

derstand how competing entrepreneurs can manage to sell the entire product of labor including the surplus product for so much more than the natural cost of production. Here again that "force" of his which, in his estimation, is the very evil thing, comes into play. According to Marx, the surplus product does not have any cost of production, it is the part of the product which costs the capitalist nothing. If the entrepreneurs were to sell the surplus product at its real cost of production they would have to give it away. Is it not a fact that the competing entrepreneurs really sell the product of labor every day at its natural cost of production? According to Herr Duehring the cost of production consists "in the expenditure of labor or force and therefore in the last analysis must be measured by cost of maintenance," and therefore, in present day society, is to be estimated at the cost of the raw material, instruments of labor and actual wages paid in distinction to taxation, profit and compulsory raising of prices. It is well recognised that in modern society the competing entrepreneurs do not sell their wares at the natural cost of production but calculate on a profit and generally get it. This question which Herr Duehring fancies will level the walls of Marxism as the blast of Joshua did those of Jericho is a question which the economic doctrines of Duehring have to meet also.

"Capitalistic property," he says, "has no practical value and only realises itself because it implies the exercise of indirect power over man. The testimony to the existence of this force is capitalistic profit, and the amount of this latter depends upon the extent and intensity of the power of 'force.' . . . Capitalistic profit is a political and social institution which manifests itself very strongly as competition. **The entrepreneurs**

LANDMARKS OF SCIENTIFIC SOCIALISM

take their stand on this relation and each one of them maintains his position. A certain amount of profit is a necessity of the dominant economic condition."

We know quite well that the entrepreneurs are in a position to sell the products of labor at a cost above the natural cost of production. Surely Herr Duehring does not think so meanly of his public as to hold the position that profit on capital stands above competition as the King of Prussia used to stand above the law. The proceeding by which the King of Prussia reached his position of superiority to the law we all know, the methods by which profit has come to be mightier than competition is just what Herr Duehring has to explain and what he stubbornly refuses to explain. It is no argument when he says that the entrepreneurs trade from this position and each one of them maintains his own place. If we take him at his word, how is it possible for a number of people each to be able to trade only on certain terms and yet each one of them to keep his position? The gildmen of the Middle Ages and the French nobility of 1789 operated from a decidedly superior position, and yet they came to grief. The Prussian army at Jena occupied an advantageous position and yet it had to abandon it and surrender piecemeal. It is not enough to tell us that a certain measure of profit is a necessary concomitant of domination in the economic sphere, it is necessary to tell us why. We do not get a step further by the statement of Duehring. "Capitalistic superiority is inseparable from landlordism. A portion of the peasantry is transformed in the cities into factory hands and in the final analysis into factory material. Profit appears as another form of rent." This is a mere assertion and only repeats what should have been explained and proved. We can come to no other conclusion, then,

POLITICAL ECONOMY

except that Herr Duehring does not like to tackle the answer to his own question how the capitalists are in a position to sell products of labor for more than the natural cost of production, in short Herr Duehring shirks an explanation of profit. He takes the only path open to him, a short cut, and simply declares that profit is the product of " force." This has been stated by Herr Duehring in his economic theory under the statement " force distributes." That is all very well; but the question still persists what does force distribute? There must be something to distribute otherwise force cannot distribute it. The profit which the competing capitalists pocket is something actual and tangible. Force may take but it cannot create. And if Herr Duehring still obstinately persists in his statement that " force " takes the profits for the entrepreneurs he is as silent as the grave as to whence it takes it. Where there is nothing the Kaiser, as all other " force," ceases to operate. From nothing comes nothing, particularly nothing in the shape of profits. If capitalistic private property has not practical actuality, and cannot realize itself, except by the exercise of indirect force over men, the question still persists, on the first place, how did the capitalist government come into possession of this " force " and in the second place how has this force been transformed into profits, and in the third place where does it get these profits?

(The remainder of this section is merely further elaboration of this idea with more caustic satire at the expense of the antagonist of Engels.)

LANDMARKS OF SCIENTIFIC SOCIALISM

IX. Natural Economic Laws — Ground Rent.

(In this chapter Engels proceeds to examine what Herr Duehring called the "fundamental laws" of his theory of economic science.)

LAW No. I. The productivity of economic instruments, natural resources and human force are capable of being increased by invention and discovery."

We are amazed. Herr Duehring treats us like that joke of Moliere on the parvenu who was informed that he had talked prose all his life without being aware of it. That inventions and discoveries increase the productive force of labor in many cases (but in many cases not, as the patent records everywhere show) we have been for a long time aware.

LAW No. II. "Division of Labor. The formation of branches of work and the splitting up of activities increases the productivity of labor."

As far as this is true it is a mere commonplace since the time of Adam Smith. How far it is true will appear in the third division of this work.

LAW No. III. "Distance and transportation are the most important causes of the advance or hindrance of the organization of productive forces.

LAW No. IV. The industrial state has incomparably greater capacity for population than the agricultural state.

LAW No. V. "In economics only material interests count."

These are the natural laws on which Herr Duehring founds his new economics. He remains true to his philosophic methods.

(Hereupon Engels proceeds to the discussion of Duehring's opinions on ground-rent.)

POLITICAL ECONOMY

Herr Duehring defines ground-rent as "that income which the landowner as such derives from ground and land." The economic idea of ground-rent, which Herr Duehring undertakes to explain to us, is transformed right away into the juristic concept so that we are no further than at first. He compares the leasing of a piece of land with the loan of capital to an entrepreneur but finds, as is so often the case, that the comparison will not hold. Then he says " to pursue the analogy the profit which remains to the lessee after the payment of ground-rent, answers to that portion of the profit on capital which remains to the entrepreneur who operates with borrowed capital after the interest on the borrowed capital has been paid."

(To these arguments Engels replies:)

The theory of ground-rent is a special English economic matter, and this of necessity because only in England does a mode of production exist by which rent is separated from profit and interest. In England there prevail the greater landlordism and the greater agriculture. The individual landlords lease their lands in great farms to lessees who are able to cultivate them in a capitalistic fashion and do not, like our peasants, work with their own hands, but employ laborers just like capitalistic entrepeneurs. We have here then the three classes of bourgeois society, and the income which each receives — the private landlord in the form of ground-rent, the capitalist in that of profit and the laborer in the form of wages. No English economist has ever regarded the profit of the lessee as Herr Duehring does and still less would he have to explain that the profit of the lessee is what it indubitably is, profit on capital. In England there is no use to discuss this question for the question as well as its answer are obvious from the facts

LANDMARKS OF SCIENTIFIC SOCIALISM

and, since the time of Adam Smith, there has been no doubt at all about it.

The case in which the lessee cultivates his own land, as the rule in Germany, for the profit of the ground landlord does not make any difference in this respect. If the landlord cultivates the land for his own profit and furnishes the capital he puts the profit on capital in his pocket as well as the ground-rent for it cannot be otherwise under existing conditions. And if Herr Duehring thinks that rent is something different when the lessee cultivates the land for himself it is not so and only shows his ignorance of the matter.

For example:—

"The revenue derived from labor is called wages; that derived from stock by the person who manages or employs it is called profit. The revenue which proceeds from land is called rent and belongs altogether to the landlord. The revenue of the farmer is derived partly from his labor and partly from his stock. . . . When those three different sorts of labor belong to different persons they are readily distinguished, but when they belong to the same they are sometimes confounded with one another at least in common language A gentleman who farms part of his own estate, after paying the expenses of cultivation, should gain both the rent of the landlord and the profit of the farmer. He is apt to denominate, however, his whole gain, profit, and thus confounds rent with profit, at least in common language. The greater part of our North American and West Indian planters are in this situation. They farm, the greater part of them, their own estates, and accordingly we seldom hear of the rent of a plantation but frequently of its profit. . . . A gardener who cultivates his own garden with his own hands, unites in his own per-

POLITICAL ECONOMY

son the three different characters of landlord, farmer, and laborer. His produce, therefore, should pay him the rent of the first, the profit of the second and the wages of the third. The whole, however, is commonly considered as the wages of his labor. Both rent and profit are in this case confounded with wages."

This passage is in the sixth chapter of the first book of Adam Smith. The case of the landholder who tills his own land has been examined a hundred years ago and the doubts which perplex Herr Duehring so much are caused entirely by his own ignorance.

X. With Respect to the "Critical History"

This which is the concluding portion of the Second Division of the work and which deals with Herr Duehring's estimates of economic writers is omitted as being of too limited and polemic a character for general interest.

PART III

CHAPTER IX

SOCIALISM

The first two chapters of this Division, which deal respectively with the historical and the theoretical sides of Socialism, are omitted. They have been already translated. The well known pamphlet " Socialism, Utopian and Scientific " contains both of them. The second has also been translated by R. C. K. Ensor and published in his " Modern Socialism."

Production

For him (Herr Duehring) socialism is by no means a necessary product of economic development, and, still less, a development of the purely economic conditions of the present day. He knows better than that. His socialism is a final truth of the last instance, it is " the natural system of society." He finds its root in a " universal system of justice." And if he cannot take notice of the existing conditions which are the product of the sinful history of man up to the present time in order to improve them that is so much the worse, we must look upon it as a misfortune for the true principles of justice. Herr Duehring forms his socialism as he does everything else on the basis of his two famous men. Instead of these two marionnetes, as heretofore, playing the game of lord and slave they are converted to that of equality and justice and the Duehring socialism is already founded.

SOCIALISM

Clearly in the view of Herr Duehring the periodic industrial crises have by no means the same significance as we must attribute to them. According to Herr Duehring they are only occasional departures from normality and furnish a splendid motive for the institution of a properly regulated system.

(Duehring attributes crises to underconsumption; to which Engels replies:)

It is unfortunately true that the underconsumption of the masses and the limitation of the expenditures of the great majority to the necessities of life and the reproduction thereof is not by any means a new phenomenon. It has existed as long as the appropriating and the plundered classes have existed. Even in those historic periods where the condition of the masses was exceptionally prosperous, as in England in the fifteenth century, there was underconsumption; men were very far from having their entire yearly product at their own disposal. Although underconsumption has been a constant historical phenomenon for a thousand years, the general break down in trade, due to overproduction, has appeared, for the first time, within the last fifteen years. Yet the vulgar political economy of Herr Duehring attempts to explain the new phenomenon, not by means of the new factor of overproduction, but by means of the exceedingly old factor of underconsumption. It is just as if one were to try and explain a change in the relation of two mathematical quantities, one of which is constant and the other variable, not from the fact that the variable quantity has varied, but that the constant has remained constant. The underconsumption of the masses is a necessary condition of all forms of society in which robbers and robbed exist, and therefore of the capitalist system. But it is the capitalist system which

LANDMARKS OF SCIENTIFIC SOCIALISM

first brings about the economic crisis. Underconsumption is a prerequisite of crises and plays a very conspicuous role in them, but it has no more to do with the economic crisis of the present day than it had with the former absence of such crises.

· · · · · · · ·

In every society in which production has developed naturally, to which class that of to-day belongs, the producers do not master the means of production but the means of production dominate the producers.

In such a society every new leverage of production is converted into a new means of subduing the producers beneath the means of production. This was the cause of that instrument of production, the mightiest up to the time of the introduction of the greater industry, the division of labor. The first great division of labor, the separation of the city and country, doomed the inhabitants of the rural districts to a thousand years of stupidity and the people of the towns to be the slaves of their own handiwork. It denied the chance of intellectual development to the one and of physical development to the other. If the peasant had his land and the town dweller his handiwork, it is just as true to say that the land had the peasant and the handiwork the townsman. As far as there was a division of labor there was also a division of man. The rise of one single fact slaughtered all former intellectual and bodily capacities. This annexation of man grew in proportion as the division of labor developed and reached its culmination in maufacture. Manufacture distributes production into its separate operations, makes one of these operations the function of the individual worker, and imprisons the worker for his whole life to a given function and to a given tool. "It forces the workingman to become an abnormality,

SOCIALISM

since it makes him concentrate his efforts on detail at the expense of the sacrifice of a world of forces and capacities. . . . The individual himself becomes subdivided, he is transformed into the automatic tool of the division of labor" (Marx). This tool in many cases finds its perfection in the literal crippling of the worker, body and soul. The machinery of the greater industry degrades the workingman from a machine to being the mere appendage of a machine. "From the lifelong specialization of looking after a machine there comes the lifelong specialization of serving a part of a machine. The abuse of machinery transforms the worker from childhood into a portion of a part of a machine" (Marx). And not only the workingman but the classes which indirectly or directly plunder the workingman are also themselves involved in the division of labor and become the slaves of their own tools. The spiritually-barren bourgeois is the slave of his own capital and his own profit-getting, the jurist is dominated by his ossified notions of justice which rule him as a self-contained force; the "refined classes" are dominated by the local limitations and prejudices, by their own physical and spiritual astigmatism, by their specialised education and their lifelong bondage to this specialty, even though the specialty be doing nothing.

The Utopists were thoroughly aware of the effects of the division of labor, of the effect on the one hand of crippling the worker and on the other of crippling the work, the unavoidable result of the lifelong, monotonous repetition of one and the same act. The rise of the antagonism between town and country was regarded by Fourier as well as Owen as the beginning of the rise of the old division of labor. According to both of them the population should be divided into groups of

LANDMARKS OF SCIENTIFIC SOCIALISM

from six hundred to three thousand each, distributed over the country. Each group has an enormous house in the midst of its territory and the housekeeping is done in common. Fourier occasionally speaks of towns but these only consist of four or five of the big communal houses in close proximity to each other. By both of them the work of society is divided into agriculture and industry. According to Fourier, handwork and machine manufacture were both included in the latter while Owen made the great industry play the most important part, and the steam engine and machinery performed the work of the community. But both in agriculture and manufacture the two writers named gave the greatest possible variety of occupation to individuals, and accordingly the education of the young provided for the most universal technical training. Both of them think that there will be a universal development of the human race as a result of a universal practical participation in practical work, and that work will recover its old attractiveness, which has been lost as a result of the division of labor, by virtue of this variety and the shortening of the time expended upon it.

. . . . .

Just as far as society obtains the domination of the social means of production in order to organize them socially it abolishes the existing servitude of man to his own means of production. Society cannot be free without every member of society being free. The old methods of production must be completely revolutionized and the old form of the division of labor must be done away with above all. In its place an organization of production will have to be made in which, on the one hand, no single individual will be able to shift his share in productive labor, in providing the essentials of human

SOCIALISM

existence, upon another, and on the other hand productive labor instead of being a means of slavery will be a means towards human freedom, in that it offers an opportunity to everyone to develop his full powers, physical and intellectual, in every direction and to exercise them so that it makes a pleasure out of a burden.

This is no longer at the present time a phantasy, a pious wish. Owing to the present development of the powers of production, production has proceeded far enough, provided that society endows itself with the possession of the social forces and abolishes the checks and impediments, as well as the waste of products and productive forces, which springs from the capitalistic methods, to make a general reduction of labor time, to an amount, small as compared with present day ideas.

The abolition of the old method of division of labor is not an advance which would not be possible except at the expense of the productivity of labor, quite otherwise. It is a condition of production which has come about spontaneously through the great industry. "The machine industry does away with the necessity of constantly distributing groups of workmen at the different machines by keeping the worker constantly at the same task. Since the total product of the factory, proceeds not from the worker but from the machine, a continual changing about of individuals could not exist, without an interruption of the labor-process. Finally the speed with which work at the machine is learnt even by children does away with the necessity of training a distinct class of workmen exclusively as machine laborers." But while the capitalistic method of use of machinery does away with the old limited particularity of labor, and, in spite of the fact, that technique is rendered superfluous, machinery itself rebels against the anachronism.

LANDMARKS OF SCIENTIFIC SOCIALISM

The technical basis of the greater industry is revolutionary. "Through machinery, chemical processes and other methods, the functions of the working class and the social labor process are revolutionized along with the technical basis of production. The division of labor is also revolutionized and masses of capital and labor are hurled incontinently from one branch of industry to another. The nature of the greater industry demands mobility of labor, a fluidity of functions and a complete adaptibility on the part of the laborers. We have seen how this absolute contradiction shows itself in the continual sacrifice of the working class, the most complete waste of labor force, and the dominance of social anarchy. But if the mobility of labor now appears to be a law of nature beyond human control which realizes itself, in spite of all obstacles, it also becomes a matter of life and death for the greater industry, owing to its catastrophic character, to recognise the mobility of labor and hence the greatest possible adaptibility of the working class, as a universal law of social production, and to accommodate circumstances to its normal development. It becomes a question of life and death for the greater industry to keep an enormous number of people on the edge of starvation always in reserve, in order that they may be able to be placed at the disposal of the needs of capital as these vary.

While the greater industry has taught us how to transform molecular movement into mass movement in order to fulfill technical needs, it has, in the same measure, freed industrial production from local limits. Water power was local, steam power is free. If water power belongs to the country, steam power is by no means limited to the town. It is capitalistic practice which causes concentration into cities and which makes manu-

SOCIALISM

facturing towns of manufacturing villages. But thereby at the same time it undermines the essentials of its own motive force. The first requisite of the steam engine and a prime requisite of all branches of motive power is a sufficient quantity of pure water. The factory town transforms all water into evil smelling sewage. Therefore, in proportion as the concentration into cities is the foundation of capitalistic production, each individual capitalist tries to get away from the towns which have been necessarily produced to the motive forces of the country. This process may be individually observed in the textile districts of Lancashire and Yorkshire. The greater industry creates new towns in the course of its progress from the town to the country. The same phenomenon was to be observed in the districts of the metal industry where somewhat different causes produce identical results.

The capitalistic character of the greater industry is responsible for this aimless blundering and these new contradictions. Only a society which organizes its industrial forces according to a single great harmonious plan, can permit industry to settle itself in such a manner throughout the land as to secure its own development and the retention and development of the most important elements of production.

The abolition of the antagonism between town and country is now not only possible, it has become an absolute necessity for industrial production itself. It has also become a necessity for agricultural production, and is, above all, essential to the maintenance of the public health. Only through the amalgamation of city and country can the present poisoning of air, water, and localities, be put at an end and the waste filth of the

LANDMARKS OF SCIENTIFIC SOCIALISM

cities be used for the cultivation of vegetation rather than the spreading of disease.

The capitalistic industry has made itself relatively independent of local limitations for its raw materials. The textile industry works with imported raw materials for the most part. Spanish iron ores are worked up in England and Germany, and South American copper ores in England. Every coal field supplies a yearly increasing number of places beyond its own confines. The whole coast of Europe has steam engines driven by English and, occasionally German and Belgian, coal. A society freed from the limits of capitalistic production could make still further advances. While it makes a sort of all round skilled producers, who are acquainted with the scientific requirements of general industrial production, and by whom every new succession of branches of production is completely developed from beginning to end, it creates a new productive force which undertakes the transportation of a superabundance of raw material or fuel.

The abolition of the separation between town and country is no Utopia, it is an essential condition of the proportionate distribution of the greater industry throughout the country. Civilization has left us a number of large cities, as an inheritance, which it will take much time and trouble to abolish. But they must and will be done away with, however much time and trouble it may take. Whatever fate may be in store for the German nation, Bismarck may have the proud consciousness that his dearest wish, the downfall of the great city, will be fulfilled.

And now we can see the childishness of Herr Duehring's notion that society can obtain possession of the means of production without revolutionizing the old

SOCIALISM

methods of production from the ground up and above all doing away with the old form of the division of labor.

It is easy to see that the revolutionary elements which will abolish the old division of labor together with the separation of town and country and will revolutionize production as a whole are already in embryo in the methods of production of the modern great industry and their unfolding is only hindered by the capitalistic methods of production of to-day. But to see all this, it is necessary to have a broader outlook than the mere limitations of the Prussian Code, the country where schnapps and beet sugar are the staple industries, and you have to study industrial crises by way of the booktrade. (This is a sneer at one of Duehring's illustrations: Ed.) One has to understand the history and the present manifestations of the greater industry particularly in that land where it has its home and where it has had its classic development. It must not be imagined that modern scientific socialism can be done away with by the specific Prussian Socialism of Herr Duehring.

Distribution.

We have seen that Duehring's economics depend upon the statement that the capitalistic method of production is good enough and can be kept up, but that the capitalistic method of distribution is bad and must be done away with. We now discover that the " sociality " of Herr Duehring is merely the imaginary putting into force of this statement. In fact it appears that Herr Duehring has nothing to declare respecting the method of production as such in a capitalistic society, and that he will maintain the old division of labor in all

LANDMARKS OF SCIENTIFIC SOCIALISM

its essential features. So he has hardly a word to say about production in his social state. Production is too dangerous a ground for him to tread on. On the other hand, in his estimation, distribution is not bound up with production but can be settled by an act of the will.

Let us consider all the ideas of Herr Duehring as realized. Let us then assume that the society pays each of its members for his work a sum in gold in which are incorporated six hours of labor, say twelve marks. Let us now imagine that prices and values are in full accord, so that under our hypothesis only the cost of raw materials, the wear and tear of machinery, the use of tools and wages are comprehended. A society then of a hundred working members produces daily goods of the value of 1200 marks, and in a year of three hundred working days three hundred and sixty thousand marks and expends the entire amount on its working members and thus each member has his share of three thousand six hundred marks a year. At the end of the year and at the end of a hundred years the society is no better off than it was at the beginning. Accumulation is entirely overlooked. Worse than that, since accumulation is a social necessity and the hoarding of gold is an elementary form of accumulation, the organization of a society on this basis will necessitate private accumulation on the part of its members and consequently the destruction of the society.

How can this difficulty with respect to the economic society be overcome? Refuge might be taken in a forcible raising of proceeds and the produce of the society sold at four hundred and eighty thousand marks instead of for three hundred and sixty thousand. But all other

SOCIALISM

economic societies would be in the same fix and each would have to make it out of the other with the result that they would only be extorting tribute from their own members.

Or it might find an easy way out by paying for six hours work less than the product of six hours work, eight marks a day instead of twelve, prices remaining the same. It accomplishes in this way plainly and openly what formerly it did secretly, it adopts the Marx surplus value notion to the amount of one hundred and twenty thousand marks a year, since it pays the members under the value of their work and reckons the goods which they are only able to buy by its means at their full value. His economic society therefore can only get a reserve fund by adopting the truck system. Therefore one of two things is certain, either the economic society practices "equal work for equal work" and then it can get no funds for the maintenance and development of industry except through private sources, or it does create such a fund and ceases to practice "equal work for equal work."

This is the fact about the exchange in the economic society, but what about the form of it? According to Herr Duehring in his economic society money does not function as money between the members of the society. It serves merely as a labor certificate; it corresponds with the expression of Marx "only the share of the individual of the common labor, and his individual claim to the consumption of a certain portion of the common product" and in this function, says Herr Duehring, it is just as little money as a theater ticket. In short it functions in exchange like Owens "labor-time money." As far as the mere calculating between amount due for production and the amount to be expended in consumption of the individual member of the society is concerned, paper markers or gold would serve the purpose equally well. But it would not do for other purposes as will appear.

If the specie does not function as money among the members of a given society, but as a mark of labor, it functions still less as money in the exchange between different economic societies. According to the theory of Herr Duehring, therefore, specie as money is entirely superfluous. In fact it would be mere bookkeeping to set off the products of equal labor against the products of equal labor, according to the natural measure of labor-time, taking the labor-hour as a unit — if the labor hours are first translated into terms of money. Exchange is in reality only simple exchange; all surpluses are easily and simply equalized by means of bills of exchange on other societies. But when one community has a deficit in its dealings with another community it can only make it up by increasing its labor output, if it is not to suffer disgrace in the eyes of other communities. The reader will notice here that this is no attempt at social reconstruction. We are simply taking the notions of Herr Duehring and showing their unavoidable conclusions.

Therefore neither in exchange among the individual members of a society nor in exchange between different economic societies can gold realize itself as money. Yet Herr Duehring says that the function of money is carried out even in his "sociality." We must therefore discover another field of activity for this money function. Herr Duehring predicates a quantitatively equal consumption. But he cannot compel that. On the other hand, he prides himself that in his community one can do with his money as he will. He cannot prevent one

SOCIALISM

man, therefore, from saving money and another from not making his wages sufficient. This is indisputable, for he recognises the common property of the family in inheritance and talks about the duty of parents to provide for their children. Thereby his quantitatively equal consumption comes a cropper. The young unmarried man can get along splendidly on twelve marks a day, but the widower with eight young children has a hard time of it. On the other hand the community, since it takes money in payment without ceremony, lets money be acquired otherwise than by individual labor when the opportunity offers. *Non olet*. It does not know whence it comes. But now arises the chance for money which has up to now played the role of a standard of work performed to operate as real money. The opportunities and the motives arise for saving money on the one hand and squandering it on the other. The needy borrows from the saver. The borrowed money taken by the community in payment for means of living becomes again, what it is in present day society, the social incarnation of human labor, the real measure of labor, the universal means of circulation. All the laws in the world are powerless against it, just as powerless as they are against the multiplication table or the chemical composition of water. And the saver of money is in a position to demand interest so that specie functioning as money again becomes a breeder of interest.

So far as we have only dealt with the operation of specie inside of Herr Duehring's economic society. But beyond the confines of that society the world goes peacefully along its old way. Gold and silver remain in the world-market, as world money, as the universal means of purchase and payment, as the absolute social incorporation of wealth. And in this ownership of the

LANDMARKS OF SCIENTIFIC SOCIALISM

precious metals the individual societies find a new motive for saving, for getting rich, for increasing their supply,— the motive of becoming free and independent of the communities beyond their borders and of converting into money their piled up wealth in the world market. The profit hunters transform themselves into traders in the means of circulation, into bankers, into controllers of the means of production, though these may remain forever as the property of the economic and trading communties in name. Therewith the savers and profit mongers who have been converted into bankers become the lords of the economic and trading communes. The "sociality" of Herr Duehring is very distinct from the "cloudy ideas" of the earlier socialists. It has no other end than the resurrection of the high finance.

The only value with which political economy is acquainted is the value of commodities. What are commodities? Products produced in a society composed of more or less separated private producers and therefore private products. But these private products first become commodities when they are made not for private use but for the use of someone else, that is for social use. They are converted into objects of social use by means of exchange. The private producers are therefore in a social relationship, they constitute a society. Their private products, while the private products of each individual, are at the same time, unconsciously and indeed involuntarily, social products also. Wherein does the social character of these private products consist? Plainly in two properties, in the first place because they satisfy human needs but have no use-value for the producers, and in the second place that, while they are the products of individual private producers, they are at the same time plainly the products of human labor,

SOCIALISM

of human labor in general. In so far as they have a use value for other people they can be exchanged; in so far as they all possess the common quality of human labor in general, they can be mutually compared in exchange by means of this labor. In two similar products under identical social conditions there may be unequal amounts of private labor, but equal amounts of human labor in general. An unskillful smith might take as long to make five horeshoes as it would take a skillful smith to make ten. But society does not fix the price according to accidental lack of skill of the one, it recognises only human labor in general, the human labor of the ordinary normal skilled smith. Each of the five horseshoes then made by the first does not have any more value than each of the other ten which were made in the same time as the five. Only so far as is socially necessary does private labor comprehend human labor in general.

Therefore I maintain that a commodity has a certain value, 1st. because it is a socially useful product, 2nd. because it is produced by a private individual for private profit, 3d. because while it is a product of private labor, it is, at the same time, unconsciously and involuntarily a social product and exchanges socially according to a definite social standard. 4th. this standard is not expressed in terms of labor, in so many hours, but in another commodity. If, therefore, I say that this clock is worth this piece of cloth and that they are both worth fifty marks, I say that in the clock, the cloth and the gold there is an equal amount of social labor. I also affirm that the amounts of social labor time in them are socially measured and found to be equal, not directly and absolutely however, as one measures labor time in hours or days, but in a round about fashion, relatively, by means of exchange. I cannot therefore express this certain amount of labor-time in labor hours, since their number is not known to me, but I can express it relatively in terms of another commodity, which has the same amount of labor time incorporated in it. The clock is worth as much as the piece of cloth.

But while the production of commodities and the exchange of commodities compel the society resting upon them to take this roundabout course, they are impelled to a shortening of the process. They separate from the mass of commodities one sovereign commodity, in which the value of all other commodities can be universally expressed, a commodity which is the complete incarnation of social labor, and, against which, all other commodities may be set in direct comparison — gold. Gold already germinates in the idea of value, it is only developed value. But since the commodity value exists in gold also, itself being a commodity, a new factor arises in the society which produces and exchanges commodities, a factor with new social functions and operations. We can now examine this a little more closely.

The economy of the production of commodities is by no means the only science which has to reckon with relatively known factors. Even in physics, we do not know how many single gas molecules there are in a given volume of gas, pressure and temperature being given. But we know, as far as Boyle's law is correct, that a given volume of that gas has as many molecules as a similar volume of another selected gas at the same pressure and the same temperature. We can therefore compare the different volumes of different gases with respect to their molecular content, and, if we take one litre of gas at 0° Fahrenheit as the unit we can refer the molecular content of each to this standard. In

SOCIALISM

chemistry the absolute atomic weights of separate elements is unknown to us. But we know them relatively when we know their mutual conditions. And just as the production of commodities and their economy has a relative expression for the unknown quantities of labor existing in commodities, since it compares these commodities according to the relative amounts of labor which they contain, so chemistry makes a relative expression for the amounts of atomic weights unknown to it, since it compares the separate elements according to their atomic weights and expresses the weight of the one as multiples or factors of the other. And just as the production of commodities elevates gold to the position of an absolute commodity, to the universal equivalent for other commodities, the measure of values, so chemistry elevates hydrogen to the position of a chemical gold-commodity, since it fixes the atomic weight of hydrogen at 1 and reduces the atomic weights of all the other elements in terms of hydrogen and expresses them as multiples of its atomic weight.

The production of commodities is by no means the exclusive form of social production. In the ancient Indian communities and the family communities of the Southern Slavs products were not transformed into commodities. The members of the community were directly engaged in social production, the work was distributed as custom and circumstances required as were the products as they came into the realm of consumption. Direct social production and direct social consumption exclude all exchange of commodities and hence the transformation of products into commodities (at least within the confines of the society) and therewith their transformation into value.

As soon as society comes into direct possession of the

LANDMARKS OF SCIENTIFIC SOCIALISM

means of production and undertakes production as a society, the labor of each, however distinctive its special useful character may be, becomes direct social labor. The amount of social labor existing in a product does not then have to be established in a roundabout way, daily experience shows the average amount of human labor necessary. Society can easily determine how many hours of labor there are in a steam engine, how many in a hectolitre of wheat of last harvest, how many in a hundred square yards of cloth of a given quality. It cannot therefore happen that the quantities of labor embodied in commodities, which will then be absolutely and directly known, will be expressed in terms of a measure which is only relative, fluctuating, inadequate and absolute, in a third product, and not in their natural, adequate and absolute measure, time. This would not happen any more than in chemistry. One would express the atomic weights indirectly by means of hydrogen if it were possible to express them absolutely in their adequate measure, that is in real weight, that is in billions or quadrillions of grammes. Under the foregoing conditions, then, society ascribes no value to products. The simple fact that a hundred yards of cloth have taken a thousand hours in their production need not be expressed in any distorted or foolish fashion, they would be worth a thousand labor hours. Society would then know how much labor each object of use required for its creation. It would have to direct the plan of production in accordance with the means of production to which labor-force also belongs. The advantageous effects of the different objects of use and their relations to each other and the creation of the necessary means of labor would be the sole determinants of the plan of production. People make things

SOCIALISM

very easily without any interference on the part of the much discussed "value."

The value idea is the most universal and the most comprehensive expression of the economic conditions of the production of commodities. In the idea of value there is not only the germ of gold but also of those more highly developed forms of commodity production and exchange. Since value is the expression of the social labor incorporated in individual products, there lies the possibility of a difference between this and the individual labor embodied in the same product. This difference becomes very apparent to a private producer who abides by an old fashioned method of production while the social method of production has taken a step forward. It then appears that the sum of all the private manufacturers of a given commodity produce an amount in excess of the social needs. Then, since the value of a commodity is expressed only in terms of other commodities and can only be realised in exchange with them, the possibility arises that either exchange will cease or that the commodity will not realise its full value. Finally, the specific commodity labor-force finds its value like that of other wares in the social labor time necessary for its production. In the value form of the product there is already in embryo the entire capitalistic form of production, the antagonism between the capitalists and the wage-workers, the industrial reserve army, the crisis. The capitalistic system will be abolished by the restoration of true value (just as Catholicism will be abolished by the restoration of the true Pope), or by the restoration of a society in which the producer finally dominates his product, by the doing away of an economic category which is the most comprehensive expression of the slavery of the producer to his own product.

When the society producing commodities has developed the inherent value form of the commodities, as such, to the gold-form, various germs of value hitherto hidden thereupon begin to sprout. The next substantial step is the generalising of commodity forms. Gold makes objects directly produced for use into commodities by driving them into exchange. Thereupon the commodity and the gold smite the community which is engaged in social production, break one social tie after another and finally dissolve the society into a mass of private producers. Gold establishes, as in India, individual cultivation of the land in the place of communal cultivation, then it destroys the system of regular distribution of communal lands among individuals and makes ownership final, and lastly it leads to the division of the communal wood land. Whatever other causes arising from the industrial development may work along with it, gold is always the most powerful instrument for the destruction of the communal society.

The State, the Family, and Education

(Herr Duehring says " In the free society there will be no religion, since, in all its degrees, it tends to destroy the originality of the child, in that it places something above nature or behind it, which may be affected by means of works or prayers " also " a properly constituted socialist state will do away with all the paraphernalia of spiritualistic magic, and all the actual forms of religion." Engels proceeds—)

Religion will be forbidden. Now, religion is nothing but the fantastic reflection in men's minds of the external forces which dominate their every day existence, a reflec-

SOCIALISM

tion in which earthly forces take the form of the supernatural. In the beginning of history it is the forces of nature which first produce this reflection and in the course of development of different peoples give rise to manifold and various personification. This first process is capable of being traced, at least as far as the Indo-European peoples are concerned, by comparative mythology, to its source in the Indian Vedas and its advance can be shown among the Indians, Greeks, Persian, Romans, and Germans, and, as far as the material is available, also among the Celts, Lithuanians, and Slavs. But, besides the forces of nature, the social forces dominated men by their apparent necessity, for these forces were, in reality, just as strange and unaccountable to men as were the forces of nature. The imaginary forms in which, at first, only the secret forces of nature were reflected, became possessed of social attributes, became the representatives of historical forces. By a still further development the natural and social attributes of a number of gods were transformed to one all-powerful god, who is, on his part, only the reflection of man in the abstract. So arose monotheism, which was historically the latest product of the Greek vulgar philosophy, and found its impersonation in the Hebrew exclusively national god, Jahve. In this convenient, handy and adaptible form religion can continue to exist as the direct, that is, the emotional form of the relations of man to the dominating outside, natural, and social forces, as long as man is under the power of these forces. But we have seen over and over again in modern bourgeois society that man is dominated by the conditions which he has himself created and that he is controlled by the same means of production which he himsel has made. The fundamental facts which give rise

LANDMARKS OF SCIENTIFIC SOCIALISM

to the reflection by religion therefore still persist and with them the reflection persists also. And just because bourgeois economy has a certain insight into the relations of the original causes of this phenomenon, it does not alter it a particle. Bourgeois economy can neither prevent crises, on the whole, nor can it stop the greed of the individual capitalists, their disgrace and bankruptcy, nor can it prevent the individual laborers from suffering deprivation of employment and poverty. Man proposes and God (to wit, the outside force of the capitalistic method of production) disposes. Mere knowledge even though it be broader and deeper than bourgeois economics is of no avail to upset the social forces of the master of society. That is fundamentally a social act. Let us suppose that this act is accomplished and society in all its grades freed from the slavery to the means of production which it has made but which now dominate it as an outside force. Let us suppose that man no longer merely proposes but that he also disposes. Under such conditions the last vestiges of the external force which now dominates man are destroyed, that force which is now reflected in religion. Therewith, the religious reflection itself is destroyed owing to the simple fact that there is nothing more to reflect.

But Herr Duehring cannot wait until religion dies a natural death. He treats it after a radical fashion. He out Bismarcks Bismarck, he makes severe "May laws" not only against Catholicism but against all religion. He sets his gendarmes of the future on religion and thereby gives it a longer lease of life by martyrdom. Wherever we look we find that Duehring's socialism has the Prussian brand.

After Herr Duehring has blithely got rid of religion he says "Man can now, since he is dependent upon him-

SOCIALISM

self and nature alone, intelligently direct the social forces in every way which open to him the course of things and his own existence." Let us look for a little while at that course of things to which the self-reliant human can give direction.

The first in the course of things by which man becomes self-reliant is being born. Then during the time of his immaturity his education is in the hands of his mother. "This period may, as in the old Roman law, reach to the age of puberty, that is to about fourteen years of age." Only where the older boys do not respect the authority of the mother does the father's assistance play a part and the public method of education robs this of all harm. With puberty the boy comes under the natural care of his father, where this is exercised in a truly fatherly manner, in other cases society takes charge of his education.

As Herr Duehring has already maintained the position that it is possible to convert the capitalistic methods of production into social methods without disturbing the mode of production itself, so he here seems to think that one can separate the modern bourgeois family from its entire economic foundations without any change in the whole form of the family. This form is so permanent in his estimation that he thinks of the old Roman jurisprudence, in an "improved" form, as the model of the family for ever, and he does not conceive of the family otherwise than as a permanent unit. The Utopists have the superiority over Herr Duehring here. In their estimation a really free mutual condition would arise in all the family relations as a result of the free association and the public ownership of the instruments of production together with the institution of a system of public education. And Marx has shown furthermore

LANDMARKS OF SCIENTIFIC SOCIALISM

in his " Capital " how " the greater industry, which takes widows, young persons and children of both sexes from the home, and employs them in organized social productive processes, lays the foundation for a higher form of the family and better conditions for people of both sexes."

LANDMARKS OF SCIENTIFIC SOCIALISM

APPENDIX

The foregoing pages will have given the reader some idea of the infinite care which Engels expended in order to keep abreast of the chief scientific discoveries of his times. He was as painstaking as a genius. On the other hand, his modesty was almost absurd, for he never ventured to claim anything for himself, and such ability as was displayed in the laying of the economic political foundations of the socialist movement was invariably credited by him to the superior talent and comprehension of Marx.

There is no question that the work constitutes a most effective reply to the arguments of Duehring, with whom, poor fellow, we need no longer trouble ourselves. It constitutes, moreover, a very formidable answer to all those who seek for a justification of the socialist movement in those abstract conceptions which the average man finds it so hard to escape. In fact, so removed is the point of view of the writer of the foregoing pages from that of the man in the street that it is doubtful whether it is possible for more than a comparatively few students thoroughly to grasp the significance of the dialectic and to apply it in a satisfactory and effective fashion. Still, there is no question that this understanding of the socialist movement, as a movement, is absolutely required of all who can be

LANDMARKS OF SCIENTIFIC SOCIALISM

considered as taking an intelligent and useful attitude with regard to social and political questions.

The possession of this key gave the two founders of the modern socialist movement such a comprehension of the tendencies of modern civilization as enabled them to make those economic and political predictions which have been so completely fulfilled.

There is little need to call attention to the fact that much of Engels' argument is now antiquated in face of the growth of science and the almost incredible development of mechanical invention and the material progress consequent upon it. It could not have been otherwise. The wonders of Engels' day are the commonplaces of our existence. The machines, which he considered so wonderful and so change-compelling have already been "scrapped" for new machines of greater power and capacity for production. The remark that the battleship had in his time arrived at a point where it was as expensive as it was unfit for fighting sounds almost ridiculous in face of the tremendous development of the engines of naval warfare since he wrote, and the invention and use of the submarine. Still it must be remembered that there has been no really great test of ships of war since Engels' day and that the expense of modern navies is worrying the governments to distraction. Only a few weeks ago Lord Charles Beresford refused to accept the command of the Channel Squadron unless provided with an equipment the expense of which seemed almost intolerable to Great Britain, wealthy as that country is and dependent as she is on the maintenance of the sea power. Great armies are still on the increase and the expense of their support combined with the unsatisfactoriness of their performances is by no means reassuring to those who

APPENDIX

have the responsibility for national military organization. The Boer War proved the unreliability of the armed forces of one power, at all events, and the performances of great masses of trained men in the Russo-Japanese conflict have not inspired any very great respect for the effectiveness of these colossal and expensive fighting machines. Together with the breakdown of armies and navies, as a material fact, there has grown up a strong prejudice against their employment, and the anti-war attitude of the international proletariat has been supplemented and strengthened by the distinct growth of an international peace spirit in certain sections of the middle class. So that in spite of superficial appearances it does not seem to be so very unlikely that the action of the dialectic will be manifest in the destruction of modern armaments, at least as far as the greater nations are concerned, though there is little doubt that military forces will still be maintained for the purpose of bullying and overawing the smaller and weaker peoples.

Mention has already been made of the fact that Engels never really divested himself of the old "forty-eight" spirit. The notion that a revolution would break out somewhere in the near future finds a curiously fixed, if unexpressed, lodgment in his mind. One cannot help feeling that he expected things to mature earlier than they have done and that he anticipated that changes in the mode of production and the development of industry would have made a stronger impression upon the mind of the proletarian than history shows to have been the case. This latent, but still persistent, notion is in curious contrast to the almost detached way in which, particularly in his later years, he views the course of economic and political events. He never

LANDMARKS OF SCIENTIFIC SOCIALISM

really in fact divested his mind of the notion of the imminence of social revolution, for in his 1892 preface to "The Condition of the Working Class in England in 1844" he says, "I have taken care not to strike out of the text the many prophecies, amongst others that of an imminent social revolution in England, which my youthful ardor induced me to venture upon." His youthful ardor seems never to have really abated in that respect. The dreams of boyhood seem to have haunted him and the old fighter stirred uneasily in his study chair at the echoes of past conflicts in which he also heard the bugles of the coming fight. To those who have watched the development of Engels' thought, as shown in his works, this philosophic, unemotional way of looking at things proves the effect of experience and age upon the fighter. He started with a heart inflamed with the wrongs of the suffering, as the damning pages of the work above cited show; he ends with a calm and dispassionate enquiry (apart from what he considered to be the exigencies of controversy) into the fundamental causes of economic and social progress. The burning enthusiasm and white-hot indignation had died down in him ere he reached the stage of the Duehring controversy. He finds that although not everything that is real is reasonable, to use the phrase against which he has fulminated in "Feuerbach," nevertheless every step in human progress has been an essential step and it is impossible to hurry things. To the proletarian he looks of course as the next great actor in the drama of social development. But the proletarian, while his destiny is indubitable, is still not a being apart from existing conditions. He exists in the conditions, is in fact part of the conditions, and, while at war with them, takes on the color of his surroundings. The facts of life

APPENDIX

have driven him to an unconscious rejection of old faiths and old philosophies but they have not forced him to take up the sword against the actual realities of modern life, to which he appears, in fact, to submit himself with a humility which is at least provoking to the eager and enthusiastic revolutionist.

What wonders of economic organization, what triumphs in mechanical production have been achieved since Engels gave the last revision to this book in 1894 we in the United States at least have cause to know. The entire structure of production has been modified from top to bottom, the old individual doctrine has fallen victim to its dialectic, and concentrated industry and collective capital now rise supreme over the ruins of that individualism which gave them birth and to which they owe their existence. In the name of the individual the individual is denied. The courts hand down decisions in the name of individual liberty which have for their result the dethroning and extermination of the individual. The conglomeration of individual states which was considered the very foundation of the American government, and the outward and visible sign of collective sovereignty is already in its death throes. The dialectic of the United States is in course of develment and there comes about in consequence the birth of the United Imperial Republic, a republic which is so only in name, which is, in fact, as little of a republic as were those oligarchies of the Middle Ages whose very existence defamed the name of republic. The old things have passed away, all things have become new.

Still there is one factor which has not really appreciably changed, one factor which is always confronted by the same necessity, the necessity of maintaining its existence. This factor is the working class.

LANDMARKS OF SCIENTIFIC SOCIALISM

The dialectic is at work with the working class also, and that which according to the individualistic notion consisted of isolated units seeking their daily bread in meek conformity with the laws of contract and property will disappear into that great collective organized body of labor which spurns the theories of contract and thereby makes itself no longer subject but master.

AUSTIN LEWIS.